Passing Time Across the Water

Passing Time Across the Water: Irish Clockmakers in America

By Killian Robinson

Library of Congress Control Number: 2020901875

© 2020 by Killian Robinson and National
Association of Watch & Clock Collectors, Inc.
All rights reserved. No part of this publication may be stored in a
retrieval system, reproduced, or transmitted in any form by any
means, electronic, mechanical, photocopy, recording, or otherwise,
without written permission of the publisher and the author.

Publisher: The National Association of Watch & Clock Collectors, Inc.,
514 Poplar Street, Columbia, PA 17512
Editor: Christiane Odyniec
Designer: Keith Lehman
Copy Editor: Gillian Radel

ISBN 9780961498412
Printed in the United States of America

To Jackie Yew Ming, Síofra and Ríoghnach

Table of Contents

Foreword ix
Acknowledgments xi
Introduction 1

Chapter 1

Pennsylvania and Delaware 3

Chapter 2

Massachusetts, New Hampshire, Connecticut, Vermont, and Maine 31

Chapter 3

New York, New Jersey, Ohio, and West Virginia 41

Chapter 4

Maryland, Kentucky, and Missouri 61

Chapter 5

Virginia, North Carolina, and South Carolina 91

Chapter 6

Miscellaneous and Summary 113

Appendix 1..119
Appendix 2..123
Appendix 3..124
References 125
Index 143
About the Author 153

FOREWORD

The author's stated goal was to identify and document clock and watchmakers from Ireland who came to America in the 18th and 19th centuries and, where possible, to describe their lives and production here. His painstaking and thorough research has resulted in an authoritative publication that far exceeded his goal.

Killian Robinson is perhaps uniquely qualified to research and write on this topic. Born in Ireland and trained as a Cardiologist, he moved to the United States in 1993 to join the faculty of the Cleveland Clinic, where he practiced until 2000. At that time he moved to Winston-Salem, North Carolina to join the faculty of Wake Forest University. Perhaps serendipitously this move to NC placed him at the home of the Museum of Early Southern Decorative Arts (MESDA). Their extensive research library on Early American craftsmen already contained a vast database with details of tradesmen who settled in the US in the 18th & 19th centuries. This sparked the author's interest in researching Irish clock and watchmakers who came to the US and he saw the potential to publish this data.

The next twenty years Dr. Robinson spent compiling information from many resources, scouring previously published sources of horological names. To these he has added those found in local newspapers, obituaries, census records, court records and city directories. The first six chapters cover the Irish craftsmen located in sixteen eastern states, one chapter each for Pennsylvania, one for the New England states, and the remaining four for the Atlantic, mid-Atlantic, and Southern states.

The inclusion of historic paintings, engravings, and maps of locations on both sides of the Atlantic help bring the story alive. It makes this book more than a valuable research tool, but also a handsome presentation of data and photos. It is copiously illustrated with color photos of clocks and watches. Many contemporary newspaper advertisements are also illustrated. All this gives flavor and life to the list of names.

I recommend this book to all collectors, students, and horologists with an interest in 18th and 19th century Irish clocks and watches. Even if Irish clocks and watches are not of particular interest to you, this book provides considerable background detail of clockmaking in the Eastern United States and it should be read by all with an interest in the social and cultural history of the time.

Not only is Dr. Killian Robinson the author of dozens of papers and books in the field of Cardiology, he is well known for his previously published scholarly articles on Irish clockmakers and watchmakers. Now semi-retired, he moved back to Ireland in 2018.

As a descendant of Irish immigrants myself, I found personal enjoyment in the author's research.

—Paul J. Foley

Acknowledgments

I am deeply grateful to the following who provided local historical information, images, moral support, encouragement, or anything else. Aidan Fee, Stewartstown and District Local History Society, Co. Tyrone; Jennifer Cunningham, Coleraine Historical Society; Dennis Rainey, Comber Historical Society; Bill Weschler, Weschler Auctions Inc. Washington DC www.weschlers.com; Linda Greenwood, Belfast Public Libraries; Grace Moloney, Clogher Historical Society; Martina Aherne, Mallow Historical Society; Stella Cherry Cork Museum; Samantha Melia, Cork Museum; James McAdam, Lisburn Cathedral; Ed Chichirichi, Historical Society of Delaware; Karen McQueen, Historical Society of Montgomery County, Pennsylvania; Wes Sollenberger, Chester County Historical Society, Pennsylvania; Jeanne Solensky, Winterthur Museum, Wilmington, Delaware; Martha Rowe, Martha Ashley, Kim May, Michelle Doyle, Museum of Early Southern Decorative Arts, Winston Salem, North Carolina; Donal Quigley, Waterford Public Library; Brenda Collins, Lisburn Historical Society, Lisburn, Co Antrim; Lesley Whiteside, The King's Hospital, Dublin; Stacy Wood, PA; Stephen Kramer NY (Photographer Stacy Wood Book); John Bachman, Bachman Funeral Home (Burrowes clock). Tom Spittler, Ohio; Dr Máire Kennedy, The Gilbert Library, Dublin Corporation, Dublin; Ed and Virginia LaFond; Doug Cowen; Doug Caulkins; Doug Smyth, Dublin; Bernadette Cunningham, Librarian, Royal Irish Academy; The National Museum Dublin; John Delaney, Massachusetts, www.delaneyantiqueclocks.com; Larry Walsh, Curator, Limerick Museum; Paul Foley, Norwell, MA, Author "Willard's Patent Time Pieces"; Dr Raymond Refaussé and Dr Susan Hood, Asst. Archivist, Representative Church Body, Library, Dublin; Tom Harris Auctions, Marshallstown, IA 50158 tomharris@tomharrisauctions.com; Mike Maguire, Limerick City Library; Niall Smith Antiques New York; Dave Dungan of www.Buyanticks.com; Johnny Wachsmann Pieces of Time http://www.antiquewatch.com; John Tkachuk. New York; The Trustees of the Guildhall Museum of the Worshipful Company of Clockmakers of London; Skinner Inc. Auctioneers, Boston www.skinnerinc.com; Pictures of Kinkead clock Courtesy Delaware Division of Historical and Cultural Affairs; Catherine Rogers Arthur, Director and Curator, Homewood Museum, The Johns Hopkins University for pictures of Bigger Clocks and Warner & Hanna's Plan of the City and Environs of Baltimore, engraved by Francis Shallus, Philadelphia, 1801, gift of Mr. & Mrs. Arthur J. Gutman; Elizabeth Hoy, Local Studies, Central Library, Ballymena; The Preservation Society of Newport County, Newport, RI 02840; Yale Art Gallery; The Frick Library and Art Reference Gallery, New York; The Representative Church Body Library, Dublin; David Sperling; Nigel Barnes, www.oldclocks.ie; The Orr family especially David, Roger and Alison Stewart; Kate Hesseldenz, Curator & Development Assistant, Liberty Hall Historic Site, Frankfort, Kentucky. I would also like to thank Christiane Odyniec and Laura Taylor, editors of the NAWCC for skilled and decisive direction of this project, Keith Lehman for the expert layout and design, and Gillian Radel for punctilious editorial assistance especially with the reference section, which was itself a gargantuan task. A special thanks to my very patient wife and daughters.

Introduction

For centuries America has been a haven for the Irish. Survival was certainly the motive for the masses from Ireland to seek sanctuary across the Atlantic. The Great Famine pushed droves of poor, if not derelict, immigrants across the water in the middle of the 19th century. Many left for other reasons, however, including avoidance of religious persecution or under political pressure for revolutionary activity. Crime, social instability, wanderlust, or just greater opportunity were other motives. Although the immigrant from Ireland is most often depicted as impoverished, this image derives from the destitute and hunger stricken of the mid-1800s. Until about 1835, however, the Irish immigrant was often one of modest means but at least self-sufficient.[1]

Many craftsmen arrived in the 18th and early 19th centuries to the growing cities of the East. While Boston, New York, and Philadelphia are well-known destinations, other towns such as Annapolis, Baltimore, and Charleston also found favor. The craftsmen were of different types: cabinet makers, carpenters, jewelers, as well as silver and goldsmiths. There were also clock and watch makers. There are some works, such as *Six Quaker Clockmakers*, documenting the Irish origins of some clock makers but most information about these craftsmen who came to America is widely and sparsely scattered.[2-8]

The aim of this book was to identify clock and watch makers from Ireland and, where possible, to document their biographical details and their artifacts. A perfect craftsman for inclusion would have been a well-documented maker from Ireland, apprenticed there, who came to America and left a marked and original stamp on a clock, dial, or case design, and of whose endeavors many images and artifacts have survived. Alas, very few fit this very demanding bill. We shall see that any characteristic features of clocks from Ireland must of necessity have been diluted, but not entirely lost, by the size of America and the relative paucity of the number of makers from Ireland. We shall also see that collaboration with other, non-Irish, makers produced hybrid cross-cultural works with varied features sometimes resulting in characteristic contributions to an early American style.

Identification of these craftsmen in America has been described as a "maddeningly elusive task."[9] This is at least partly because of the non-Gaelic names of many. They often had a Scottish, English, or Welsh background and even occasional French or German names are to be found. This was because in the early days of the watch- and clock-making industry, native Irish Catholics were excluded from learning trades; under ordinances in 1652–53, only Protestants were admitted to guilds and apprenticeships in the city of Dublin while the majority Catholic population were referred to as "Irish Papists" and "enemies."[10] In 1699, "....several Papists have been imployed in the citty....to the great scandall of poor Protestants, who might get a livelyhood......"[10] Thereafter, for failure to take the oath of allegiance or even to employ a Catholic apprentice, the punishment was severe and could result in loss of freedom of the city[10] and the ability to make a living. This practice was alive and well not just in Dublin but also in Ulster many years later (see the *Belfast Newsletter* advertisement by John McCabe for 1769).

For this book, material was gathered from a number of sources. Published lists of names were used[2, 5-8] to identify makers in Ireland. These included material gathered by the late Messrs Wilfred Seaby and William Stuart.[5,6] Seaby's notes were deposited by him in the Belfast Museum and were kindly made available for the purpose of this study. These were cross-referenced with various American sources, particularly *American Clockmakers and Watchmakers* by the Spittlers and Chris Bailey[4] and other works.[11-17] In many cases, when the name of a clock maker was found in Irish and American sources, an Irish date preceding an American date was taken as evidence of a move to America. Most of the traffic was into America and only rarely was in the opposite direction. Other sources consulted included newspaper advertisements, notices of deaths or marriages, court records, and city directories all of which contributed substantially to biographical detail. The author had the most serendipitous good fortune to have the facilities of the Frank L. Horton Center for Research in the Museum of Early Southern Decorative Arts (MESDA) at his disposal in Winston-Salem, NC. A massive amount of work had already been done in this extraordinary organization combing many early American newspapers and directories and cross referencing occupations, locations, and origins of craftspeople. Biographic details were also found in published nonhorological sources as many watch and clock makers were also involved in the manufacturing and/or selling of silverware.[18-21]

More recently, electronic sources were accessed. The influence of this form of investigation on access and gathering of information has already been profound but is still an infant technology. Street directories, census records, birth and death records, newspapers, travel records, and more, are now readily available at the push of a button. This author believes, however, that great care must still be used as electronic searches may fail to identify specific individuals for a variety of reasons ranging from image clarity of scans to variations in spelling of names and contemporary abbreviations (e.g., wtchmkr, watchmaker, watch maker).

The historian E. Milby Burton, writing of the craftsmen of South Carolina in 1942, could have known nothing of the Internet and the allied electronic resources that have burgeoned in the last few years. Despite these great advances, his comments are still prescient and applicable: "names … are not easy to recover. No doubt a great number … will be overlooked … any … could almost be spoken of as itinerant … Since they did not stay long … in one place … the modern investigator can have little hope of identifying them all …"[22] On the bright side, of one particular maker, John McKee of County Down who moved to South Carolina, he wrote: "… practically nothing has been found about McKee … "[22] Now, however, we have a biography and many records of his clocks and other artifacts.

The current work has uncovered the identities of others who found their way from Ireland to America revealing some of the detail and color of their lives in their New World. The range of experiences was very wide from accumulation of fabulous wealth to ruin and even the debtors' prison. There were early deaths due to the scourges of infectious diseases so prevalent in the 18th and 19th centuries and there were long and healthy lives. Their personalities were anything but dull and, in their midst, you will find rebels, robbers, revolutionaries, and rogues. There were cantankerous wiseacres unashamed to decry their competitors in public as well as an occasional bigamist and toper thrown in for good measure. The author hopes this work has provided a narrative framework of their lives, illustrating their place in a new environment, and that it will also serve as a reference point for others working in the fields of horology and allied trades.

Chapter One
Pennsylvania and Delaware

INTRODUCTION

The influence of the Irish on Pennsylvania has been aptly described as "deep, pervasive and lasting." Since the connections between Ireland and this state stretch back to the 17th century,[23] it is appropriate that our story should begin here. Some of the earliest names in American clock-making are to be found in Pennsylvania to where many craftsmen went to avail of the freedom of religion.

Born on October 14, 1644, to Anglican parents, William Penn was expelled from Oxford and studied law at Lincoln's Inn. His father had estates in Ireland, which William managed. He was converted to Quakerism in Cork by the minister of Oxford, Thomas Loe.[24] In financial difficulties, he called in a debt owed to his father by Charles II, which was repaid by a grant of land. Thus, on March 4, 1681 he obtained the charter for Pennsylvania. His "Concessions and Agreements" argued that "no men. . . hath power or authority to rule over men's consciences in religious matters," ensuring many Europeans persecuted for their faith would flock there.

IRISH QUAKERS

So it was with the Quakers and other non-conformist Protestants from Ireland often imprisoned for failure to pay tithes and other dues. Irish Quakers came mostly from the provinces of Leinster in the east and Ulster in the north, but some also came from the southern province of Munster arriving in considerable numbers between 1680 and 1750. As well as religious freedom offered by the new state, they could also enjoy greater economic opportunity. Penn died in 1718 marking the end of a period of emigration of many early Quakers from Ireland but the influx of the Irish continued long after for many other reasons as we shall see.

If only for historical reasons, therefore, it is worth mentioning the Chandlees and another group of clock makers, the Jacksons, two well-known Quaker families in the history of American clock-making.

THE CHANDLEES

This family is well documented in *Chester County Clocks and their Makers* by Arthur E. James.[25] Benjamin Chandlee was born in 1685 in Kilmore, County Kildare. He arrived in Philadelphia in 1702, almost 150 years before the Great Famine. He moved to Nottingham, MD, in 1712[4] and was apprenticed to the Englishman Abel Cottey, whose daughter Sarah he married. He moved to Chester County, Pennsylvania and, in 1741, to Delaware where he died about four years later.[24, 26] His business was continued by his sons Benjamin Jr, Ellis, and Isaac.[27] During a 30-year career, he made some 40 clocks.[25] Often in a simple Quaker style, some are more ornate like this one of walnut with highly decorated spandrels (Figures 1 and 2).

Figure 1. Long case clock by Benjamin Chandlee, Jr., 1755–75 of Nottingham, PA. Wood types: walnut, and tulip poplar. Museum purchase with funds provided by the Henry Francis du Pont Collectors Circle, 2003.32. Images Courtesy, Winterthur Museum, Delaware.

THE JACKSONS

Anthony Jackson emigrated to Ireland from Lancashire in 1649,[25] settling in Lurgan, Co Armagh. He was an early convert to Quakerism in Ireland and, in 1654, he became a member of the first Friends Meeting to be established there.[25] He moved to nearby County Cavan in 1655 but, like many Quakers in Ireland at the time, was persecuted for nonpayment of tithes.[28] His son, Isaac, born in 1665, lived in County Meath and emigrated to Delaware in 1725.[25] There he seems mainly to have been occupied as a weaver[25] as were many of the Quakers who left Ireland.[28] He later moved to Chester County, Pennsylvania. His grandson Isaac, was born in 1734 and may have learned the clock-making trade from Benjamin Chandlee[25] or John Jackson of Marlboro, who was his cousin.[29]

Many of his long case clocks have survived which, predictably, show Quaker features of simplicity in design and rudimentary, if any,

Figure 2. Detail of the dial of the clock of Benjamin Chandlee. The spandrels are highly decorated and the central boss in the arch reads, "B Chandlee Nottingham."

4 passing time across the water

decoration. The composite brass dial clock shown here (Figure 3), which was originally in a Quaker style case has applied mid–18th-century spandrels and a silvered chapter ring.

Other Chester County clock makers by the name of Jackson can also claim Irish descent, including John, Isaac's first cousin, and the later George, born before 1778, whose grandfather was also born in Ireland in 1703.[25]

Jackson was not simply a clock maker but had other skills as a craftsman. In addition to clocks he was also a watch maker, silversmith, pewterer and brass caster. A snuffbox of his has also survived with masonic symbols (Figure 4).

Philadelphia

Although the Chandlees and Jacksons were early arrivals from Ireland, they learned their trade in America. Later tradesmen would bring these skills with them. Philadelphia was certainly a popular destination (Figure 5). Indeed, by about 1850, 80-90% of Pennsylvania immigrants from Ireland were to be found there.[1] Many were tailors, boot and shoemakers, bricklayers, or painters.[1] A good living could be made by a journeyman and many cities had a book of prices that had established pay rates toward the end of the 18th century. Retail prices were about 3.5 times the price of labor and a cabinet maker was paid about a dollar per hour for an 11 hour day.[30] Making a clock case took about eight days.[30]

Figure 3. Clock dial by Isaac Jackson the boss engraved with, "Is Jackson, Newgarden." Several such clocks are known from there and London Grove, PA. He also made one-handed and 30-hour clocks uncommon in America[25] and often engraved "Time passeth swiftly away" on the spandrels.

Figure 4. Inscribed "I. Jackson," this snuffbox is engraved with illustrations of Masonic symbols including the eye, a symbol of the Supreme Being and eternal watchfulness, and the swords, the symbols of Justice.

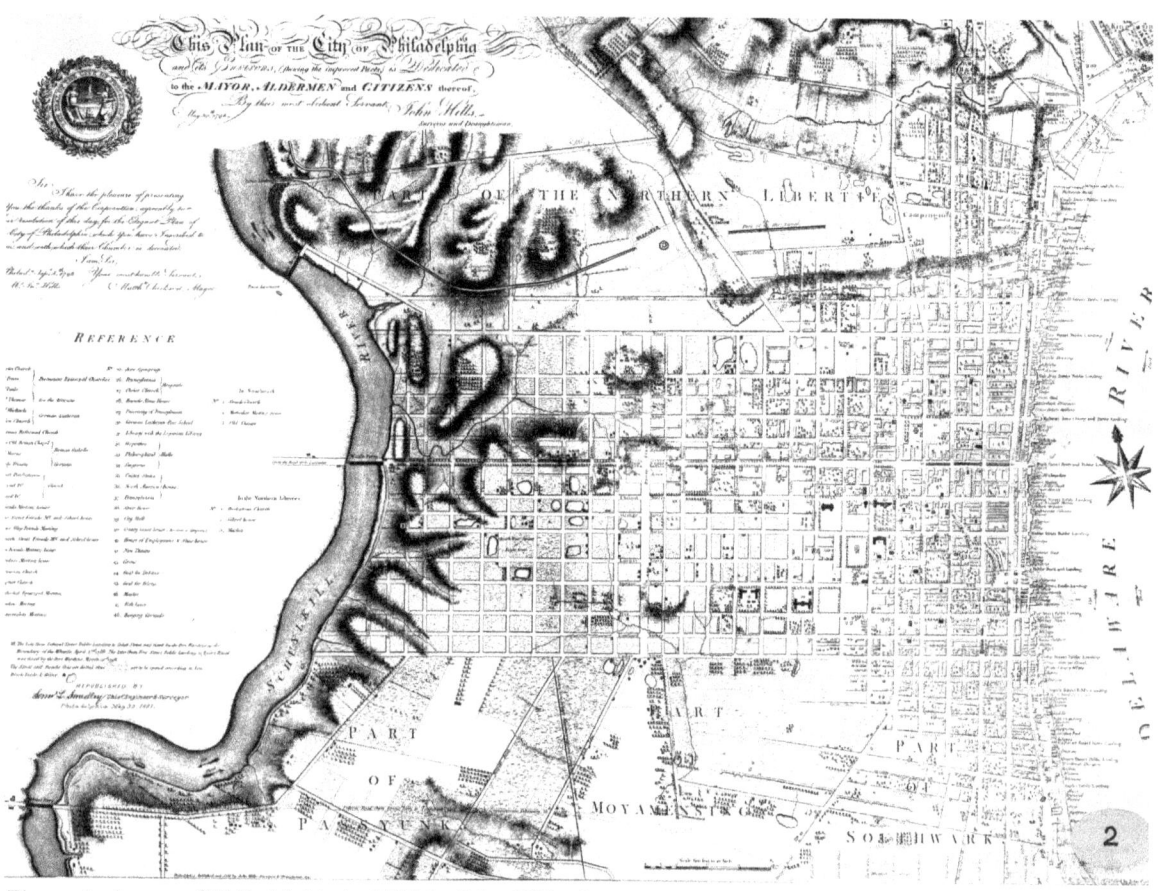

Figure 5. A map of Philadelphia in 1796 by John Hills the surveyor and draughtsman showing the grid structure of the city. Second Street is the first straight vertical street on the right side of the map and Front Street is almost parallel to its right.

PHILIP SYNG

Philip Syng Jr. was born in Cork in 1703, the son of Philip Syng and Abigail Murdock (Figure 6). His father was active as goldsmith in Cork in 1712[31] but emigrated with his wife and three children, arriving in Philadelphia in 1714. They stayed there for several years before moving to Annapolis, MD. Philip Senior died in 1739.

Presumably Philip Junior had learned his trade as a silversmith from his father. He moved to Philadelphia, probably around 1726. He was a member of the first Masonic Lodge in America, which was constituted there in 1727.[32] The many other institutions with which he was associated include the American Philosophical Society and The Public Academy, later to become The University of Pennsylvania (Figure 7). He became an intimate associate of Benjamin Franklin and, being interested in the sciences, participated in Franklin's electrical experiments.[33] Philip Syng had 18 children including a daughter Abigail, who married Edward Physick.

Front Street

Philip Junior was in business in Front Street[34] for many years, retiring in September 1772 when Richard Humphreys became his successor. The notice in the *Pennsylvania Gazette*, September 23, 1772[35] read: "...Having taken the house in which Philip Syng, lately dwelt, hereby

Figure 6. Philip Syng Jr. silversmith, goldsmith, and watch maker. Image courtesy Historical Society of Pennsylvania.

informs his friends and the public, that he now carries on the Goldsmith's Business in all its branches at the aforesaid place, a few doors below the Coffee house, where he has for sale, a neat and general assortment of Gold and Silver Ware..." Syng's endorsement of his successor was generous: "The subscriber having lately removed into Upper Merion township, hereby informs his friends and former customers, that they may be supplied as usual, at his late dwelling, by the above-named Richard Humphreys, whom he hereby recommends to them, as a person qualified to serve them on the best terms, and whose fidelity in the above business will engage their future confidence and regard. —Philip Syng."

Writing Paraphernalia

Although described as a watch maker,[4, 6, 36] how many watches he made is unknown. His father was a goldsmith in Cork, not a watch maker,[31, 37] and the entry in the Philadelphia Directory is for a silversmith. In *The Cost of Old Silver*[34] and *American Silversmiths*[35] he is a "silversmith" (see also Figure 8). Perhaps his best known piece (Figure 9) was the writing paraphernalia used to sign the Declaration of Independence.[38] Many items have survived but in an exhibition of Philadelphia Silverware in 1956, with what was described as an "outstanding collection" of over 50 items of his work, there were no watches or watch cases.[39] He died in 1789.[34, 36]

LAURENCE BIRNIE

Laurence Birnie's grandfather, John Birnie, died in 1763 or before, and was survived by four sons William, John, Alexander, and Samuel.[40] The eldest brother, William, Laurence's father, also made clocks and worked in Templepatrick, in the most northeasterly county of Antrim, in Ireland, from the middle of the 18th century. Laurence served his apprenticeship with William in Templepatrick and then established his own business (Figure 10) in Ballymoney about 20 miles to the north in 1767.[41] He moved to Dublin and England shortly after, appearing in Philadelphia in 1774,[42] where he opened shop on Arch Street around October 1774[27, 42] (Figure 11) but moved to Second Street a year later.[27, 43]

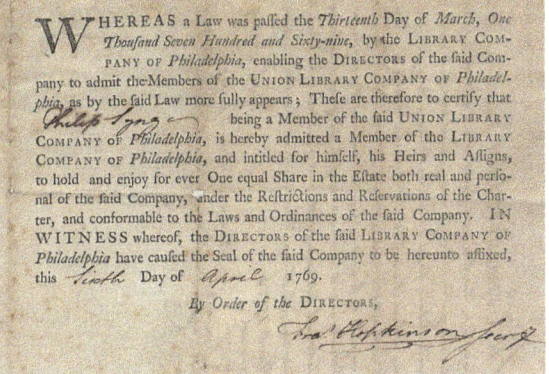

Figure 7. Syng's membership to the Library Company of Philadelphia founded by Franklin in 1731. Syng designed the Company seal. The Union Library, founded in 1746, merged with the Library Company in 1769. He later sold his interest to his son-in-law Edward Physick. Edward's son, Philip Syng Physick, Professor at the University of Pennsylvania, is sometimes called the Father of American Surgery.

Philadelphia, May 5. 1748.

RUn away, laſt Thurſday, from Philip Syng, of this city, ſilverſmith, a Negroe man, named Cato, about 20 years old, a ſhort, well-ſet fellow, and ſpeaks good Engliſh ! Had on when he went away two jackets, the uppermoſt a dark blue halfthick, lined with red flannel, the other a light blue homeſpun flannel, without lining, ozenbrigs ſhirt, old leather breeches, yarn ſtockings, old ſhoes, and an old beaver hat. When he went away he had irons on his legs, and about his neck; but probably has cut them off, as he has done ſeveral times before on the like occaſion ; he generally ſkulks about this City. Whoever brings him home, ſhall have *Twenty Shillings* reward, and reaſonable charges. paid by PHILIP SYNG.

Figure 8. Philip Syng seeks the return of his "negroe" (sic) Cato in the Pennsylvania Gazette for May 1748.[545] Many of the Founding Fathers were influenced by the Romans of whom Marcus Porcius Cato (95 BC–46 BC) was one. Note that here Syng is styled a silversmith and not a watch maker.

Figure 9. The Declaration of Independence and the Constitution of the United States were signed using this inkstand and writing paraphernalia by Syng. Picture by RD Smith via http://commons.wikimedia.org/wiki/File:Syng_inkstand.jpg.

He both made, and repaired, repeating and horizontal watches in gold and silver.[42] In 1775, he sought a journeyman[27] and was still at Second Street nearly three years later.[27,44]

He was a willing participant in the American Revolutionary War and his talents, which extended well beyond clock-making to construction and engineering, were put to good use. He petitioned for,[45] (Figure 12) and was advanced, £300 by the Committee of Safety in 1776 to erect an air furnace and mill. This was located in Hummelstown[14] and cut files for a gun factory.[36]

In the same year, he was the captain of a company of the Philadelphia militia. The distinguished American artist Charles Willson Peale saw his first active service as Birnie's lieutenant. Peale was also a watch and clock repairer and painted a miniature of Birnie in December 1776. Unfortunately, the location of this is unknown.

Birnie was unwell at this time and apparently took no active part in the campaign to cross the Delaware River. This duty fell to Peale, who assumed the captaincy from him.[46] On April 17, 1777, the Pennsylvania War Office in Philadelphia appointed Birnie as a member of a Committee to oversee the removal of provisions and stores from Philadelphia that might be useful "to our enemies" (i.e., the British).[47] Although it

LAURENCE BIRNIE, who ſerved his Time with his Father William Birnie, of Templepatrick, Watch-maker, hath now ſet up in Ballymoney, where he reſolves to carry on the Buſineſs of making and repairing Watches in the beſt Manner, and at the moſt reaſonable Prices, ſo as to give Satisfaction to Gentlemen and Ladies who pleaſe to employ him; not only in the neat and elegant Appearance of the Work, but, as he was always taught; to take faithful Care in the Performance thereof.

Ballymoney, 10th Auguſt, 1767.

Figure 10. Laurence Birnie establishes business in Ballymoney as advertised in the Belfast Newsletter for August 1767.

LAWRENCE BIRNIE, WATCH and CLOCK MAKER, from the city of Dublin,

BEGS leave to acquaint his friends, and the Public in general, that he ſerved a regular apprenticeſhip to his father William Birnie, late of Temple Patrick, and afterwards experienced a conſiderable ſhare of knowledge with ſome of the moſt eminent Watchmakers in England and Ireland; and as he has opened a ſhop at his lodgings in the houſe of Mrs. Fauces, in Arch-Street, near Second Street, where he intends carrying on ſaid buſineſs in all its various branches, particularly making and repairing all ſorts of repeating, horizontal and plain gold and ſilver Watches, he therefore flatters himſelf (from his care and cloſe application to buſineſs) to meet with the encouragement of the Public; and at all times he will be particular in trying his accounts out to merit their eſteem and a continuance of their favour.

Figure 11. Now in the New World, Birnie announces his appearance in Arch Street in The Pennsylvania Packet for October 3, 1774.

THE PETITION OF LAURENCE BIRNIE, 1776.

To the Honorable Committee of Safety.

Humbly Sheweth,

That your Petitioner being Master of the business of Filecutting, a branch much wanted and absolutely necessary for the carrying on with success, the important and usefull manufactory of Gunlocks as well as all other branches in Iron work, &c.

The necessity of this work being done, has induced those whome your honors has imployed to oversee the Gunlock factory to make application to me on this head. From a willingness to serve this Country as well in Particular as the Grand cause for which I have alredy associated induces me to offer the following proposals for your Consideration.

First, That your Honors will advance the sum of £300 for the erecting an air furnace, mills, &c., for this purpose.

Secondly. That your petitioner will ingage in 18 months to Return the said sum in files manufactured at the said works: or in cash if required.

That your Petitioner's endeavours shall not be wanting to carry this usefull branch into execution, with the utmost dispatch and alacrity if properly encoraged by this Honorable Committee, and your Petitioner as in duty bound will ever Pray, &c.

LAUR. BIRNIE.*

Figure 12. Laurence Birnie's petition to the Pennsylvania Committee for Safety for funding a factory.

LAWRENCE BIRNIE, of Ballyclover, in the County of Antrim, ever willing, as far as in his Power, to give his Creditors that Satisfaction which Justice requires of him, proposes attending at the following Places on the following Days, and lay a State of his Affairs before them, when he expects to point out a Mode of Payment, which he hopes will meet with their Approbation,

At Belfast, on Tuesday 12th June inst.

At Antrim, on Thursday 14th June inst.

At Ballymena, on Saturday 16th June instant.

Ballyclover, 5th June, 1780.

Figure 13. From the Belfast Newsletter, September 1780.

has been said that he may have changed sides and have taken refuge behind British lines,[46] he was still at Second Street in February 1778.[27]

He returned to Antrim around this time, seriously indebted and his farm at Ballyclover was offered for sale in Belfast.[48] In order to find a way to clear his debts, he appeared in Belfast, Antrim, and Ballymena in June 1780[49] (Figure 13). Subsequently, he and his wife left their property in the hands of trustees in 1780 to settle his finances. It is said that he returned to Philadelphia and advertised in the *Pennsylvania Evening Herald* on February 5, 1785.[14] This may be erroneous as he is not listed in the Philadelphia directories for that[50, 51] or for the following years.[52-68]

Fusee

A verge fusee watch with the low serial number of 38 has survived from his Philadelphia period (Figures 14 and 15). It has late 18th-century features including beetle and poker hands, Roman numerals with an Arabic minute track, scroll work, a grotesque mask on the balance cock, and a Tompion regulator. Whether the movement was made, or only finished, by Birnie is unclear and it is also unknown if it was made in Philadelphia or was brought with him from Dublin or England.

A number of his long case clocks have survived. One, from 1778,[69] gives a fascinating insight into the interactions between different ethnic groups in the world of Philadelphia crafts in general, and clock-making in particular, at the time (Figures 16 and 17). The brass dial, silvered in the center, is signed, "Lawrence Birnie, Philadelphia." The movement is signed, "G Owen" below which is the number four. This may have been the fourth clock made by Griffith Owen, an apprentice of Jacob Godshalk, another Philadelphia clock maker.[69] This suggests that Birnie may have received additional movements from Godshalk or others. Godshalk was probably trained by a German, and his movements show German characteristics.[69] Another clock by him descended through the Van Wagenen family of New York.[70] Standing 8'6" high, it is 17½" wide and 9" deep (Figure 18). The primary wood is mahogany and the secondary wood is poplar. There is a swan-neck pediment with dentils and a single central finial. Blind fretwork is seen below the pediment and above the door. Fluted columns flank the hood door, there are quarter columns in the trunk, and there is a raised panel in the base. The clock stands on ogee feet. The arched white dial has a rolling moon. Hours are indicated by Roman numerals while Arabic numbers illustrate the minutes at intervals of five.

It has been suggested that Birnie may have focused on watch-making, rather than clock-making. His advertisement in 1775, however, specifically stated that he intended "making........eight-day, spring, chime and repeating clocks."[27] Surviving watches such as the one above, and clocks, are, unfortunately, rare.

JOHN RILEY

A John Reily (also Riley) is noted in the *Philadelphia Directories* from 1785 to 1814.[71] Conceivably, he might be the same as John Reilly recorded in the Passenger and Immigration Lists Index as arriving in Philadelphia in 1773[72] the year in which John Riley watch and clock maker is noted.[4] He sought an apprentice in 1783[73] (Figure 19) and worked between 1785 and 1813 as a repairer of equation clocks and clocks of unusual construction.[38] Located at Second (Figure 20) between Market and Chesnut Streets (sic), he was listed as a clock and watch maker in 1785[50] but by 1805 had branched out into the bottling business.[63]

Wine and liquor

By 1811, his premises at 11 South Second Street had become a liquor store[74] later adding wine.[75] Watch-making is not mentioned and wine and liquor may have been more lucrative than clocks and watches. By 1816, Mr. Riley had gone.[65] There may have been three (or even four) makers of this name in Dublin of whom two

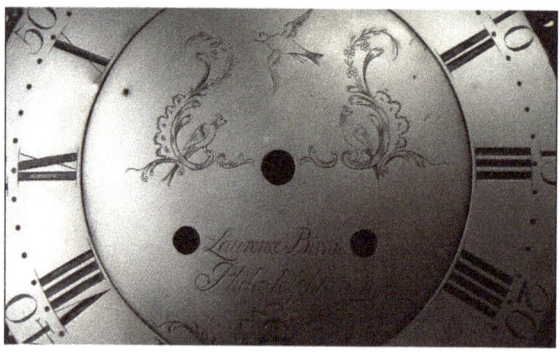

Figures 14-17. Several items of horological interest relating to Laurence Birnie. Figures 14 and 15 above: a verge fusee watch with the low serial number of 38 the signature "Laur. Birnie Philad." Contemporary features include beetle and poker hands, Roman numerals with an Arabic minute track and a Tompion regulator. Figures 16 and 17 below: the dial and movement of a Birnie clock made in conjunction with Griffith Owen himself an apprentice of Jacob Godshalk a Philadelphia clock maker of German extraction. Photographs for Figures 14 and 15 very kind courtesy John N. Tkachuk, New York. Photographs for Figures 16 and 17 very kind courtesy of John Spencer.

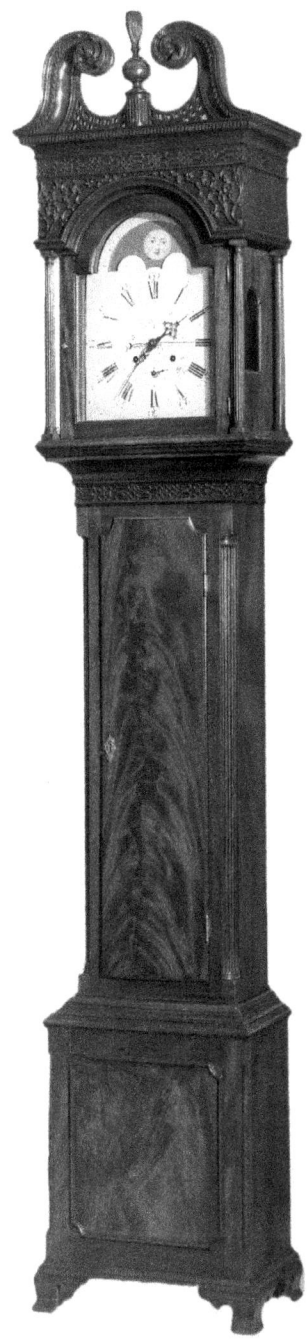

Figure 18. *The long case clock that descended through the Van Wagenen family of New York.*[70] *Photograph courtesy of Bernard & S. Dean Levy, Inc., New York.*

Came in the laſt VESSELS from LONDON, and to be SOLD by

John Riley,

Clock and Watchmaker,

Seven doors below Market-ſtreet, on the eaſt ſide of Second ſtreet,

A neat ASSORTMENT of

Capped and plain Silver Watches,

with a Variety of Chains, Seals, Keys, &c.

Likewiſe ſecond-hand Gold and Silver WATCHES.

CLOCKS and WATCHES repaired, as uſual.

, A ſmart active BOY, who can be well recommended, will be taken as an Apprentice.

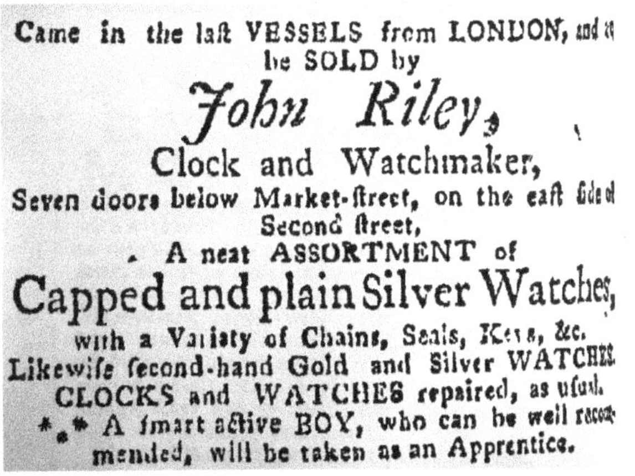

Figure 19. Located below Market on the East side of Second, business looked auspicious for Riley as evidenced by his desire for an apprentice. He stayed at this address for many years before undertaking a new enterprise.[73]

John Riley,

Clock & Watchmaker, ſeven doors below the Market, on the eaſt ſide of Second-ſtreet, has for Sale,

MOON clocks, plain arch month and thirty hour ditto with and without mahogany caſes, a variety of ſilver watches warranted good; with a quantity of watch tools and materials, ſuch as chryſtals, blow pipes, large and ſmall framed ſaws, adjuſting tools, tail vices, callappers with and without bars, ſcrew drivers, ſmall hammers, ſcrew plates, bench vices, cutting nippers, ſcrew keys, pendants, ſcrew wheels, magnifying glaſſes of different kinds, watch ſcrews, fuzes chains, motion wheels, cannon pinions, chains, ſeals, ſtrings, keys and trinkets; likewiſe, a ſmall invoice of jewellery, &c. &c. 3tf.

N. B. Clocks and watches repaired as uſual.

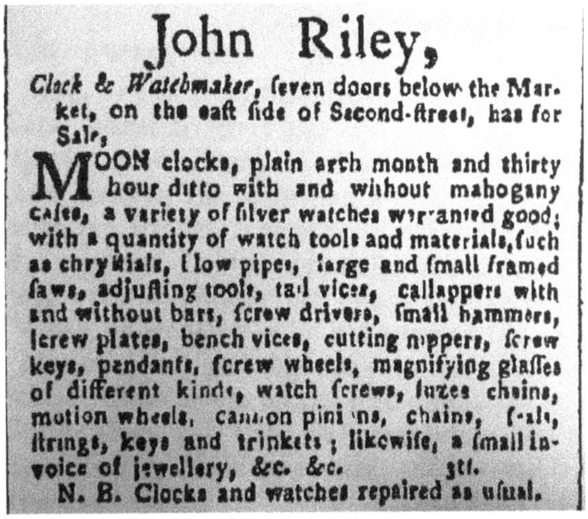

Figure 20. An advertisement from the Pennsylvania Packet and General Advertiser for May 15, 1784 shows the range of goods for sale. Mr. Riley was not only a retailer of clocks and watches but also a supplier of tools to the trade.[547]

found new homes in Pennsylvania and Virginia (see later). The variant spellings make it difficult to trace makers of this name: Reilly, Reily, Riley, Rielly. The maker Reiley and Co. is also known from Kentucky.[71]

ANDREW CALDERWOOD

Chilling circumstances were sometimes a cause for tradesmen to quit their Irish homeland in the 18th century. "We the Subscribers hereof, Inhabitants of the Town and Parish of Ballymoney, in the County of Antrim, have ... with .. Indignation considered the unhappy Tendency of...the most horrid Murders, Robberies, burning of Houses.... We do hereby pledge ....at the Risque .. of our Lives, ... in the due Execution of the Laws, by arming ourselves and repelling Force by Force, ... to re-establish Peace, Safety, and good Order" (Figure 21). Published in *The Belfast Newsletter* on April 7, 1772, one of the signatories to this notice was Andrew Calderwood.[76] In Stewartstown from about 1780,[5] he appeared in the *Philadelphia Directory* at 22 Strawberry Alley in 1800.[59] He stayed until around 1809, when he is found on the Germantown Road.[64] There was also a nearby William Calderwood, who was a gunsmith. He may possibly been a relative, who had gone by 1819.[67] Andrew remained at least until 1820[68] or 1822.[4] He is known to have made brass dial clocks.[5]

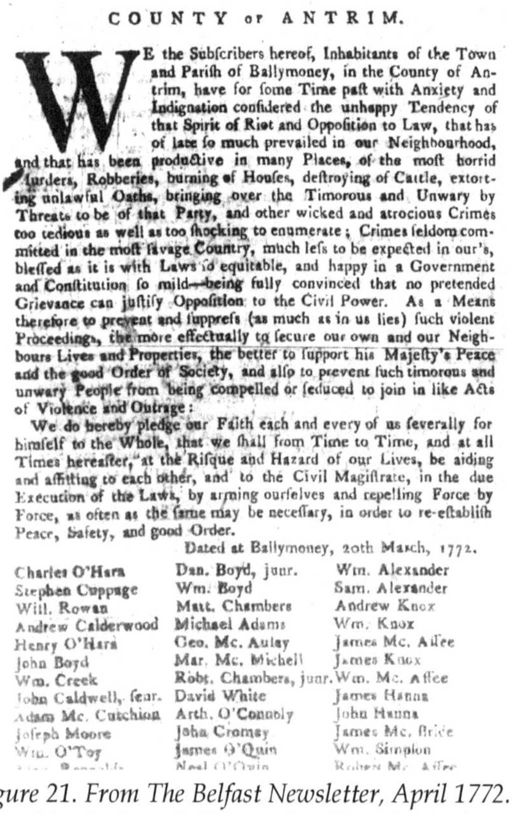
COUNTY OF ANTRIM.

WE the Subſcribers hereof, Inhabitants of the Town and Pariſh of Ballymoney, in the County of Antrim, have for ſome Time paſt with Anxiety and Indignation conſidered the unhappy Tendency of that Spirit of Riot and Oppoſition to Law, that has of late ſo much prevailed in our Neighbourhood, and that has been productive in many Places, of the moſt horrid Murders, Robberies, burning of Houſes, deſtroying of Cattle, extorting unlawful Oaths, bringing over the Timorous and Unwary by Threats to be of that Party, and other wicked and atrocious Crimes too tedious as well as too ſhocking to enumerate; Crimes ſeldom committed in the moſt ſavage Country, much leſs to be expected in our's, bleſſed as it is with Laws ſo equitable, and happy in a Government and Conſtitution ſo mild—being fully convinced that no pretended Grievance can juſtify Oppoſition to the Civil Power. As a Means therefore to prevent and ſuppreſs (as much as in us lies) ſuch violent Proceedings, the more effectually to ſecure our own and our Neighbours Lives and Properties, the better to ſupport his Majeſty's Peace and the good Order of Society, and alſo to prevent ſuch timorous and unwary People from being compelled or ſeduced to join in like Acts of Violence and Outrage:

We do hereby pledge our Faith each and every of us ſeverally for himſelf to the Whole, that we ſhall from Time to Time, and at all Times hereafter, at the Riſque and Hazard of our Lives, be aiding and aſſiſting to each other, and to the Civil Magiſtrate, in the due Execution of the Laws, by arming ourſelves and repelling Force by Force, as often as the ſame may be neceſſary, in order to re-eſtabliſh Peace, Safety, and good Order.

Dated at Ballymoney, 20th March, 1772.

Charles O'Hara	Dan. Boyd, junr.	Wm. Alexander
Stephen Cuppage	Wm. Boyd	Sam. Alexander
Will. Rowan	Matt. Chambers	Andrew Knox
Andrew Calderwood	Michael Adams	Wm. Knox
Henry O'Hara	Geo. Mc. Aulay	James Mc. Affee
John Boyd	Mar. Mc. Michell	James Knox
Wm. Creek	Robt. Chambers, junr.	Wm. Mc. Affee
John Caldwell, ſenr.	David White	James Hanna
Adam Mc. Cutchion	Arth. O'Connoly	John Hanna
Joſeph Moore	John Cromey	James Mc. Bride
Wm. O'Toy	James O'Quin	Wm. Simpſon
[illegible]	Neal O'Quin	Robert Mc. Affee

Figure 21. From The Belfast Newsletter, April 1772. Signed by Andrew Calderwood and hundreds of others willing to form a local militia for "....Peace, Safety, and good Order."

UNITED IRISHMEN

Apart from crime in his native Ulster, Calderwood may have had an even more compelling personal reason to leave Ireland. He was one of the United Irishmen, the revolutionaries conspiring to take up arms against the British whose seat of power in Ireland was Dublin Castle (Figure 22). Inspired by America, there was even a "Yankee Club of Stewartstown" which, in 1784, had sent a public message of congratulations to George Washington: "Viewing with regret the oppressive scenes of misery under which our native country has long groaned without hopes of redress....we rejoiced to hear that the spirit of America had risen .... to .. royal... oppression ... and had thrown off.... the fetters that were to bind her.....".[77] Stewartstown was certainly the place for disturbances against the crown. Mr. Newton, a contemporary magistrate, noted in a letter that "the United Irishmen were determined to batter and abuse every Loyalist..."[77]

SPIES

The British had a network of spies and informers. Two, James Baxter and John Henderson, members of the Royal Irish Invalides Regiment, described Calderwood as one of the "Chiefs and leaders .... in and about Stewartstown."[77] By December 1797, the British had

Figure 22. The focus of the Revolutionaries' attention, Dublin Castle was the center of British power in Ireland in the 18th century. This scene from 1792 by James Malton shows the Great Courtyard. In the background is St Werburgh's Church, the spire of which, not surprisingly, was removed after (yet another) insurrection in 1803.[548] The clock for the church was supplied by Joseph Blundell (1703-32)[31, 481] and paid for by a usurious banker, James Southwell[549] who bequeathed on his death in 1729 "£45 for a clock and £386 for the bells."[550]

had enough of this particular United Irishman and the redoubtable watch maker was arrested and confined in Charlemont Castle[78] (Figure 23). There he remained for about four months and was released on a surety of £300 to leave Ulster.[77] Although the clampdown brought some stability to the locality, the main rebellion would still take place the following year. By this time, however, the United Irishmen had already been proscribed and their leaders hunted for several years. Indeed, many had already left for America.[79] Calderwood was not alone in Ulster clock-making circles to have been involved in this uprising. Joseph Castles or Cassels "... a watchmaker of Aughnacloy ... at Omagh Jail ....a very leading man" was another[78] as was Ambrose Moore in the records of the United Irishmen[80] and who was found at various addresses in Dublin including Skinners Row and Dame Street from 1780.[81-94] He disappeared or died after 1797. Yet another was William Orr, a watch maker from Creevery who was - wrongly - "transported" (i.e., banished) to Australia having been refused permission to go to America. After many years he found his way back to Ireland and lived to be 86 years old.[79] Others who had earlier left for America and who subsequently had become involved with the American Revolutionary movement included John McCabe and Ambrose Clarke of whom we shall hear more later. Presumably, after the rising was crushed, Mr. Calderwood was now *persona non grata*, disillusioned–or both–and left for the greener pastures of North America.

JOHN CROWLEY

John Crowley is known as a clock maker from the Philadelphia Directories from 1803 to at least 1820[71] or 1823.[4] Whence he came is not clear but the name is not rare in Ireland. There is

pennsylvania and delaware 13

Figure 23. Charlemont Castle on the Tyrone/Armagh county border where Andrew Calderwood was held for 16 weeks in December 1796, and from which he was released on surety of £300 to leave the province of Ulster for the duration of the war with France. Information from Aidan Fee.[77]

Figure 24. Horological ephemera are scarce but this business card for John Crowley at South Front Street is still extant. Trade cards were important in the 18th and 19th centuries in Europe and America. Advertising the names and locations of craftsmen, they were portable and transferable. Like watch papers, they could provide an artistic challenge. This particular specimen was engraved by W. Kneuss. The standard of art work and engraving are high although a partially-clad lady might be deemed inappropriate today for promoting watches and clocks. Image Courtesy, Winterthur Library; Digital Arts Photographic Collection.

no watch maker of this name in the Dublin city directories[91, 92, 94-105] before the appearance of this name in 1803 in Philadelphia. Nor is his name on lists for Ulster[6], Limerick[5, 106] or Cork[37] where it is quite common.

Initially, he was located at 15 Spruce Street[61] but a year later was at 134 South Front Street.[62] There were moves to 130 South Front in 1809[64] and to 132 South Front in 1817[107] where he stayed for many years. Presumably the advertisement measuring 9" high by 11.5" wide, which has survived dates from after 1817 (Figure 24). He made and repaired clocks and watches and sold keys, seals and chains as well as "jewellery."

He is occasionally referred to as Crawley[36,71] in the Philadelphia directories although beside others with the name Crowley.[68] His clocks and a will are signed Crowley.

Bracket clocks

Several bracket or shelf clocks have survived and at least one tall case clock. One mahogany clock stands about 17½" high, 12¾" wide and some 6¾" deep (Figure 25). There is a bail handle on an arched and molded top, a door with an astragal top, oval sidelights, molding at the bottom, and ogee bracket feet which are either metal or gilded. The dial is painted with Roman hour numerals and there is a strike/silent selector in the arch. It has an 8-day movement and is signed, "John Crowley, Philadelphia." This is similar to other surviving bracket clocks although one with time and strike with a moon arch dial and a subsidiary calendar dial is also known.[29]

Long case clock

A long case painted dial clock standing almost 71" high has also survived (Figure 26). The hood is adorned by a central metal finial flanked by swan necks, which lack rosettes. Similarly, the turned hood pillars are quite simple. There is some inlay to the hood and the trunk door and the trunk has chamfered edges. The paneled

Figure 25, above. Names found inside clocks by Crowley include John Pickering and EW Schurman contemporary Philadelphia clock makers. They may have been responsible for cleaning and/or repairing the clock but might have been part of a construction team. The maker of the case is unknown but it is not unlike another attributed to M. H. Heckscher mentioned in the records of Winterthur Museum. Image Courtesy, Winterthur Library; Digital Arts Photographic Collection.

Figure 26, right. A note inside this long case clock by John Crowley reads, "makers are Patton and Jones" (cf Hardin and Jones) but it is unclear what part(s) they may have made. Patton and Jones were on Market Street, from ca.1798 to 1814 and also had a large supply business.[135] Image Courtesy, Winterthur Library; Digital Arts Photographic Collection.

base is supported by French bracket feet. The dial, with Arabic numerals for both minutes and hours, is signed, "John Crowley Philadelphia." There is a subsidiary seconds dial below 12 and a calendar aperture below center. The maps in the arch are simple in outline and, unusually for an American clock, the spandrels are quite "full."

Partnership

Mr. Crowley may have formed a partnership with John Farr (1824–40) after 1825.[4] He was listed in the *Philadelphia Directory* as John Crawley in 1822[108] and as Crowley in 1823.[109] Curiously, in that year, while he was still at 132 South Front, another Crowley was listed in partnership with John Farr at 106 High Street.[109] This liaison may have been brief, as by 1828, Farr was listed alone again.[110] In 1825, John Crowley was still alone[111] but from around 1828 until at least 1833 he was in another partnership, this time as Somers and Crowley.[110, 112] They were no longer listed in 1837.[113]

JAMES MALCOLM ORR

Philadelphia continued to be journey's end for Irish clock makers until well into the 19th century. James Malcolm Orr, born in County Antrim on November 26, 1853, went there too. The following biographical details are from his family, who are expert genealogists.[114, 115] His father was Thomas Orr, a weaver who became a watch maker.

Belfast

James Orr probably learned from his father initially but moved to Belfast between 1870 and 1875 to work for two of the principal jewelers and watch makers there. He worked with William Gibson then located at 36 Castle Buildings and Donegall Place[116, 117] and also with John Pyper at Bridge and North Streets.[116, 117] In 1875, he married Jane Stewart in the Baptist Church, Shankill, Belfast. Unfortunately, Thomas died shortly thereafter from smallpox and

JAMES ORR,
PRACTICAL WATCHMAKER AND JEWELLER,
75, CHURCH STREET, BALLYMENA,
(Late of J. Pyper's, Bridge Street, and formerly of W. Gibson's, Donegall Place, Belfast).

EVERY description of English and Foreign Watches, Clocks, Jewellery, &c., carefully cleaned and repaired, at moderate charges.

A SELECT STOCK OF
WATCHES, CLOCKS, GENT'S AND LADIES' CHAINS,
FINE AND BRIGHT GOLD EAR-RINGS,
BROOCHES, PENDANTS, LOCKETS, NECKLETS, GEM RINGS,
WEDDING RINGS AND KEEPERS.

Also, a Large Assortment of the most fashionable
SILVER JEWELLERY,
AT LOWEST PRICES.

Please Note the Address:—
75, CHURCH STREET,
(Opposite Bryan-st.,) (36)

Figure 27. Watches, clocks, chains, and silver jewelry could all be had from Orr. Sadly, business closed after a few short years following personal and financial tragedies. From the Ballymena Observer.[553]

the business was listed in the name of J Orr the following year[118] as James had moved back to Ballymena immediately to take it over. James took his younger brother Samuel, then about 15 years old, under his tutelage. Business seemed to be going quite well, at least according to the *Ballymena Observer* for April 30, 1881 (Figure 27).

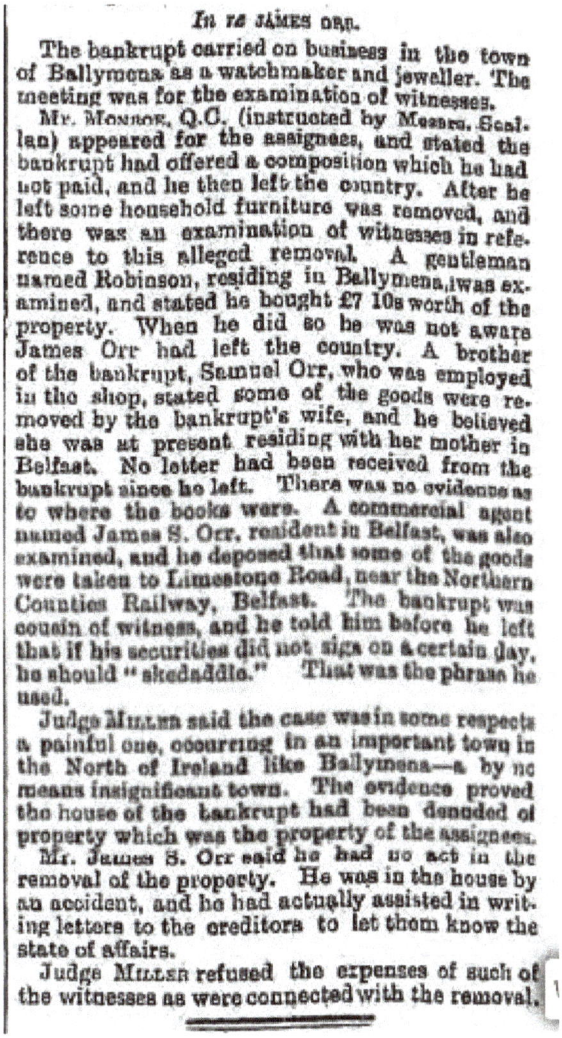

In re JAMES ORR.

The bankrupt carried on business in the town of Ballymena as a watchmaker and jeweller. The meeting was for the examination of witnesses.

Mr. Monroe, Q.C. (instructed by Messrs. Scallan) appeared for the assignees, and stated the bankrupt had offered a composition which he had not paid, and he then left the country. After he left some household furniture was removed, and there was an examination of witnesses in reference to this alleged removal. A gentleman named Robinson, residing in Ballymena, was examined, and stated he bought £7 10s worth of the property. When he did so he was not aware James Orr had left the country. A brother of the bankrupt, Samuel Orr, who was employed in the shop, stated some of the goods were removed by the bankrupt's wife, and he believed she was at present residing with her mother in Belfast. No letter had been received from the bankrupt since he left. There was no evidence as to where the books were. A commercial agent named James S. Orr, resident in Belfast, was also examined, and he deposed that some of the goods were taken to Limestone Road, near the Northern Counties Railway, Belfast. The bankrupt was cousin of witness, and he told him before he left that if his securities did not sign on a certain day, he should "skedaddle." That was the phrase he used.

Judge Miller said the case was in some respects a painful one, occurring in an important town in the North of Ireland like Ballymena—a by no means insignificant town. The evidence proved the house of the bankrupt had been denuded of property which was the property of the assignees.

Mr. James S. Orr said he had no act in the removal of the property. He was in the house by an accident, and he had actually assisted in writing letters to the creditors to let them know the state of affairs.

Judge Miller refused the expenses of such of the witnesses as were connected with the removal.

Figure 28. Details of the court case concerning the bankruptcy of James Orr. By this time Orr had left Ulster for America leaving his wife and family to follow. From the Belfast Newsletter of October 1st, 1884.[554]

Hardships

The year of 1883 was particularly bad for Jane and James as they lost three of their children to various illnesses in only six months. They moved business to Church Street, Ballymena and, although it was still listed there in 1884,[119] there followed a serious downturn in business and subsequent bankruptcy. *The Belfast News-letter* for Wednesday, October 1, 1884 published the court proceedings (Figure 28).

His cousin James S. Orr, told the court that the unfortunate watch maker said he should "skedaddle." A week later, the paper reported that his wife Jane believed her husband was in Philadelphia, but she that she not heard from him. In fact, at that point, Mr. Orr was at 3 Museum Buildings, Troy, NY.

There were industrial connections between Ballymena and Troy in the linen industry at that time so he might have had a network of support there until he could recover financially. He stayed from 1885 to 1887 and later moved to Philadelphia where he enjoyed great success. In 1889, he was at 2031 Germantown Avenue in

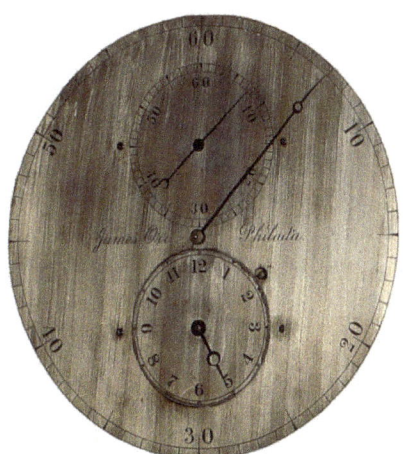

Figure 29. The silvered dial has a typical regulator layout showing minutes on the outside of the main dial with subsidiary dials for seconds above and hours below.

Philadelphia and had various later addresses. James M. Orr died in 1938 but Jane Orr was still alive aged 85 some years later.

Wall clock

A fine clock of his has come down to us (Figures 29 and 30). Dating from circa 1885, it is 94" tall and weighs approximately 165 pounds, so it should not be hung on the average domestic wall. Ruggedly built, the back plate is almost 3/4 inch thick. It is a timepiece only and runs 90 days. It has a gravity escapement, which together with its compensated pendulum ensures great accuracy. The pendulum weight and beat scale are marked, "James Orr Philadelphia." Such clocks were used where time needed to be not only precise and accurate but uniform throughout large stores, railway stations and other institutions. In such circumstances, as in this case, a master clock was connected electrically to drive other so-called slave clocks.

The case with beveled glass is of walnut and is in the Eastlake style with symmetric bas-relief carving, and lightly incised lines. In this style, moldings and other features are modest and restrained as are the curves and geometric designs. Much of the surface is flat so the whole case does not appear overworked.

Other Orr Clock Makers

The clock-making gene was transmitted through the Orr family (Figure 31). One of James and Jane's children, William Stewart Orr, was born in 1876 and had himself a pendulum-like movement across the Atlantic. When his parents left for America, he chose to stay in Ireland with his paternal grandmother. He then went to Philadelphia but returned to Ireland in 1898. He was subsequently noted on the Philadelphia census for 1900 but was back in Belfast in 1901. He later became a watch maker himself and may have learned from his uncle Samuel, James's brother. Samuel had remained in Ballymena and started his own business there. He was at Bridge Street in 1890[120] and at Church

Figure 30. The clock has a beautiful and sophisticated pendulum. It is a variant of the gridiron compensation pendulum constructed of steel and zinc. There are four bridges and five rods. The central rod is of zinc while the outer rods are of steel creating two frames. Zinc expands more than steel with rising temperature. When this happens, one frame expands downward while the zinc rod lifts the other frame to cancel out any temperature-related changes in pendulum length ensuring a constant frequency.

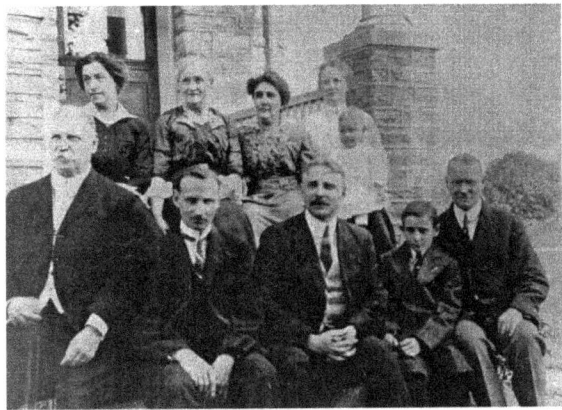

Figure 31. James Malcolm Orr and his family from left to right: Front: James Malcolm, Walter Francis, James Alexander, Arthur, Thomas Edwin; Back: Nettie, Jane Stewart Orr, Lucy, Maggie Stewart and David H. Picture very kind courtesy of David and Roger Orr.

Street until the end of the century.[121-125] He was in business at least until 1911 perhaps moving to Belfast to be with his nephew William Stewart Orr.[114] William Stewart Orr died in 1922 and Samuel in 1923 in Belfast. James Armstrong Orr, Samuel's son, also became a watch maker and extended the tradition to another generation.

MATTHEW MAHVE OR MAHER

Maher may be a relatively common name in Ireland although the names Mahva or Mahve, which are also associated with this maker,[4] are certainly not. Whatever his name and its variants, he advertised in the *Penna Journal and Weekly Advertiser* on November 19, 1761 that he was in Philadelphia on 2nd Street.

He made and repaired all sorts of watches having "wrought for some of the most iminnant (sic) watch makers of both London and Dublin."[13, 126] The estate inventory of Matthew Maher, possibly the same, then of Georgetown, SC, dated May 13, 1768, included watch makers tools, gold scales, and weights.[128] Little is known about his work.

SIX DOLLARS REWARD.

RUN away from the ſubſcriber, on Thurſday evening laſt, an indented Iriſh ſervant man, named *Charles Dogood*, about 35 years of age, 6 feet 7 inches high, a little marked with the ſmall-pox, brown h[illegible] ned [illegible]hind, talks a little on the Iriſh accent, by trade a watch maker, and lately lived a ſervant in Lancaſter, has about 10 months to ſerve; had on a light brown coat, a little tarred behind, blue waiſtcoat, black knit breeches, and black ſtockings, ſuppoſed to have ſilver buckles in his ſhoes; took with him, two white ſhirts, and ſundry other things; he is much given to drink and the company of ſoldiers. Whoever takes up and ſecures ſaid run-away, ſo that his maſter may have him again, ſhall have the above reward and reaſonable charges paid, by SAMUEL JEFFERYS, watch-maker in Second-ſtreet.

N. B. He has been uſed to the ſea, and may poſſibly offer himſelf to maſters of veſſels, who are forbid to take him off at their peril.

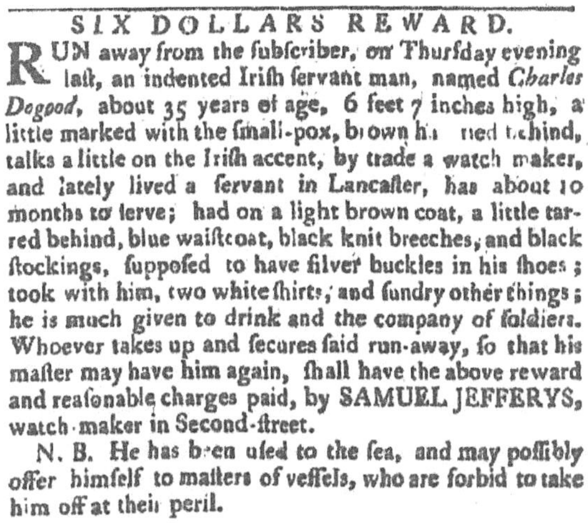

Figure 32. From The Pennsylvania Chronicle, Philadelphia for Monday, May 6, 1771 a notice similar to that from the Maryland Gazette concerning Mr Dogood.

CHARLES DOGOOD

In 1771, *The Maryland Gazette* carried the notice by Samuel Jefferys, a watch maker in Philadelphia, regarding the unfortunate-sounding Charles Dogood, who had run away. The Pennsylvania Chronicle carried a similar notice in the same year (Figure 32).

He was a servant man "....marked with the Small-Pox, a down looking fellow...round shouldered, long Visage....talks with the Irish Accent, and waddles much in his walk ... by Trade a Watchmaker."[27]

The notice calls for his return to his master; running away was a serious matter for indentured servants and apprentices and was akin to deserting but it was not uncommon for many reasons including the greater opportunities to be found elsewhere compared with the limited benefits of a servant. Dogood may also have been in Lancaster around the same time[4] but there are no records in Ireland.[129]

EDWARD McKINLEY & JAMES McELWEE

Other Irish clock makers in Pennsylvania include Edward Mackinley or McKinley.[6] From Dublin, he was at 122 High Street, Philadelphia from at least 1830[130] possibly until 1837[126, 127] but he was not in the city directory that year.[113] His date of arrival is unclear but he is not listed in the directories for 1818–20.[66-68] He is not on the apprentice lists[31] or in the Belfast directories.[131-134] By whom he was trained is unknown.

James McElwee may have been a partner with Benjamin Ferris on Front Street Philadelphia circa 1813–14[135] and may be the same as noted in Derry in 1774.[5]

HARRISBURG

GEORGE BEATTY

George Beatty, born January 4, 1781, in Ballykeel Edenagonnel, County Down[136] was the youngest son of James and Alice Ann Beatty. They emigrated to America in 1784. George's sister Nancy married Samuel Hill, an English clock maker who instructed George. The latter started business in Harrisburg, PA, in 1808 and worked there for nearly 40 years in the clock and watch business and also as a silversmith and sword mounter.

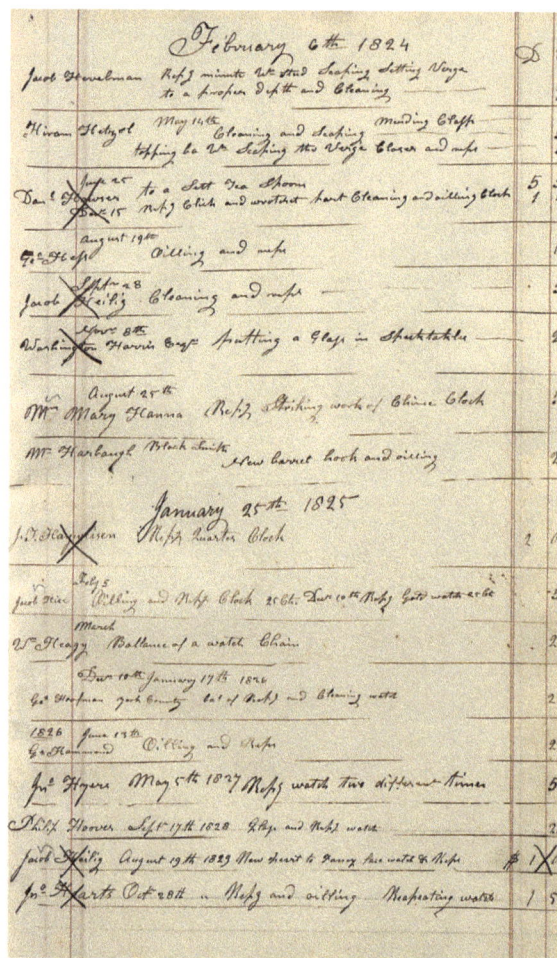

Figure 33, above. A rare glimpse into the working life of a craftsman and his fees. Most of Beatty's work consisted of repairing and cleaning watches at least during the time this book was kept (ca. 1811-1829) but there are references to an 8-day "long seconds" clock presumably a center sweep seconds hand, a wooden clock in 1815 and a 30-hour clock in 1823.

Figure 34, right. Notice in the Pennsylvania Republican, November 17, 1812 for payment of debt. Perhaps he made more from sword-mounting than clocks; the United States and Britain were again at war until the Treaty of Ghent in 1814.

Account books

His account book covering dates between 1811 and 1829 has survived (Figure 33) and gives a detailed insight to his work on timekeepers, jewelry, chains, rings, seals, and specktakles (sic). Among the more expensive items in his ledger were two 8-day clocks for $50 and $52 while English watches were available for around $18.

These prices accord well with those of Jabez Baldwin of Salem, MA, whose accounts have also survived, and of John Hoff of Pennsylvania, who likewise charged about $50 for an 8-day clock, or about £20 at the time.[137] Watches by Dublin makers for prices ranging from $16.50 to $18.50 are also recorded in Baldwin's book. The makers were John Cunningham, William Gregory and Charles Williams, the last not noted before.[129] For cleaning a watch, George Beatty charged 25–50 cents and for mending a fusee chain and repairing a click 60–70 cents.

Most of his documented work concerned repair and sale of watches and only a little clock repair. This is quite surprising, if not a little odd, as he was referred to as an "ingenious mechanician," and was noted for his clocks of "peculiar and rare invention."[138] Presumably, the ledger is not representative of all his horological endeavors. There were relatively few entries in his account book for 1812 but business may have been poor that year because of the war. In the Pennsylvania Republican (Figure 34) he urged his debtors "to make immediate payment, or the most prompt means will be taken to compel them."[14] Like other clock makers we will meet, he was also of a military disposition and he was orderly sergeant of Captain Thomas Walker's Harrisburg Volunteers.[136] Conceivably, his duties in this regard might also have been interfering with business.

Success

By 1835, his finances had improved and he had become a wealthy man, renting a house and land to one Thomas McQuaide for $210 annually. Perhaps he had a sweet tooth or was even a fruit-seller, because he reserved the right to half the apples from the trees on the property.

In another enterprise, Mr. Beatty and a certain John Heimer later formed a partnership in March 1843 in the brick-making business.[138] Heimer was responsible for digging clay and making bricks, while Beatty furnished the yards and machinery. Mr. Beatty continued successfully in business until his retirement in about 1850.

Not of a liberal disposition he wrote to the Rev. John F. Mesick of Harrisburg's Reformed Congregation:

Harrisburg: March 11, 1846

Dear Sir,

> On last Sabbath evening, 8th inst, you preached a sermon to our congregation on "The Evils of Dancing." ..... we would esteem it as a favor if you would furnish us with a copy ..... for publication ..... (so that people may) ..... learn its evil consequences, and abstain from its practice hereafter....... its use is not in character with the present ..... whatever may have ..... commended it in former days.[139]

Almost to the day 16 years later, on March 10, 1862, George Beatty died. He is buried at Harrisburg Cemetery (Figure 35).[136]

Figure 35, above. The gravestone of George Beatty in Harrisburg cemetery. Beatty married three times: to Elizabeth White, in 1815 who died at only 20 years old in 1817; to Sarah Smith Shrom, who died at the age of 32 in 1828 and lastly, in 1830, to Catharine Shrom who died August 11, 1891, in Harrisburg, PA, at age 83[551] some 30 years after Mr. Beatty.

Figure 36, above. Loan office certificates were sold by the Government to the public to fund various projects including the War of Independence. They paid a rate of interest and could also be cashed in. They were clearly not enough to satisfy Mr. Hemphill. The dispute did not hurt Murphy—he was still in Northampton many years after this appeared in the Pennsylvania Gazette on March 12, 1783. Note the currency is still the pound; Congress did not authorize the dollar until 1785 and it took several more years for the first coins to be minted. The name of Northampton was changed to Allentown in 1838.

Figure 37, right. A long case clock dated 1789 on the hood with five finials and a swan neck pediment terminating in rosettes. The hood has turned columns and side windows. Note extensive dentils on the upper trunk and fluted quarter columns.[29] Courtesy, The Winterthur Library; Digital Arts Photographic Collection

Allentown

JOHN MURPHY

John Murphy "from Ireland,"[29] was, according to the early 20th-century Pennsylvania historian Charles Roberts, the earliest clock maker in Lehigh county.[140] He was in Allentown from 1775 until at least 1790[140] being in some financial trouble in 1783 (Figure 36). A clock he made was purchased by the great-great-grandfather of Roberts in 1787 for the sum of £18.[140] He may be the same as Johannes Morphy at Allentown mentioned by Orr,[141] who also mentions John Murphy "following from vicinity of Easton, Pennsylvania."[141]

Several examples of his clocks are known, including three with walnut cases. One has five finials and a swan neck pediment terminating in rosettes (Figure 37). The hood has four turned columns and side windows. The trunk has dentils, an inlaid door, and fluted quarter columns.

There is a raised panel on the front of the base which also has fluted quarter columns and stands on ogee feet. The dial is painted, with a picture of a gentleman in the arch. The light and airy representation of flowers in the corners is in keeping with the date on the hood as is the pattern of inner Roman numerals for hours and outer Arabic numerals at five minute intervals.[29]

Two other clocks are also known, one with a brass dial and an arch boss, going 30 hours and another, a painted dial also going thirty hours and similar to the above.[29] It is interesting that Murphy was making 30-hour clocks so late in the 18th century. At this period, they must have been very rare in Ireland, or at least have not survived, as 8-day clocks were the norm.

There was, evidently, another John Murphy in Charlestown, PA, who also made a 30-hour clock circa 1790 with an enameled dial in a walnut case with quarter columns.[126]

Strasburg

THOMAS BURROWES

Thomas Burrowes was born in Killigoan, County Cavan, Ireland.[14,142] The year of his birth is disputed as either 1770 [14,142] or 1764.[143] The earlier date seems more likely; he would certainly have been young to have completed an

Figure 38. The portrait of Thomas Burrowes, by Jacob Eichholtz, who was born soon after the Declaration of 1776 in Lancaster, PA. Thomas's son, Thomas H Burrowes, entered politics "....it was only when ... the late Hon Thomas H Burrowes became ... Secretary of the Commonwealth ... that Eichholtz got his right place as painter at the "Republican Court" in Harrisburg." Shortly preceding Christmas 1836, Burrowes appears as giving him a large commission including "... separate portraits of Mr. Burrowes father, mother and uncle ...."[546] Picture very kind Courtesy LNP Media Group Inc., Lancaster, PA. The locations of the other portraits—Mrs. Burrowes and Dr. Isaac B Burrowes—are unknown to the author.

> **Thomas Burrows,**
> Watch and Clock-maker, from Dublin,
> TAKES this opportunity to acquaint his friends, and the publick, That he has Commenced Business in Market-street, Wilmington, next door to William Hemphill's store, where he hopes, by a strict attention, to merit the countenance of those ladies and gentlemen who please to honour him with their commands. All kinds of work, in his way, done on the most reasonable terms.

Figure 39. Although arrived in Delaware in 1784, this commencement of business in Market Street, Wilmington dates from 1787 - from the Delaware Courant.[145] Thomas had wanderlust, returning to Ireland, thence to Quebec, again to Ireland and, finally, settling in Lancaster County, Pennsylvania.

apprenticeship and to start his own business at only 17 years old (see below). He was the older brother of Isaac Bredin Burrowes, also a clock maker, and came to Delaware in 1784, settling in Strasburg, Lancaster County, Pennsylvania in 1787.[144] He lived at what is now West Main Street.[142] He had been educated for the Episcopal ministry in Ireland but never took holy orders.[143] He married Ann Smith from adjoining County Monaghan in 1787 and had 13 children, of whom seven survived to maturity including Thomas Henry Burrowes, the founder of the public school system in Pennsylvania.[143] A fine portrait of him by Jacob Eichholtz has survived (Figure 38).

In Business

*T*he Courant Delaware and Wilmington Advertiser announced in May[27] and July 1787[145] that he had commenced business (Figure 39). Where he learned his clock-making skills is unclear and he is not on the list of apprentices, quarter brothers or freemen in Dublin around this time.[31]

Isaac and Thomas were on the tax lists from 1797 until 1809 when Isaac was constable. In

Figure 40. Thomas Burrowes clock. Image Courtesy, The Winterthur Library; Digital Arts Photographic Collection.

1810, they returned to Ireland to take care of family affairs after the death of an uncle. They remained in Ireland for about seven years and then went to Quebec from 1817 until 1822.[143] They are not on the list of Canadian makers[146, 147] and presumably were not working as such. They returned again to Ireland[143] for a further three years and, having disposed of some property, finally settled in Lancaster County in 1825.[143] Isaac Burrowes died in 1837 and Thomas in 1839.[135]

James Spence,
Clock and Watch Maker,
BROWNSVILLE.
(Late from the City of Belfast.)

Takes this method of informing his friends and the public generally, that he has commenced the above business next door to the Rising Sun tavern, at present occupied by Mr. T. Norfolk, & formerly by Mr. Noble, & nearly opposite Messrs. Jacob's and Co's store; where he intends carrying on the same in all its various branches—he hopes by his attention & experience to give general satisfaction to those who may favour him with their custom.

Patent Lever, Horizontal, Virgule, Duplex, Vertical, Repeating, & Plain Watches, carefully repaired.

☞ All orders for clocks, thankfully received and promptly attended to.

June 5, 1816. E.83

Figure 41. James Spence was in Brownsville at least until January 1818. The town, situated on the Monongahela river about 40 miles south of Pittsburgh, was first settled in 1785 after the defeat of the Iroquois by Major General John Sullivan, a descendant of the O'Sullivan Beare clan. The terms patent lever, virgule, and duplex refer to the escapements, or regulatory mechanisms of watches that control the release of power. Repeating watches were those that could be activated to strike again at will.

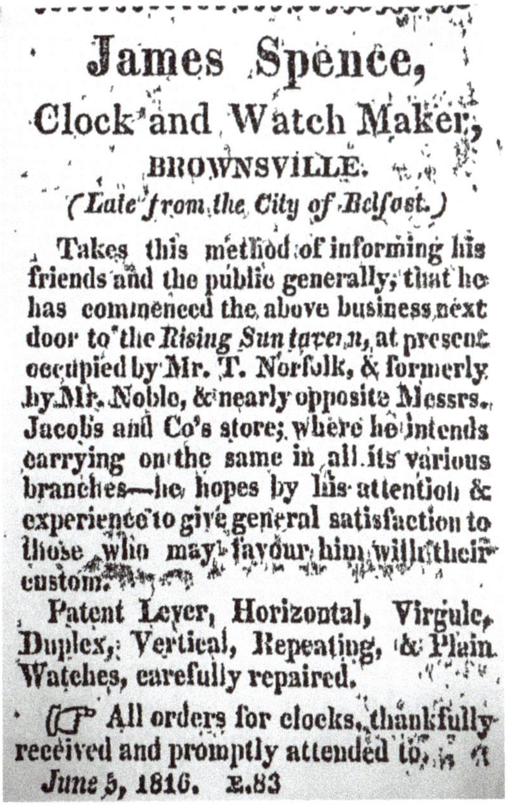

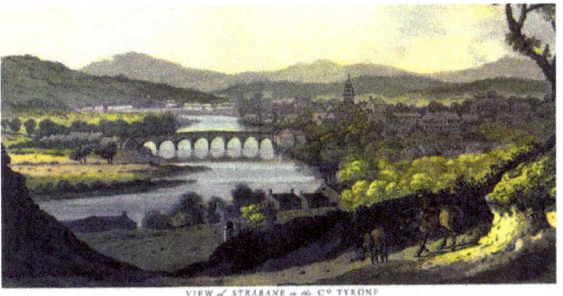

Figure 42. Strabane on the east bank of the River Foyle in the 18th century showing the bridge over the river. Today, the Foyle marks the border between the counties of Tyrone in Northern Ireland and Donegal in the Republic of Ireland. On the other side of the river is the smaller town of Lifford in County Donegal. Engraved by Jonathan Fisher. Published in the Scenery of Ireland, London, 1795 in a series of select views.

Clocks

Several of Thomas Burrowes clocks have survived usually with arched white dials and rolling moon automations. The dial styles are simple with lightly painted floral spandrels in the style of the turn of the 18th and 19th centuries and a simple, if not rudimentary, style of inscription and artwork. The numerals are Arabic for minutes and Roman for hours. One has a central calendar indicator, while others show the date on "short-mouth" apertures above six. This feature does not seem to have progressed to the advanced "full" decorations of the type seen on later British or Irish white dial clocks.[148] Several types of hands are used consistent with the proliferation of different styles at this time.[148] The case work is typical for Pennsylvania with rapidly rising swan neck pediments terminating in multi-leafed rosettes in layers, and turned finials. Relatively, the trunks are short and the bases large giving a squat appearance.

An 8-day clock standing 86¾" high, in a flat top walnut case is also known. The brass movement has rack and snail striking, anchor escapement, and the date 1800 appears on the movement.[149] This has no automation but has a rather simple floral design in the arch.

Chippendale Case

Another in a fine Lancaster County Chippendale case and dating circa 1790–1810 is also known (Figure 40). The hood is topped by swan necks which terminate in multiple rosettes.

There are three carved finials. Below this, the hood is quite plain. The trunk is short with a narrow door and is flanked by quarter columns. The plinth has an applied front panel with leaf-like carving at the corners.

The dial is in the "Burrowes style," with

From Strabane, in Ireland, but late of Salisbury Township, Chester County,

NOW follows his Business at Emanuel Rouse's, Clock and Watch-maker, in Front-street, near the Drawbridge, Philadelphia.

Figure 43, above. James Kinkead's advertisement in the Philadelphia Pennsylvania Gazette for March 14, 1765. Image Courtesy Chester County Historical Society.

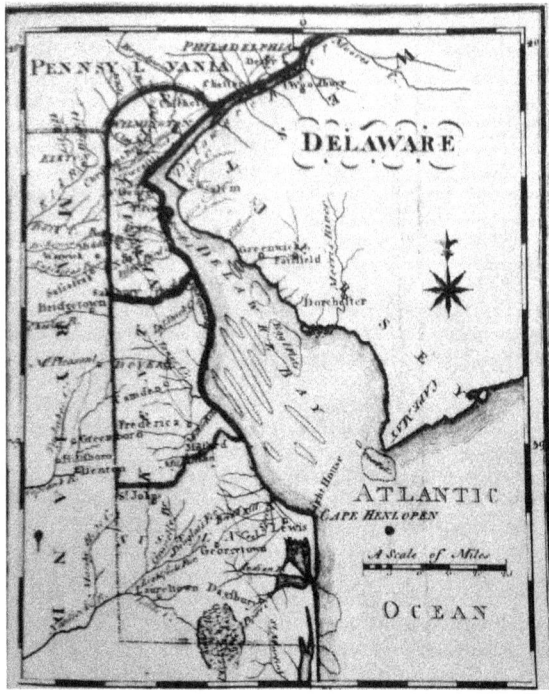

Figure 44, above. Delaware and the adjoining states from a map published by Joseph Scott in his 1807 Description of the States of Maryland and Delaware. Christiana Bridge can be seen just southwest of Wilmington at top left.

simple, almost naive, painting and crude hemisphere maps below the arch. The 8-day movement is of good quality with rack and snail striking and deadbeat escapement.[150]

How many clocks he made is unknown and no watches are recorded.

BROWNSVILLE

Brownsville, PA became the workplace of James Spence in June 1816 according to the American Telegraph (Figure 41). He was next door to the Rising Sun Tavern until January 1818. The American Telegraph went out of business later that year and what became of Mr. Spence is unknown. Late of Belfast, he was not mentioned in Joseph Smyth's Directories for that city in 1807–08, although a David Spence was trading in High Street there as a haberdasher.[131]

THE KINKEADS

The Pennsylvania Gazette (Figure 43) of March 14, 1765, describes James Kinkead "....Clock and Watchmaker from Strabane, in Ireland, but late of Salisbury (sic) Township, Chester County,.." as working with Emanuel Rouses, also a clock and watchmaker in Front Street..., Philadelphia.[126, 151] It is unclear when he came to America.

FAMILY

He may have come with his whole family since the will of John Kinkead of Sadsbury of 1770/1 mentions James and four brothers Charles, David, John and Samuel.[25, 152] A bond for 1 pound, 6 shillings and 6 pence borrowed by James Kinkead of Sadsbury Township from one John Taylor of Thornbury Township, Chester County dated October 2, 1740[153] would make him at least legal age (21 years) and possibly born about 1719 or 1720 or before.[153] Like other provincial clock makers in Ireland such as Laurence Birnie or John McKee, he may have had a local apprenticeship perhaps to a family mem-

JA·MES KINKEAD,
WATCH AND CLOCK MAKER,
At Chriſtiana, nearly oppoſite to Mr. Dunn's ſtore,
CONTINUES to carry on his buſineſs in as extenſive a manner as ever, and hopes to merit the favour of all thoſe that pleaſe to employ him; He returns thanks to all thoſe Ladies and Gentlemen that have favoured him with their cuſtom; and gives them caution that there is another perſon who follows the ſaid buſineſs at the ſign of the Boot and Shoe, a little below his ſhop, where ſome watches have been carried, through miſtake of the meſſengers, which the owners intended for ſaid Kinkead.

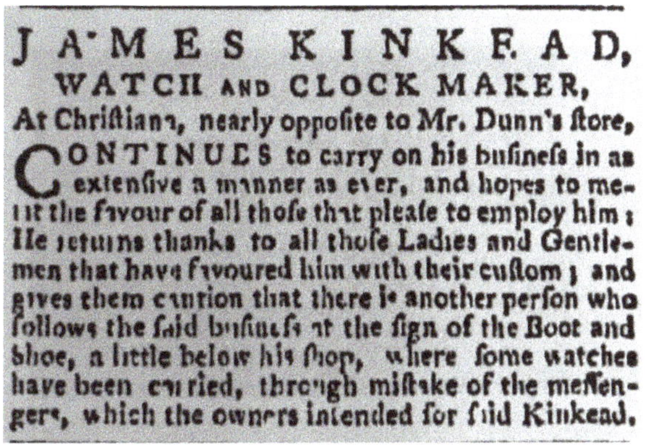

Figure 45. By February 7, 1774, Kinkead was now in Christiana, DE. From Dunlaps Pennsylvania Packet or the General Advertiser.[552]

ber in his native County Tyrone. He is not on the lists of apprentices, freemen or quarter brothers of the Dublin Goldsmiths Company from 1730 onwards.[31] He had been a freeman (i.e., was unmarried) of Sadsbury Township in 1765 and presumably moved from there to Philadelphia in that year (Figure 43).

PHILADELPHIA

The list of letters remaining uncollected in Philadelphia Post Office published in *The Pennsylvania Gazette* for January 30, 1766 contains the name of James Kinkead and he may still have been there at that time. In January 1770, however, *The Gazette* also reported the sale of "...household furniture, horses, cattle...." late the estate of James Kinkead, seized and taken in execution and to be sold by the Sheriff.[154] It is not known how long he stayed in Philadelphia, but by February 1774 he was at Christiana "nearly opposite to Mr. Dunn's store"[27] (Figures 44 and 45). This name is mentioned in Brix's Philadelphia Silversmiths and Allied Artificers, for 1774 and tax records from Southwark, Philadelphia County also list James Kinkead (Kincaid) from 1774 to 1780.[14] The resignation of James Kinkead "of the offices of Register of wills &c and Recorder of deeds, in and for the county of Westmoreland" is found in *The Pennsylvania Gazette* for April 26, 1786. If this is the

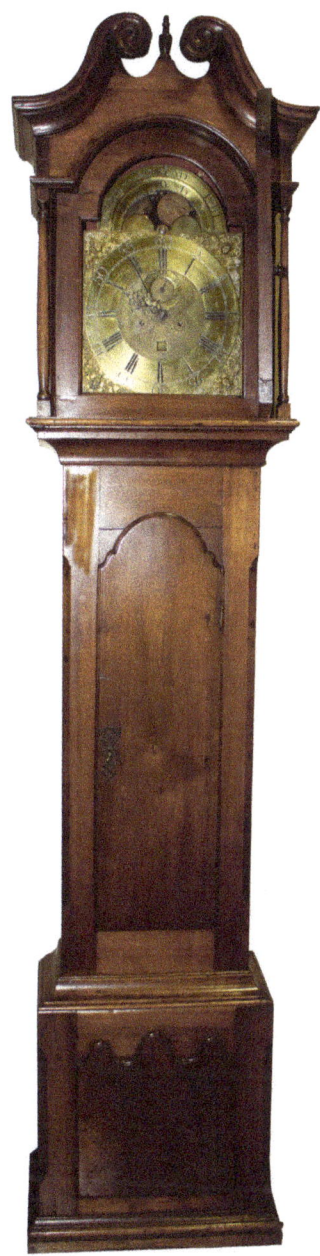

Figure 46. The long case clock from his Philadelphia period. There is a rolling moon automation in the arch and composite brass dial with silvered chapter ring signed, "James Kinkead, Phil." The clock dates from ca. 1765. See text for description. Image Courtesy Delaware Division of Historical and Cultural Affairs.

same Kinkead, he may have forsaken the watch and clock business for the somewhat more mundane, but less risky, life of the bureaucrat.

CLOCKS

Several of his clocks are extant including a handsome brass dial longcase clock from his Philadelphia period with a rolling moon in the arch which now graces the Governor's Mansion in the State of Delaware (Figure 46). The composite brass dial has a silvered chapter ring lacking half-hour or half-quarter marks. Inner Roman numerals mark the hours and relatively large Arabic numerals mark the minutes. Hour and minute numerals are separated by a double track with individual minute marks. The center of the dial is lightly engraved with a floral motif rising upwards and outwards from the winding holes. There is a seconds hand below 12 and a square date aperture above six. Above the rolling moon is the name of the maker, James Kinkead, Phil.29 The clock has been dated to circa 176529 although the spandrels resemble those from earlier times.155 The mahogany case stands 94½" high. The hood has a swan neck pediment with carved terminals and a small centrally placed wooden finial. Turned pillars flank the hood door. The chamfered trunk is quite wide lending a bulky touch to the piece. Concave molding separates the trunk from the plinth which is also chamfered and on which there is an elevated molded panel.

Another survivor (see Figure 47) stands 91" tall in a walnut case with differences in the shape of the finials, the ends of the turned pillars flanking the glass door and the degree of molding. The dial is of pewtered brass with Roman numerals, a date aperture, and subsidiary seconds dial. A scrolling foliate chased lunette reads, "Jas. Kinkead/Christiana Bridge." The two-train movement strikes a bell on the hour.

Figure 47. A tall case clock by James Kinkead, Christiana Bridge, Delaware. Picture very kind courtesy Bill Weschler, Weschler Auctions Inc. Washington, D.C. www.weschlers.com

WALNUT CLOCKS

Two walnut tall case clocks signed, "James Kinkead, Christiana Bridge," have survived. The style and the biographical details suggest a date of 1770–80. One has a brass arch dial with black Roman hour numerals, Arabic minute numerals, a subsidiary seconds dial below 12, and a date aperture above six. There are decorative foliate brass spandrels. The circular boss which adorns the arch is inscribed, "Jas. Kinkead/ Christiana/Bridge." The two train movement strikes a bell on the hour. Standing at 93½" in height, the case has a simply molded swan neck pediment terminating in rosettes and topped by three turned finials. Turned columns flank the hood door. The trunk is relatively plain and is separated from the hood and plinth by concave molding and has an arched door. The clock stands on ogee feet.

A white dial clock is also known by this maker,[5] but its whereabouts are unfortunately unknown to the author.

ALEXANDER KINKEAD

Another clock-making Kinkead family from Ireland was also represented in Delaware. Alexander Kinkead, originally from the same county of Tyrone as James above, but from the more centrally located town of Omagh, arrived with his brother around 1770.[156] He was about 18 years old at this time and also settled in Christiana Bridge where he became well known as a clock maker. About 1781 he was in partnership with a Joseph Kinkead[156], the latter being known as the "clockmaker of Christiana Bridge." Joseph was the son of William and Sarah Kinkead of nearby Iron Hill and may have been a possible kinsman.

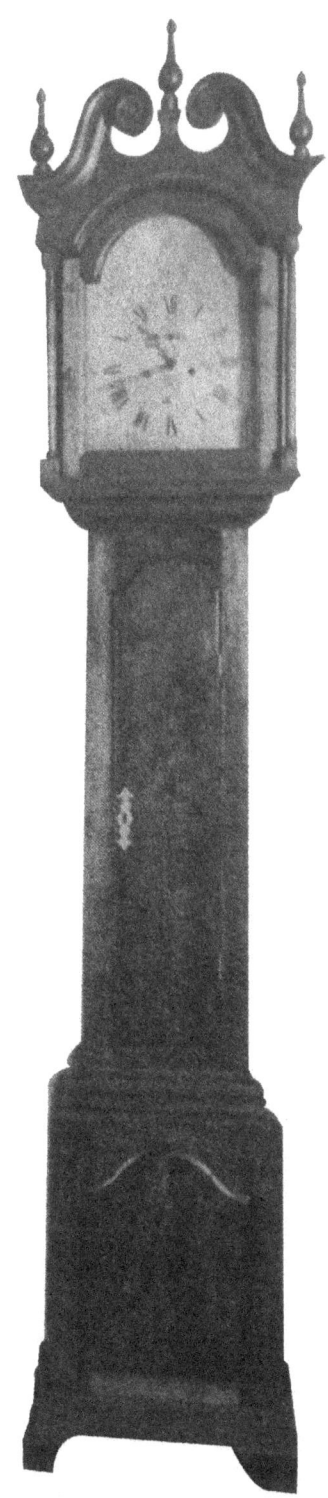

Figure 48, right. A long case clock by Alexander Kinkead of Delaware. There were several makers by this name in the state. At least some may have been related since they came from the same county of Tyrone in Ireland.

WHITE CLAY CREEK HUNDRED

It is not known where Alexander learned clock-making, although this trade was being practiced in Omagh around this time[6] and it is conceivable that he had some instruction prior to arriving in America. It has also been suggested that he (and Joseph) might have had training by the Chandlees[156], who were themselves also of Irish extraction. Alexander might even have learned from Joseph.

In any event, the two remained together for several years but Joseph married and moved to Newark, DE,[156] where he became known as the "Watchmaker of White Clay Creek Hundred," an area near Newark.[26]

In 1796,[4] he sold up and moved from Newark to Mifflintown, PA.[27] Alexander married and moved to North Milford Hundred in Cecil County around 1790. He had several children and, apparently, one slave, and continued to make clocks at least until 1818. Until 1839 he was appointed as a Justice of the Peace and was apparently still alive in the summer of 1840 living to a ripe old age.[156]

Joseph and Alexander Kinkead produced several clocks together and at least two, bearing the numbers 15 and 17 are known.[156] One is illustrated in *The Kinkeads of Delaware as pioneers of Minnesota, 1856-1868: contemporary account of experiences in the Sioux Uprising, 1862*, by Clara Janvier Kinkead. The arch dial, (Figure 48) has black Roman hour numerals, subsidiary seconds dial below 12 and a date aperture above six. There is a two-train movement.

The case has a simply molded swan-neck pediment terminating in rosettes and topped by three turned finials. Turned columns flank the hood door. The relatively plain trunk, separated from the hood and plinth by convex molding, has an arched door. The plinth has a raised panel.

The case is similar to the tall case clock by James Kinkead, Christiana Bridge. It has been said that the cases for some of these Delaware clocks may have been made by Charles Allen[157] and perhaps these are examples of his work.

THOMAS KINKEAD

There is another clock maker by the name of Thomas Kinkead also from Christiana Bridge, who may have been Joseph's brother. We know little about his life or his clocks. He may have died around 1832.[156]

Chapter Two
Massachusetts, New Hampshire, Connecticut, Vermont, and Maine
Boston

The earliest American clock makers were found in Boston where the first town clocks were located as early as the 17th century.[158] By 1687, clock maker William Davis and the watch maker David Johnson were there,[158] as were others.[159] Joseph Allen, who was probably from Dublin, was working in Boston circa 1691–1728 and was paid 6 shillings by Samuel Sewall[135] for "cleansing ye clock and making it work."[160]

While some makers in New England had immigrated from England or Ireland,[159] their names do not appear on lists of Irish makers active at the time. Silversmiths and jewelers with possibly Irish names such as John Butler or Samuel Casey, a Dublin linen printer John Hickey, and Irish "Protestant Servants" are known, but *Dow's Arts & Crafts in New England* does not specifically mention Irish watch makers for the period 1704 to 1775.[161] In the *Heritage Foundation Collection of Silver with Biographical Sketches of New England Silversmiths*, however, several were noted from 1625 on, including Abraham Barnes who arrived from Ireland on the *Globe* circa 1716.[162] Given the prominence of Boston in Irish-American culture it seems surprising that there is such a relative dearth of makers.

JOHN McLEAN

John M'Lane, or McLean, was in Boston in 1767. A watch maker and finisher who had worked in Dublin and London, he had served his time to "one of the best Finishers" (Figure 49) in Dublin although we do not know who this was.[163] There was no watch or clock maker of this name in the Dublin directories for 1767 or before that time.[95-98] In any event, two years later he was located in King Street, Boston (Figure 50) at work on a watch "...the whole of which will be finished in the Province, except the two plates and the case."[164] He was still in Boston in October 1773 but he is not mentioned in the later Boston directories.[165-178]

Others with the name John McLean, perhaps related, are known from Lisburn,[7] Belfast,[2] and Dublin around the same time.[90, 179]

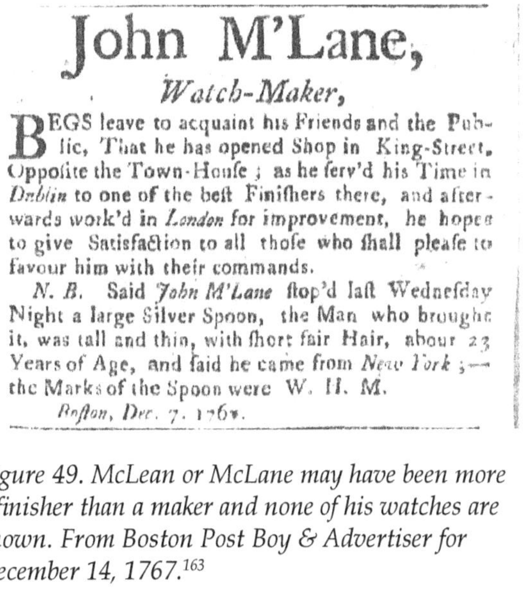

John M'Lane, Watch-Maker,

BEGS leave to acquaint his Friends and the Public, That he has opened Shop in King-Street, Opposite the Town-House; as he serv'd his Time in *Dublin* to one of the best Finishers there, and afterwards work'd in *London* for improvement, he hopes to give Satisfaction to all those who shall please to favour him with their commands.

N. B. Said *John M'Lane* stop'd last Wednesday Night a large Silver Spoon, the Man who brought it, was tall and thin, with short fair Hair, about 23 Years of Age, and said he came from *New York*;— the Marks of the Spoon were W. H. M.

Boston, Dec. 7. 1767.

Figure 49. McLean or McLane may have been more a finisher than a maker and none of his watches are known. From Boston Post Boy & Advertiser for December 14, 1767.[163]

JOHN AND JAMES DALRYMPLE

The Boston Dalrymples were related to a family of clock makers in Dublin.

Figure 50. Detail of the map of Boston, 1775 by Thomas Hyde Page. King Street, location of the premises of John McLean, is at bottom center and Ann Street, the workplace of Cornelius Doherty about a hundred years later is just above. Library of Congress G3764.B6S3 1777. P3 Faden 32. Licensed under Public Domain via Commons https://bit.ly/39W56Gy

John Dalrymple

John Dalrymple was a quarter brother in 1754–55.[31] His name suggests a Scottish origin for the family and an apprentice has been recorded in Edinburgh.[8] From 1762 until 1767[96-99] he was working in Digges Street, having taken one apprentice in the interim, a Richard Harper in 1757.[31] He moved to Aungier Street in 1768,[100, 101,180-184] where he was listed at number 42 after 1775.[182-184] He died in 1779[6] after which the business was taken over temporarily by Hannah Dalrymple, perhaps his widow.[81] By 1784, her name had been replaced by that of John Dalrymple[82] presumably the son who had been apprenticed to his father in 1768 and who became free in 1789.[31] He remained at the family business address in Aungier Street until the end of the first quarter of the 19th century.[82-94,102-105, 183-200] These dates illustrate some of the difficulties in the use of the directories as uncorroborated guides to biography; although he was listed in 1824,[201] he was recorded elsewhere as having died in 1823.[31] He had a successful career, being Warden of the Dublin Goldsmiths Co. from 1805 to 1808 and Master from 1811 to 1812.[31] Many Dalrymple clocks survive.

James Dalrymple

James Dalrymple was born in 1765 and was at 29 Capel Street from 1791 where he worked as a watch maker for several years.[88-92] *The Salem Gazette* for December 29, 1795 advertised (Figure 51) that he had taken up the business of Joseph Mulliken in Court Street, Salem.[202] Why he left Ireland is unclear but, like others, involvement in the 1798 Rising is a possibility. He moved in 1802 to nearby Essex Street[203] until 1836 (Figure 52). Over the years, his notices appeared variously in The *Salem Gazette*, The *Salem Register*, and The *Essex Register* and his business expanded from clock-making to the sale of hardware and fancy goods as well as tools and equipment for clock and watch makers.[204]

> **James Dalrymple,**
> *Watch-Maker,*
>
> HAS commenced business in the Shop formerly occupied by Mr. Joseph Mulliken, in Court-street, in Major Waldo's Brick-Store.
>
> ☞ As DALRYMPLE carried on the Watch-Making Business for several years in the City of Dublin, he presumes his experience will enable him to give satisfaction to those who favour him with their commands.
>
> He has lately received from Ireland,
> **A few Eight-Day Clocks,**
> which will be sold with or without Cases.

Figure 51. Dalrymple occupied part of Major Waldo's Brick Store from where he conducted his business. His business was in repairs, retail, importation of clocks[555] and, later, watches.[203] He imported from Dublin, and clocks could be purchased with or without cases. This not uncommon practice in the 18th and early 19th centuries in America, resulted in "hybrid" clocks - the clock from one town and the case from another or even from a different country.

> **James Dalrymple,**
> WATCHMAKER—Has removed from the shop he occupied in Dr. Stearns' brick store, to a shop in Essex street, a few doors east of the corner of Court street, and nearly opposite to the mansion of Colonel Derby—Where he offers for sale, a large assortment of warranted and low priced WATCHES, from the manufactories of England, France, and Geneva, on low terms for cash or approved credit—a profusion of Chains, Seals and Keys—and a variety of Materials and Implements, only necessary for persons engaged in the Watchmaking business.
>
> Part of a new and well finished HOUSE, in Essex street, to be let.
> Salem, Oct. 4, 1802.

Figure 52. Major Waldo's brick store changed hands to those of a Dr. Stearns and subsequently Dalrymple moved to Essex Street where he remained for over twenty years.

> **DIED**
> In Salem, James Dalrymple, Esq. a native of Ireland, aged 74; Mr Samuel Kehew, aged 71; Mr Benjamin B. Allen aged 36

Figure 53. The death notice of James Dalrymple from the Essex Gazette for April 5, 1839.

Death

James Dalrymple passed from this life in 1839 and the notice of his death (Figure 53), at the age of 74, appeared in the *Essex Gazette* for April 5 of that year.[205] He had been successful in Salem, having become a naturalized citizen in 1802.[206] He married in 1806,[126,135] and became a staunch Republican.[207] There was another John Dalrymple of Portland, ME who may have been James's brother, but this has not been confirmed and the relationship between them is unclear.[206] The John Dalrymple, Jr. of Dublin could conceivably also have been a relative, possibly even an older brother, since he was apprenticed in 1768 and presumably born circa 1754, 10 or 11 years before James. The author is not aware of any American clocks or watches by this maker.

CORNELIUS DOHERTY

Other individuals working in this area include Cornelius Doherty, born in Ireland in 1798 and who died in Boston on November 28, 1858. He was at Ann Street, Boston in 1851 and was listed as a clock maker from 1853 to 1858.[3,135] Doherty clock makers are known from Clonmel and Derry.[6]

NORTH ATTLEBORO

BERNARD McGUIRE

Bernard McGuire, clock maker and jeweler, was born in Ireland in 1830 and died in Attleboro on October 7, 1856.[3] He is not listed in Ireland.[5-7]

ROXBURY

JOHN O'CONNELL

John O'Connell was born in Ireland in 1820 and was in the Roxbury directories from 1848–60. He may have been employed at the firm of Howard and Davis.[3]

NEW HAMPSHIRE

PISCATAQUA (LATER PORTSMOUTH)

JOHN SIMNET

"A principal Manufacturer...." at least according to himself, his name is sometimes spelt Sinnet.[135] He may be the same as the John Simnel in Dublin before 1778, and one of his watches has survived.[8] He arrived in New York in 1764.[208] His extensive advertisements from there and from New Hampshire between 1768 and 1785, about 100, allow us insight into his origins and progress in America. He described himself as a watch maker and that he had worked in London and Dublin.[209]

He was born in 1728,[135] but it is unclear where. With this date, he would have been apprenticed circa 1742. During the term of apprenticeship he was "Finisher to Mr. Webster, Exchange Alley, London"[210] and in New York he said he was the only "watchmaker of the London Company."[211] Despite these claims, his name is not on the lists of apprentices or freemen for that city.[212, 213] The Webster to whom he referred may himself have been apprenticed to Thomas Tompion[8] and this connection may explain how Simnet may have rubbed shoulders with distinguished contemporary London makers. Although he stated he was in Dublin, the quarter brother or freemen lists for this period do not carry his name[31] nor do the earlier Dublin directories.[95, 96, 214-216] If he was there at all, he may not have worked independently in the city at the time. His colorful personality, with grandiose inclinations, enabled him to compliment himself on being one of the first to bring the manufacture of watches to "perfection"[217] and that he was the one who "first reduc'd the price of watchwork in this country."[210]

Figure 54. Advertisement by John Simnet in the *New-Hampshire Gazette and Historical Chronicle*, Portsmouth, NH, for March 17, 1769.

WATCHES,

As usual by J. SIMNET, Parade.

Most of those who profess this Employ in this Country, are rough Clockmakers; if Rats could speak, they would declare their Sentiments, say they we must eat, and we live by gnawing down what you endeavour to rear. I keep this Creature here, with few Cloaths to cover his Flesh, and but very little Flesh to cover his Bones; if I know him attempt to eat the Fruits of others Labour, I lash him, Rat like, confin'd I resist, he can't bite me; but Reader take care.

Near Portsmouth Stocks SHEEP G——ffi——h lives Lax!
 (A Turkey legged Youth,)
His Clocks with both Hands gives the Lye,
 His Tongue ne'er speaks the Truth,
Stand off, ye Pettyfogging Knaves;
 This can you all out do,
Long NAT, can Filch us of our Time;
 And of our Money too.

WATCHES

KEPT in REPAIR for Two Shillings and six pence Sterling per YEAR: Clean'd for those who desire them done cheap, for a Pistereen, and Repairs in Proportion. By J. SIMNET: Parade.

A SQUIB —— To the Tune of Miss Dawson's Hornpipe.

In yonder Hutt is to be seen,
A Hungry GIANT lank and lean,
With well patch'd threadbare Coat of Green;
To cover his round Shoulders,
With unfleg'd Chin, and foolish Face,
A greasy Hat, with worsted Lace,
Poor NAT, (tho' in a wretched Case)
Makes sport, for his Beholders.

Figures 55 and 56. Doggerel by John Simnet in the New-Hampshire Gazette, and Historical Chronicle for June 22 and 29, 1770,[220] referring to his competitor Nathaniel Sheaffe Griffith, another local watch maker. Portsmouth was too small for Simnet and Griffith to co-exist; shortly after these notices, the former left for New York but Griffith remained in Portsmouth until 1796.[135] A pistareen was a silver coin used in America and the West Indies in the 18th century and worth about twenty cents.

NEW HAMPSHIRE

He moved to New Hampshire in December 1768 where he worked opposite Mr. Staver's Tavern in Pitt Street, later Portsmouth[218] (Figure 54). Here, his fortunes would rapidly decline. In September 1769 a competitor, Nathaniel Sheafe Griffith, announced his newly-established clock and watch repair business.[209] Griffith, fiercely competitive, would charge half of Simnet's price — "let him mend as cheap as he will." [209] A public altercation ensued in the local newspaper which, as we shall see, was not uncommon in contemporary America. Their squabble in The *New Hampshire Gazette, and Historical Chronicle* continued for over a year culminating in June 1770 (Figures 55 and 56). A month before, Simnet had announced that most of the watches he had been employed on "had... passed through the hands of the best performers hereabout......and they had never been properly repaired."[219] In June, Griffith's diatribe accused Simnet of "....vainly flattering himself ..... that he is as great a watchmaker as he is a mountebank."[219] Simnet was, however, given to doggerel and lost little time in replying.[220] What action, if any, Mr. Griffith took to this public provocation is unknown, but two months later Simnet had left New Hampshire for New York, never to return.

NEW YORK

In August 1770, he was located on the New Dock (Figure 57) near Murray's Wharf,[221] but by June 1771 he had moved to the lower end of the Coffee House Bridge (Figure 58). By a curious coincidence, the equally loud and undyingly Royalist Irish clock maker and makebate, Isaac Heron, was near the bridge in the same year. We shall hear more of Heron's fortunes and misfortunes later. Both makers were so voluble they must surely have heard each other across the bridge. Simnet's ranting habits came with him from New Hampshire and he referred to his New York competitors–perhaps a swipe at Heron–as "watch butchers."[222] In 1773, he moved to the River Side, next to the Sign of the

Figure 57. A map of Manhattan, New York in 1776. The detail shows Murray's Wharf and the Dock as well other locations for our clock makers. "A plan of the city and environs of New York in North America" The Boston Public Library Digital Map Collection: http://maps.bpl.org/details_14193 via Wiki Commons.

Castle, also near Murray's Wharf.[223] In 1774, we find him at the Fly, Main Street, next to the corner of Beekman's Slip.[224] He continued his repair business and had in stock gold, silver, and shagreen-covered watches. He also had smaller ones, about the size of a British shilling, which had become the latest fashion of the day.[225] Later that year, he had new premises at the corner of Beekman's Slip and Queen Street[226] and moved again to a shop opposite the Coffee House in 1775.[227] He lasted another year or so in New York but had probably left around August 1775.[228] In April 1776, mail bearing his name was awaiting collection from one Elias Nixon.[229]

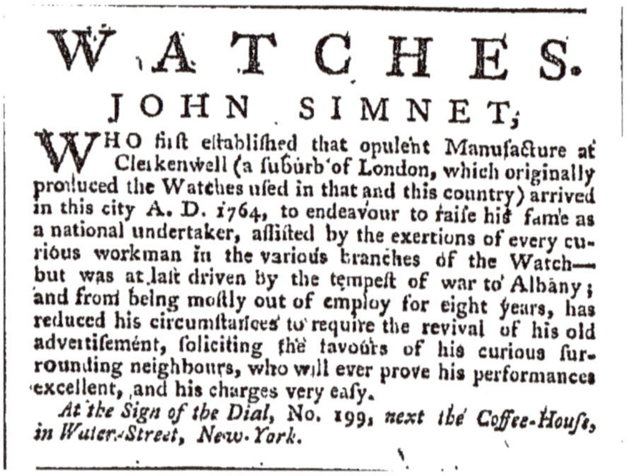

Figure 58. Simnet reestablished himself beside the Coffee House on Water Street.[208] His claim to have founded the first Clerkenwell watch factory is grand indeed as this suburb of London became a massive hub of English watch-making.

36 passing time across the water

ALBANY

Seven years later, he surfaced in Albany, NY, although yet another move was imminent[230] and, indeed, he reappears in New York in 1783.[208] In May 1785, his house at 198 Water Street was offered for rent at £40 a year.[231] He was still trading there a month later.[232] Uncommonly, these two notices detailed his clock wares, which included a regulator as well as turret and plain clocks (Figure 59). He also had astronomical and musical clocks playing either on bells or the organ "processionising both serious and comic."

Mr. Simnet died in 1786.[135] His horological productions must be rare and none are known to the author. He may have made little and just have spent much of his time finishing and/or repairing the work of others.

CONNECTICUT

NEW HAVEN

CHARLES O'NEIL

Charles O'Neil was a clock and watch repairer in New Haven[126] from circa 1802–30[4, 162] and the partner of Marcus Merriman and Zebul Bradley from 1823 to 1825.[233] Interestingly, there is also a Charles O'Neill, watch maker, of Hoey's Court, mentioned in the records of the Dublin Society of United Irishmen, the revolutionary organization founded in 1791 and suppressed by the British in 1794.[80] Perhaps the above O'Neil(l)s are the same man who, like Andrew Calderwood of Stewartstown mentioned before, thought it better to leave after the 1798 rebellion.

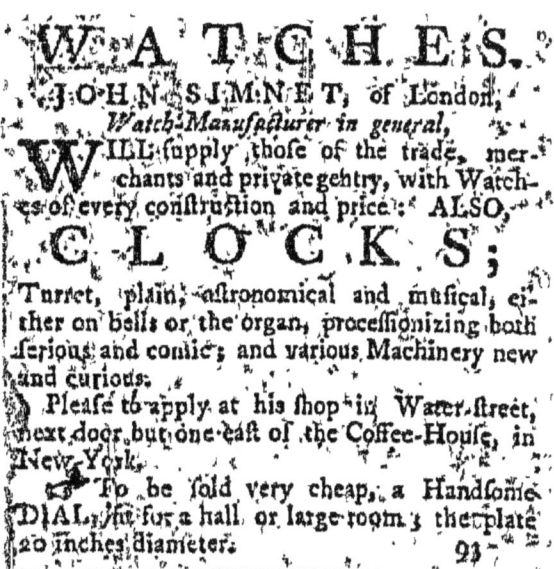

Figure 59. One of John Simnet's last advertisements published in John Loudon's New-York Packet for June 9, 1785 about a year before his death.

VERMONT

BURLINGTON AND BRANDON

JOHN JOHNSTON

Johnston was born in 1816 and served his apprenticeship in Belfast when the clock industry was thriving. There was a Thomas Johnston clock maker in Belfast in 1819[132], gone by 1835,[134] who may have been related.

In Vermont, he worked with the firm of Pangborn and Brinsmaid in Burlington before moving to Brandon[5, 234] and establishing his own premises in 1839–40. He cleaned and repaired clocks and had various items for sale including jewelry and fancy goods.

His opening advertising notice stated that he had worked for six years in America which would have meant that he arrived in the United States at age 19, so his apprenticeship was short and/or began early. Two individuals with this quite common name are noted in passenger lists, one for 1830 and the other for 1833.[72]

His career was short lived as he died of consumption or tuberculosis while only 25 years old. In his obituary, published in the *Burlington Free Press* May 21, 1841 he was noted to be of a kind and amiable disposition (Figure 60) and to have been survived by a blind mother and various brothers and sisters in his home country.[234]

FAIRHAVEN

JEDIDIAH PERKINS

Other makers in Vermont included James, also known as Jedidiah Perkins, was listed in Fairhaven from 1866 to 1878. In the U.S. Census of 1870, he stated he had been born in Ireland about 65 years previously[234] but this has not been previously documented.[129]

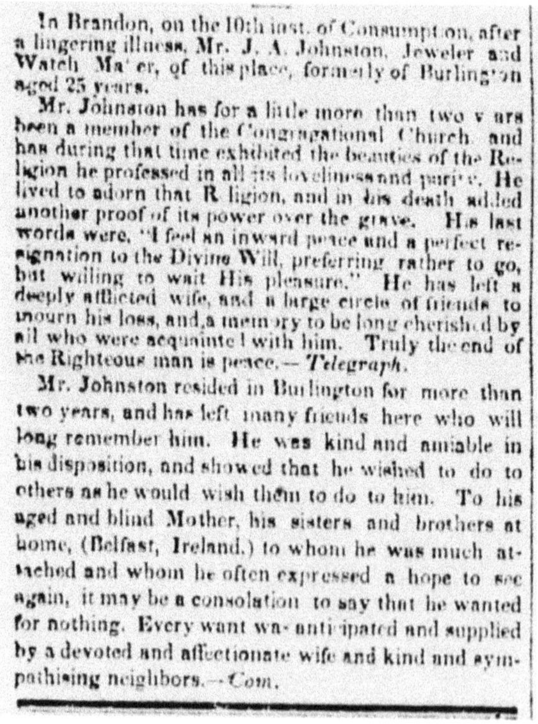

In Brandon, on the 10th inst. of Consumption, after a lingering illness, Mr. J. A. Johnston, Jeweler and Watch Maker, of this place, formerly of Burlington aged 25 years.

Mr. Johnston has for a little more than two years been a member of the Congregational Church and has during that time exhibited the beauties of the Religion he professed in all its loveliness and purity. He lived to adorn that Religion, and in his death added another proof of its power over the grave. His last words were, "I feel an inward peace and a perfect resignation to the Divine Will, preferring rather to go, but willing to wait His pleasure." He has left a deeply afflicted wife, and a large circle of friends to mourn his loss, and a memory to be long cherished by all who were acquainted with him. Truly the end of the Righteous man is peace.—*Telegraph.*

Mr. Johnston resided in Burlington for more than two years, and has left many friends here who will long remember him. He was kind and amiable in his disposition, and showed that he wished to do to others as he would wish them to do to him. To his aged and blind Mother, his sisters and brothers at home, (Belfast, Ireland,) to whom he was much attached and whom he often expressed a hope to see again, it may be a consolation to say that he wanted for nothing. Every want was anticipated and supplied by a devoted and affectionate wife and kind and sympathising neighbors.—*Com.*

Figure 60. The obituary, published in the Burlington Free Press May 21, 1841 for John Johnston, a native of Belfast who died of consumption or tuberculosis at age 25 years. He was survived by an aging and blind mother and brothers and sisters in Ireland.

MAINE

PORTLAND

JOHN DALRYMPLE

John Dalrymple possibly the brother of James of Boston[206] was on Fish Street in 1810 selling watches and sundry other goods (Figure 61).[235] In an unusual form of diversification, he became agent for Samuel D. Howe's Patent Trusses a "New and Important Discovery."[236] In 1811, he visited Charleston and brought news of the death of George III, subsequently published in The Carolina Gazette.[237] He was later in Exchange Street, at the sign of the TIME-PIECE.[238] The death of a John Dalrymple at 47 years old was reported in July 1819.[239]

Figure 61, right. John Dalrymple was in Fish Street in 1810 and had a good supply of watches as well as many other sundry goods.[235] From the Eastern Argus of February 1, 1810, Portland, Maine.

JOHN DALRYMPLE,

INFORMS the Ladies and Gentlemen of Portland, that he has for sale, a few doors above *Quincy & Baker's*, Fish-Street, nearly opposite the *Maine Bank*, a large assortment of elegant English WATCHES, second, capt, and plain; *Dutch*, day of the month and plain do.; Watch Chains, Seals and Keys, double gilt gold pattern;

A handsome assortment of JEWELRY, among which are some Filligree Work; very elegant Gold Watch-Chains & Keys; Silver Table and Tea-Spoons; Plated Castors and Candlesticks; Britannia Tea-Pots of the newest fashion; tinned, queen's metal, and pewter Table and Tea-Spoons; elegant Tortoise Shell and Horn Hair Combs; a variety of Ivory and Horn Small Tooth do.

HARDWARE— A large assortment of Knives and Forks, among which are some setts very fine; a great variety of Pocket and Penknives; a few dozen Razors of the first quality; large and small Scissors; Saws, 26 inch cast steel tenor; dovetail and wood Saws; Chissels of all kinds; Gouges, from ⅜ inch to the smallest sett; Carpenter's Squares & Compasses; Carpenter's Hammers; Lathing do.; Wood Screws; Saw Setts; Screw Drivers; Drawing Knives; fine Steel Ink Stands, pocket and desk Razor Cases; Cloth and Tooth Brushes; a good assortment of flat and round Files; Cork Screws; Snuff Boxes; Hair Brushes; a great variety of Morocco Pocket-Books, Purses, Memorandum Books, &c. together with many other articles, which he will sell cheap for Cash. Please to call and see.

He repairs and cleans Watches, and warrants his work, if the Watch be tolerably good, for one year. Every favor will be gratefully acknowledged.

☞ Willard's Patent Time-Pieces for sale.

Portland, Jan 18, 1810.

Chapter Three
New York, New Jersey, Ohio, and West Virginia

New York

New York at the beginning of the 18th century was a small colonial town on the bank of the Manhattan — now the Hudson — River, but it developed greatly within a few decades. Many people from Ireland came through this golden door, but we can identify relatively few who were clock makers. The newspapers list some but relying on this source may underestimate the number of craftsmen. For example, of 72 watch makers in the directories studied by the distinguished author and historian Rita Gottesman, only 23 advertised.[240] It is a little surprising to find relatively few makers in New York given the very vibrant trade links between Ireland and that city in the 18th century. A glance at page four of *The New York Gazette; and the Weekly Mercury* for December 31, 1770 shows just how vigorous this trade really was (Figure 62) with sailings to and from five Irish ports. From Ireland came exports of provisions of various types including beef, pork, butter, and salmon, and there was also a healthy trade in servants. In another booming 18th-century industry, British North America took over 800,000 yards of linen in 1750 and this rose to 3.5 million yards by the 1770s.[241] The Irish linen trade and New York were inextricably tied in another manner, not just by demand for finished linen product. For high-quality linen, Irish flax growers harvested before their crop went to seed. To re-sow, they imported seed — after 1740 mostly from North America — and New York was the most important port in this regard. The growth in this commercial relationship has been aptly described as "stunning."[241] That we have so few 18th-century Irish clock makers in New York, but eight or 10 in both Maryland and Pennsylvania, may reflect the tolerance of Pennsylvania and Maryland on the one hand and the conservatively British loyalism of New York on the other. This persisted to the end of the Revolution and so it was very appropriate that our most Anglophile maker should walk onto this stage around 1766 or so.

New York City

ISAAC HERON

Isaac was the son of Edward Heron of Papcastle in Cumberland, and was born in 1735.[242] His father, a seaman, retired and opened a shop in Coleraine. Isaac became apprenticed to John Davis around 1750.[242] This information comes to us from Heron's autobiography, *My own Memoirs, or the Life of I Heron, a Loyalist on Pure Genuine Principles*. Published in 1810, this rare book is only available in the National Library of Ireland and it terminates inexplicably on page 72.

Davis was active in Coleraine in 1770[6, 7] but since Heron's apprenticeship date is known we can say that Davis was working at least 20 years earlier from circa 1750 onwards. In his biography, Heron does not mention any of the

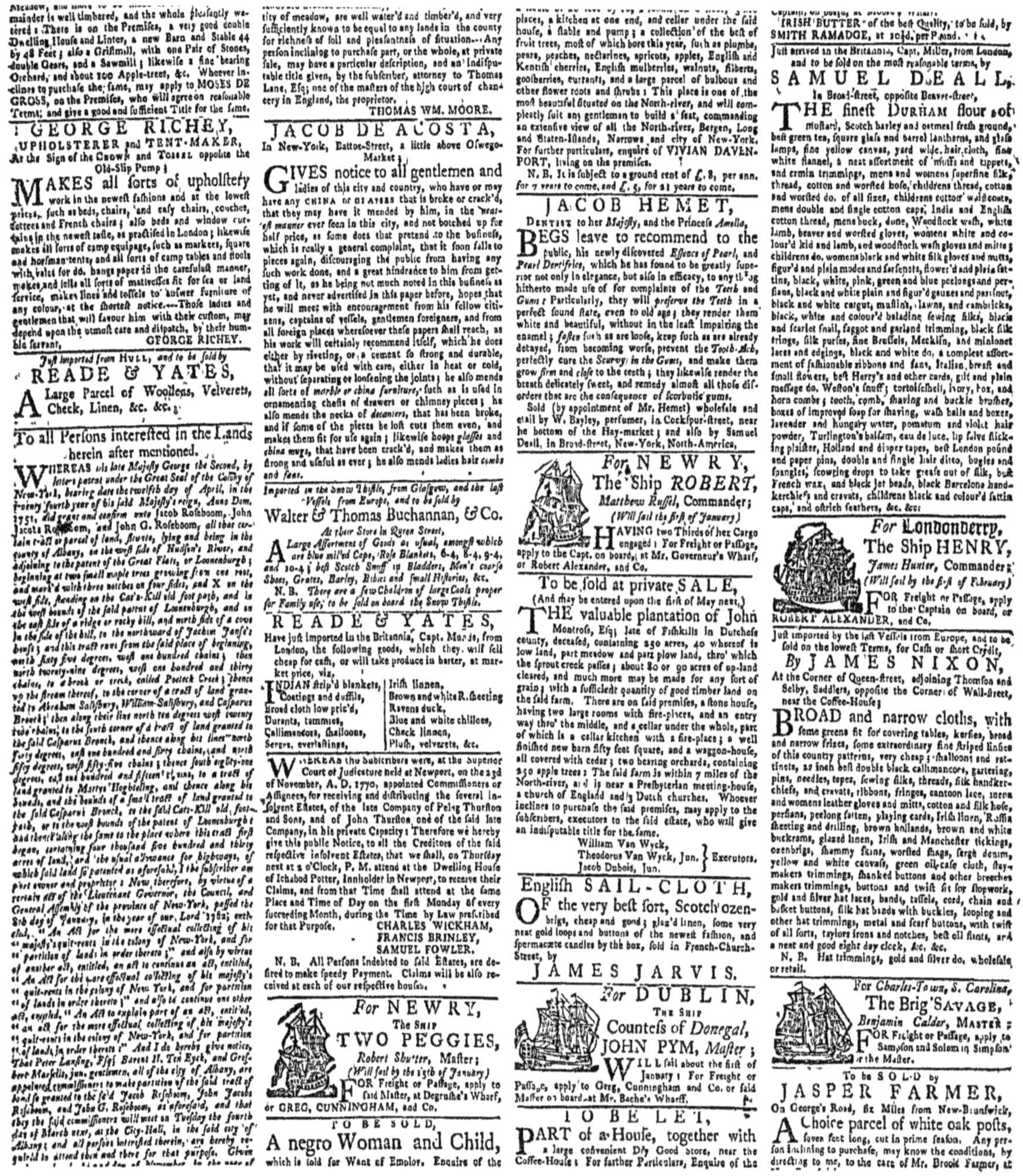

Meadow, and more to be made ... the remainder is well timbered, and the whole pleasantly watered: There is on the Premises, a very good double Dwelling House and Linter, a new Barn and Stable 44 by 48 Feet; also a Grismill, with one Pair of Stones, double Gears, and a Sawmill; likewise a fine bearing Orchard, and about 100 Apple-trees, &c. Whoever inclines to purchase the same, may apply to MOSES DE GROSS, on the Premises, who will agree on reasonable Terms; and give a good and sufficient Title for the same.

GEORGE RICHEY,
UPHOLSTERER and TENT-MAKER,
At the Sign of the Crown and Tossel opposite the Old-Slip Pump;

MAKES all sorts of upholstery work in the newest fashions and at the lowest prices, such as beds, chairs, and easy chairs, couches, settees and French chairs; also beds and window curtains in the newest taste, as practised in London; likewise makes all sorts of camp equipage, such as markees, square and horsman tents, and all sorts of camp tables and stools with valcs for do. hangs paper in the carefulest manner, makes and sells all sorts of matresses fit for sea or land service, makes lines and tossels to answer furniture of any colour, at the shortest notice.---Those ladies and gentlemen that will favour him with their custom, may depend upon the utmost care and dispatch, by their humble servant, GEORGE RICHEY.

Just imported from HULL, and to be sold by
READE & YATES,
A Large Parcel of Woollens, Velverets, Check, Linen, &c. &c.

To all Persons interested in the Lands herein after mentioned.

WHEREAS his late Majesty George the Second, by letters patent under the Great Seal of the Colony of New-York, bearing date the twelfth day of April, in the twenty fourth year of his said Majesty's reign, Anno Dom. 1751, did grant and confirm unto Jacob Roseboom, John Jacob Roseboom, and John G. Roseboom, all that certain tract or parcel of land, situate, lying and being in the county of Albany, on the west side of Hudson's River, and adjoining to the patent of the Great Flats, or Loonenburgh; beginning at two small maple trees growing from one root, and mark'd with three notches on four sides, and X on the west side, standing on the Cat's-Kill old foot path, and in the west bounds of the said patent of Loonenburgh, and on the east side of a ridge or rocky hill, and north side of a cove in the side of the hill, to the northward of Jachim Janse's house; and this tract runs from the said place of beginning, north sixty five degrees, west one hundred chains; then north twenty-nine degrees, west one hundred and thirty chains, to a brook or creek, called Poeteck Creek; thence up the stream thereof, to the corner of a tract of land granted to Abraham Salisbury, William Salisbury, and Casparus Bronck; then along their line north ten degrees west twenty two chains, to the south corner of a tract of land granted to the said Casparus Bronck, and thence along his lines north forty degrees, east one hundred and fifty chains, and north fifty degrees, west fifty-five chains; thence south eighty-one degrees, east one hundred and fifteen chains, to a tract of land granted to Martyn Hogbteling, and thence along his bounds, and the bounds of a small tract of land granted to the said Casparus Bronck, to the said Cats-Kill old foot path, or to the west bounds of the patent of Loonenburgh; and thence along the same to the place where this tract first began, containing four thousand five hundred and thirty acres of land, and the usual allowance for highways, of which said land so patented as aforesaid, I the subscriber am part owner and proprietor: Now, therefore, by virtue of a certain act of the Lieutenant Governor, the Council, and General Assembly of the province of New-York, passed the 8th day of January, in the year of our Lord 1762; entituled, "An Act for the more effectual collecting of his majesty's quit-rents in the colony of New-York, and for partition of lands in order thereto;" and also by virtue of another act, entitled, an act to continue an act, entitled, "An Act for the more effectual collecting of his majesty's quit-rents in the colony of New York, and for partition of lands in order thereto;" and also to continue one other act, entitled, "An Act to explain part of an act, entitled, an act for the more effectual collecting of his majesty's quit-rents in the colony of New-York, and for partition of lands in order thereto:" And I do hereby give notice, That Peter Lansing, Esq; Barent H. Ten Eyck, and Gysbert Marselis, jun. gentlemen, all of the city of Albany, are appointed commissioners to make partition of the said tract of land so granted to the said Jacob Roseboom, John Jacob Roseboom, and John G. Roseboom, as aforesaid, and that they the said commissioners will meet on Tuesday the fourth day of March next, at the City-Hall, in the said city of Albany; and all persons interested therein, are hereby required to attend then and there for that purpose. Given ...

... tity of meadow, are well water'd and timber'd, and very sufficiently known to be equal to any lands in the county for richness of soil and pleasantness of situation.--Any person inclining to purchase part, or the whole, at private sale, may have a particular description, and an indisputable title given, by the subscriber, attorney to Thomas Lane, Esq; one of the masters of the high court of chancery in England, the proprietor.
THOMAS WM. MOORE.

JACOB DE ACOSTA,
In New-York, Battoe-Street, a little above Oswego-Market;

GIVES notice to all gentlemen and ladies of this city and country, who have or may have any CHINA or GLASSES that is broke or crack'd, that they may have it mended by him, in the neatest manner ever seen in this city, and not botched up for half price, as some does that pretend to the business, which is really a general complaint, that it soon falls to pieces again, discouraging the public from having any such work done, and a great hindrance to him from getting of it, as he being not much noted in this business as yet, and never advertised in this paper before, hopes that he will meet with encouragement from his fellow citizens, captains of vessels, gentlemen foreigners, and from all foreign places wheresoever these papers shall reach, as his work will certainly recommend itself, which he does either by riveting, or a cement so strong and durable, that it may be used with care, either in heat or cold, without separating or loosening the joints; he also mends all sorts of marble or china furniture, such as is used in ornamenting chests of drawers or chimney pieces; he also mends the necks of decanters, that has been broke, and if some of the pieces be lost cuts them even, and makes them fit for use again; likewise hoops glasses and china mugs, that have been crack'd, and makes them as strong and useful as ever; he also mends ladies hair combs and fans.

Imported in the Snow Thistle, from Glasgow, and the last Vessels from Europe, and to be sold by
Walter & Thomas Buchannan, & Co.
At their Store in Queen Street,
A Large Assortment of Goods as usual, amongst which are blue mill'd Caps, Rose Blankets, 6-4, 8-4, 9-4, and 10-4; best Scotch Snuff in Bladders, Men's coarse Shoes, Grates, Barley, Bibles and small Histories, &c.
N. B. There are a few Chaldron of large Coals proper for Family use, to be sold on board the Snow Thistle.

READE & YATES,
Have just imported in the Britannia, Capt. Mundle, from London, the following goods, which they will sell cheap for cash, or will take produce in barter, at market price, viz.

INDIAN strip'd blankets,	Irish linnen,
Coatings and duffils,	Brown and white R. sheeting
Broad cloth low pric'd,	Ravens duck,
Durants, tammies,	Blue and white chilloes,
Callimancoes, shalloons,	Check linnen,
Serges, everlastings,	Plush, velverets, &c.

WHEREAS the Subscribers were, at the Superior Court of Judicature held at Newport, on the 23d of November, A. D. 1770, appointed Commissioners or Assignees, for receiving and distributing the several Insolvent Estates, of the late Company of Peleg Thurston and Sons, and of John Thurston one of the said late Company, in his private Capacity: Therefore we hereby give this public Notice, to all the Creditors of the said respective insolvent Estates, that we shall, on Thursday next at 2 o'Clock, P. M. attend at the Dwelling House of Ichabod Potter, Innholder in Newport, to receive their Claims, and from that Time shall attend at the same Place and Time of Day on the first Monday of every succeeding Month, during the Time by Law prescribed for that Purpose.
CHARLES WICKHAM,
FRANCIS BRINLEY,
SAMUEL FOWLER.
N. B. All Persons Indebted to said Estates, are desired to make speedy Payment. Claims will be also received at each of our respective houses.

For NEWRY,
The Ship
TWO PEGGIES,
Robert Shutter, Master;
(Will sail by the 15th of January)
FOR Freight or Passage, apply to said Master, at Degrushe's Wharf, or GREG, CUNNINGHAM, and Co.

TO BE SOLD,
A negro Woman and Child,
which is sold for Want of Employ. Enquire of the ...

... places, a kitchen at one end, and cellar under the said house, a stable and pump; a collection of the best of fruit trees, most of which bore this year, such as plumbs, pears, peaches, nectarines, apricots, apples, English and Kentish cherries, English mulberries, walnuts, filberts, gooseberries, currants, and a large parcel of bulbous and other flower roots and shrubs: This place is one of the most beautiful situated on the North-river, and will compleatly suit any gentleman to build a seat, commanding an extensive view of all the North-river, Bergen, Long and Staten-Islands, Narrows and city of New-York. For further particulars, enquire of VIVIAN DAVENPORT, living on the premises.
N. B. It is subject to a ground rent of £. 8, per ann. for 7 years to come, and £. 5, for 21 years to come.

JACOB HEMET,
DENTIST to her Majesty, and the Princess Amelia,
BEGS leave to recommend to the public, his newly discovered Essence of Pearl, and Pearl Dentifrice, which he has found to be greatly superior not only in elegance, but also in efficacy, to any thing hitherto made use of for complaints of the Teeth and Gums: Particularly, they will preserve the Teeth in a perfect sound state, even to old age; they render them white and beautiful, without in the least impairing the enamel; fasten such as are loose, keep such as are already decayed, from becoming worse, prevent the Tooth-Ach, perfectly cure the Scurvy in the Gums, and make them grow firm and close to the teeth; they likewise render the breath delicately sweet, and remedy almost all those disorders that are the consequence of scorbutic gums.
Sold (by appointment of Mr. Hemet) wholesale and retail by W. Bayley, perfumer, in Cockspur-street, near the bottom of the Hay-market; and also by Samuel Deall, in Broad-street, New-York, North-America.

For NEWRY,
The Ship ROBERT,
Matthew Russel, Commander;
(Will sail the first of January)
HAVING two Thirds of her Cargo engaged: For Freight or Passage, apply to the Capt. on board, at Mr. Governeur's Wharf, or Robert Alexander, and Co.

To be sold at private SALE,
(And may be entered upon the first of May next,)
THE valuable plantation of John Montross, Esq; late of Fishkills in Dutchess county, deceased, containing 250 acres, 40 whereof is low land, part meadow and part plow land, thro' which the sprout creek passes; about 80 or 90 acres of up-land cleared, and much more may be made for any sort of grain; with a sufficient quantity of good timber land on the said farm. There are on said premises, a stone house, having two large rooms with fire-places, and an entry way thro' the middle, and a cellar under the whole, part of which is a cellar kitchen with a fire-place; a well finished new barn fifty feet square, and a waggon-house, all covered with cedar; two bearing orchards, containing 250 apple trees: The said farm is within 7 miles of the North-river, and is near a Presbyterian meeting-house, a church of England and 3 Dutch churches. Whoever inclines to purchase the said premises, may apply to the subscribers, executors to the said estate, who will give an indisputable title for the same.
William Van Wyck,
Theodorus Van Wyck, Jun. } Executors.
Jacob Dubois, Jun.

English SAIL-CLOTH,
OF the very best sort, Scotch ozenbrigs, cheap and good; glaz'd linen, some very neat gold loops and buttons of the newest fashion, and spermacæte candles by the box, sold in French-Church-Street, by
JAMES JARVIS.

For DUBLIN,
The Ship
Countess of Donegal,
JOHN PYM, Master;
WILL sail about the first of January: For Freight or Passage, apply to Greg, Cunningham and Co. or said Master on board at Mr. Bache's Wharff.

TO BE LET,
PART of a House, together with a large convenient Dry Good Store, near the Coffee-House: For farther Particulars, Enquire of the ...

... Captain, on board, at ... Wharf.
IRISH BUTTER of the best Quality, to be sold, by SMITH RAMADGE, at 10½d. per Pound.

Just arrived in the Britannia, Capt. Miller, from London, and to be sold on the most reasonable terms, by
SAMUEL DEALL,
In Broad-street, opposite Beaver-street,
THE finest DURHAM flour of mustard, Scotch barley and oatmeal fresh ground, best green tea, square glass and barrel lantherns, and glass lamps, fine yellow canvas, yard wide, hair cloth, fine white flannel, a neat assortment of muffs and tippets, and ermin trimmings, mens and womens superfine silk, thread, cotton and worsted hose, childrens thread, cotton and worsted do. of all sizes, childrens cotton waistcoats, mens double and single cotton caps, India and English cotton thread, mens buck, doe, Woodstock wash, white lamb, beaver and worsted gloves, womens white and colour'd kid and lamb, and woodstock wash gloves and mitts; childrens do. womens black and white silk gloves and mitts, figur'd and plain modes and sarsenets, flower'd and plain sattins, black, white, pink, green and blue peelongs and persians, black and white plain and figur'd gauzes and parsinet, black and white catgut, muslins, lawns, and cambricks, black, white and colour'd balading sewing silks, black and scarlet snail, faggot and garland trimming, black silk fringe, silk purses, fine Brussels, Mecklin, and minionet laces and edgings, black and white do, a compleat assortment of fashionable ribbons and fans, Italian, breast and small flowers, best Harry's and other cards, gilt and plain message do. Weston's snuff; tortoiseshell, ivory, box, and horn combs; tooth, comb, shaving and buckle brushes, boxes of improved soap for shaving, wash balls and boxes, lavender and hungary water, pomatum and violet hair powder, Turlington's balsam, eau de luce, lip salve sticking plaister, Holland and diaper tapes, best London pound and paper pins, double and single hair ditto, bugles and spangles, scowring drops to take grease out of silk, best French wax, and black jet beads, black Barcelona handkerchiefs and cravats, childrens black and colour'd sattin caps, and ostrich feathers, &c. &c.

For Londonderry,
The Ship HENRY,
James Hunter, Commander;
(Will sail by the first of February)
FOR Freight or Passage, apply to the Captain on board, or ROBERT ALEXANDER, and Co.

Just imported by the last Vessels from Europe, and to be sold on the lowest Terms, for Cash or short Credit,
By JAMES NIXON,
At the Corner of Queen-street, adjoining Thomson and Selby, Saddlers, opposite the Corner of Wall-street, near the Coffee-House;
BROAD and narrow cloths, with some greens fit for covering tables, kersies, broad and narrow frizes, some extraordinary fine striped linsies of this country patterns, very cheap; shalloons and rattinets, 22 inch best double black callimancoes, gartering, pins, needles, tapes, sewing silks, threads, silk handkerchiefs, and cravats, ribbons, fringes, cantoon lace, mens and womens leather gloves and mitts, cotton and silk hose, persians, peelong satten, playing cards, Irish linen, Russia sheeting and drilling, brown hollands, brown and white buckrams, glazed linen, Irish and Manchester tickings, ozenbrigs, shammy skins, worsted shags, serge denim, yellow and white canvass, green oil-case cloth, staymakers trimmings, shanked buttons and other breeches makers trimmings, buttons and twist fit for slopwork, gold and silver hat laces, bands, tassels, cord, chain and basket buttons, silk hat bands with buckles, looping and other hat trimmings, metal and scarf buttons, with twist of all sorts, taylors irons and notches, best oil flints, and a neat and good eight day clock, &c. &c.
N. B. Hat trimmings, gold and silver do. wholesale or retail.

For Charles-Town, S. Carolina,
The Brig SAVAGE,
Benjamin Calder, MASTER;
FOR Freight or Passage, apply to Sampson and Solomon Simpson, or the Master.

To be SOLD by
JASPER FARMER,
On George's Road, six Miles from New-Brunswick,
A Choice parcel of white oak posts, seven feet long, cut in prime season. Any person inclining to purchase, may know the conditions, by directing to me, to the care of Mr. Brook Farmer, at ...

Figure 62. The New York Gazette and Weekly Mercury, December 31, 1770. Trade was brisk between the New World and Ireland with sailings to Dublin, Londonderry, Newry, Belfast, and Coleraine. Many of the ships spent four to six weeks or more in port before weighing anchor and setting sail from New York. With the exception of Dublin, these ports were in the northeast of Ireland and presumably there was also a connection between these sailings and the linen trade. A healthy - perhaps unhealthy by the standards of today! - interest was also seen in Irish butter. Modern non-American readers who associate slavery with the American South may be surprised to see thriving commerce in this area in New York City.

contemporary clock makers in the northeast of Ireland who shared his name and he may not have been related. He was married to the daughter of William Sharman and had four daughters.[243]

Philadelphia

He appears in *The Pennsylvania Gazette* of December 8, 1763, as a watch and clock maker (Figure 63) located on Front Street, Philadelphia although by May of the following year he had already announced his intention of leaving. This was the beginning of a career in America that would last about 15 years (Figure 64). In contrast to many Irishmen, however, the sojourn of Heron in the New World would be ended by warfare and personal financial ruin. Some of his behavior cannot have helped in avoiding this sad outcome. In 1763, he moved to Bound Brook, NJ,[4] and was still there in 1764 repairing and selling watches and clocks.[244]

By 1766, he had moved to New York (Figure 65) but had maintained contacts in the towns of New Jersey from whom he took work for repair.[244, 245] Initially, he thrived in New York trading in watches, clocks, jewelry, and silver from his location at the upper end of the Coffee House Bridge, located at the foot of Wall Street below Water Street.[246]

By 1770, he was at the high-end of the market with a musical clock and gold repeating watches as well as trinkets, snuff boxes, and plated buckles on his inventory.[247] His social standing and wealth had increased; he was elected Freeman in 1769 and had acquired 1,000 acres of land.[248]

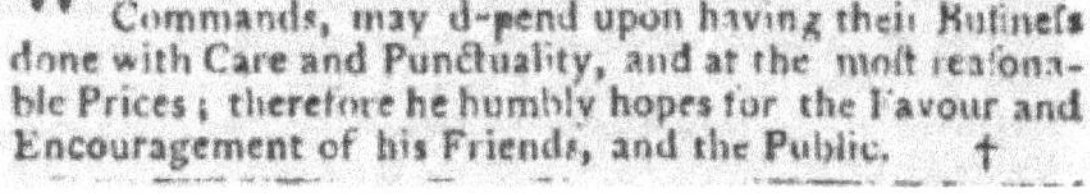

ISAAC HERON,
Repeating and plain Watch and Clock-maker, four Doors above Cheſtnut-ſtreet, in Front-ſtreet,

WHERE thoſe who pleaſe to oblige him with their Commands, may depend upon having their Buſineſs done with Care and Punctuality, and at the moſt reaſonable Prices; therefore he humbly hopes for the Favour and Encouragement of his Friends, and the Public. †

Figure 63. Isaac Heron appears in The Pennsylvania Gazette of December 8, 1763, as a watch and clock maker on Front St, Philadelphia.

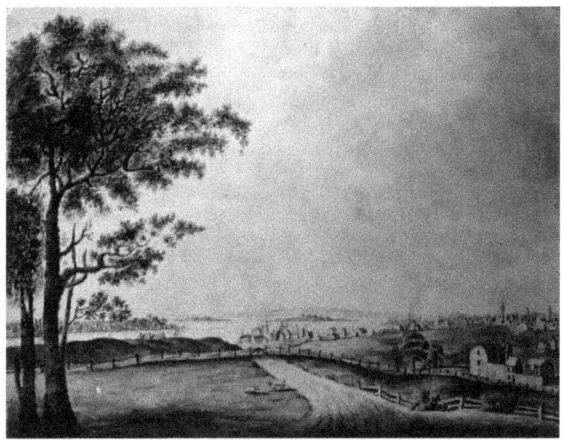

Figure 64. A view of the city and harbor of New York in more bucolic times as the outskirts might have appeared to Isaac Heron. Taken from Mount Pitt after Charles Balthazar Julien Févret de Saint-Mémin (1770–1852). Saint-Mémin fled France during the revolution, and worked as an artist in America at the turn of the 18th and 19th centuries. This work is now in the collection of The Preservation Society of Newport County and on display at Chepstow.

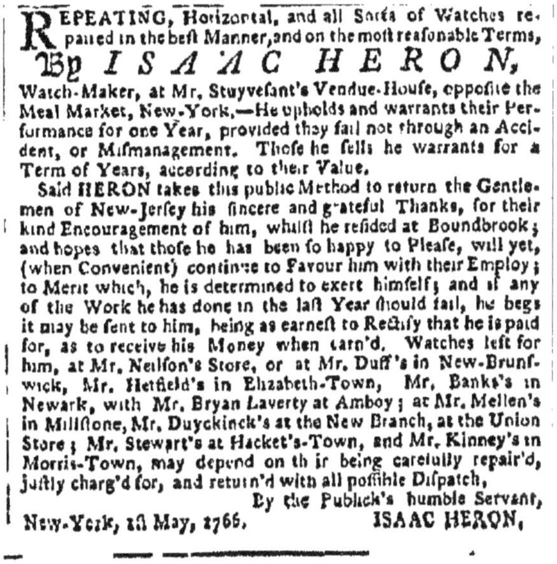

REPEATING, Horizontal, and all Sorts of Watches repaired in the beſt Manner, and on the moſt reaſonable Terms,

By ISAAC HERON,

Watch-Maker, at Mr. Stuyveſant's Vendue-Houſe, oppoſite the Meal Market, New-York.—He upholds and warrants their Performance for one Year, provided they fail not through an Accident, or Miſmanagement. Thoſe he ſells he warrants for a Term of Years, according to their Value.

Said HERON takes this public Method to return the Gentlemen of New-Jerſey his ſincere and grateful Thanks, for their kind Encouragement of him, whilſt he reſided at Boundbrook; and hopes that thoſe he has been ſo happy to Pleaſe, will yet, (when Convenient) continue to Favour him with their Employ; to Merit which, he is determined to exert himſelf; and if any of the Work he has done in the laſt Year ſhould fail, he begs it may be ſent to him, being as earneſt to Rectify that he is paid for, as to receive his Money when earn'd. Watches left for him, at Mr. Neilſon's Store, or at Mr. Duff's in New-Brunſwick, Mr. Hetfield's in Elizabeth-Town, Mr. Banks's in Newark, with Mr. Bryan Laverty at Amboy; at Mr. Mellen's in Millſtone, Mr. Duyckinck's at the New Branch, at the Union Store; Mr. Stewart's at Hacket's-Town, and Mr. Kinney's in Morris-Town, may depend on their being carefully repair'd, juſtly charg'd for, and return'd with all poſſible Diſpatch,

By the Publick's humble Servant,

New-York, 1ſt May, 1766. ISAAC HERON,

Figure 65. Heron was in Bound Brook, NJ, from 1763 until at least 1764 before moving to neighboring New York. The New York Gazette for May 5, 1766 advertised his contact details in the city and where watches could be left in towns in the state of New Jersey for collection and repair.

> Isaac Heron presents his Compliments to those Gentry, and congratulates them on their getting so *clean* off, on a Night so very *dirty* and *wet*. If they choose to return, during the *cold Season*, he will take care to provide them a *warm* Reception. And will endeavour to prevail upon them to leave behind e're they go, some Proof of their Identity; such as an amputated Limb, or, even a Snuff box full of Brains. The latter may be of Use to our very vigilant City Watch,—though, it is thought they sleep pretty sound with the few they have got.

Figure 66. The promise of retribution for the thieves who successfully burgled the premises of Isaac Heron should they return. From The New-York Journal or, The General Advertiser for January 7, 1773.

Advertising Doggerel

Compared to his first, rather meek, advertisement in Philadelphia in 1763, his public notices acquired a greater confidence and brashness with time. For example, like other early watch makers, Heron was satisfied to guarantee work for a year although by 1772, he felt confident enough to enhance his notices with doggerel:

> ISAAC HERON,
> *Coffee-House Bridge.*
> A Fresh importation of WATCHES, in silver, green skin, gray skin, *blue-skin*,* and tortoise shell cases, for either sex. Spring and house clocks, garnet hooprings, broaches, ditto for the ancient sons of peace; laced hats, purses, pen knives, pocket books; pebble, crystal and cornelian sleeve buttons, chains, seals, &c.
> * Ye Blue-skins! will you say I allude to you? Well you may, ye cursed varlets! Who can view the consequences of your baneful politicks, and not despise and detest you?---But, vain Wretches! it is not to you I advertise.
> Strangers should be informed, that in this province, the epithet *Blue-skin* was that by which, in the infancy of the rebellion, those ingrates were distinguished from Royalists, or real patriots.

Figure 67. From page 3 of The New-York Gazette and the Weekly Mercury June 9, 1777. Until he left, Heron continued to write in favor of the King and against the rebel cause, an attitude which was hardly good for business in the political climate of the day.

Should the all-sustaining hand him drop,
His Movements all springs, wheels hands must stop!
Then, like the tale of "a bear and fiddle,"
This bargain "breaks off in the middle"[244, 249]

His advertisements became increasingly strident. In 1773, thieves escaped after burglarizing his premises. In the local press he promised them a "warm reception" should they return (Figure 66). His contempt for the City Watch, who may have been asleep while his premises were being ransacked, is evident.[244, 250]

A Loyalist before the Revolution

Some of this ardor may have been explained by the tensions of the time. By 1773, plans for the Revolutionary War were already afoot and there was a serious threat to British rule. Heron had become an activist for the Loyalist cause in New York. That year he was appointed lieutenant of a company of artillery in the city of

> ISAAC HERON, DEtermines to embark in the first European fleet, and as he means to make a decent exit, he entreats those whom he has the honour to call his Debtors, THAT THEY ENABLE HIM to PUT HIS CREDITORS IN GOOD HUMOUR, by immediately discharging their several accounts. The few things remaining on hand, he will sell for first cost.

Figure 68. The indefatigable Royalist Isaac Heron bows out of America in 1778, the Revolutionaries having been victorious. Perhaps as a final swipe, this notice of his leaving appeared on September 9, 1778 in the partisan Royal Gazette.[256] The Gazette did not last long in the new political atmosphere and became defunct in 1783.

Figures 69 and 70. A rare long case clock by Isaac Heron of New York with a dial detail above right showing the arch date wheel. The clock has several idiosyncratic features - see text for details.

New York and was made captain of the militia by Lieutenant General William Tryon when British forces took over the city.[248] How much action he saw, if any, is unknown and he may have been more of a spy and gatherer of intelligence. Later, he would claim that he had passed information to the Howe brothers, an admiral and general in the British forces. They had succeeded in maintaining control of the city for seven years until the Treaty of Paris was ratified, formally ending the Revolutionary War in 1783.

In this politically unstable environment, business for Heron seemed to fluctuate; he called on his debtors in 1775 "to assist him in his...exertions to crawl from under the debt he owes"[251, 252] but had recovered somewhat by 1776 as he sought journeymen that year[253] and an apprentice in 1777.[254] His outspokenness, however, may have gone too far (Figure 67) as he referred to the "Blueskins" (revolutionaries) as "cursed varlets" with "baneful politicks" publicly in June 1777.²⁵⁵ Such ingrates were to be "distinguished from Royalists or real patriots." In the new non-Royal world of America, however, Heron's loud anti-Republicanism was hardly welcome.

It is not surprising that we find him winding up his business and leaving occupied New York for Europe in 1778.²⁵⁶ He packed his bags in September of that year (Figure 68) with the intention of sailing on the "first European fleet."²⁵⁶ The items Heron left were given to the New York watch maker, John Thompson.²⁷

Clocks and Watches

His surviving clocks and watches are now rare. One clock has been admirably described in detail by Ed LaFond, Jr. in the *NAWCC Bulletin*. Some stylistic similarities between the work of Heron and Finney of Liverpool were noted raising the possibility of a connection.²⁵² Going eight days, with rack striking on a bell, it stands 87" tall (Figures 69 and 70). It has several peculiarities, including an unhinged hood door that must be removed to allow winding. The cherry wood case is in the New Jersey style with a flat top, long door, and a plain base. The composite dial has a date wheel in the arch. The plain matted center has a seconds hand below 12, and, above six, the name of the maker, "Isaac Heron New York." The chapter ring is rather plain, with Roman numerals for hours separated from relatively large outer Arabic

Figure 71. Another Heron clock this one without spandrels. The Roman hour numerals are separated from the Arabic five-minute markers by dots indicating a later date than the clock above. Signed, "Isaac Heron, New York."

Figure 72. Watch No. 57 by Isaac Heron and signed by him for New York. Image very kind courtesy of the Guildhall Museum of the Worshipful Company of Clockmakers in London.

numerals marking five-minute intervals. Concentric circles enclose marks for the minutes. Applied spandrels of an abstract type of floral or tendril design are found in the corners and also in the arch surrounding the date wheel. Because the clock is signed from his New York period, a rough date of 1766–78 can be ascribed, consistent with the dial.

The date wheel is unusual in being located in the arch and also has an uncommon action mechanism. Most date apertures in brass dial clocks were located above six o'clock and were activated by a pin protruding from the hour wheel shaft to advance the nearby date wheel. In the Heron clock, a system of levers advances the arch wheel in two increments each of 12 hours.

This type of device has also been described in some English provincial clocks.[252] Likewise, the striking system has the peculiarity of an angled lever connecting the rack hook to the third wheel of the striking train. When the hook falls off the rack, the lever rotates interrupting the rotation of the third wheel and arresting the striking system. A movement from another long case clock by Heron is known, is now housed in an unoriginal, but geographically appropriate, case. The silvered dial (Figure 71) has an arch strike/silent mechanism, a seconds hand below 12, and a small, round date ring, above six. There are no spandrels and the Roman hour numerals are separated from the Arabic five-minute markers by dots. This indicates a later date than the clock above, although it is still signed, "Isaac Heron, New York."

Two watches signed by Heron are also known:

- No. 57, in the Guildhall Museum of the Worshipful Company of Clock makers in London (Figure 72)

- No. 58, previously in the Fraunces Tavern Museum of the Sons of the Revolution, New York[252]

Unfortunately, the latter was reported stolen sometime after 1979.[257]

Return to Ireland

Now age 43, he arrived back in Ireland in Cobh in November 1778 and settled in Waterford in the southeast of the country. His new occupation may have been as a tax collector or revenue inspector.[243] After his arrival, he applied to the Crown for assistance. In his communication to the Commission appointed by Act of Parliament for enquiring into the losses and services of the American Loyalists, he described his fall to penury in New York, the theft of his property, the threat of possible capture by the rebels, the serious injury of his daughter in America by a rebel attack on his house, and the death of his wife shortly after his return to Ireland.[258] In listening to the woes of the unfortunate but loyal Irishman it seems the Royal heart was moved. He received a stipend of £30 per annum which, with his salary of £65 per annum in the Revenue Department was felt would enable him to live comfortably[259] (Figure 73).

He tried to reestablish business again but owing to the "want of capital and the number of long established competitors……in times when… Loyalty rendered him unpopular even in his own country.." he was unsuccessful.[258] The only bright star in his sky in this dark period appears to have been the marriage of his daughter to a Mr. O'Flaherty of Grafton St in 1791.[260, 261] He was later cofounder with Worge and Smith, of a Loyalist newspaper, the *Waterford Herald*. By 1792, this was in difficulty, although it survived because of Heron, at least according to himself. "In the memorable uncommonly wet and dismal season, between the 20th of October of said 1792, and the 9th of January, 1793," he made a "… third tour of the province (of Munster) …. under vast fatigue and frequent danger…collecting *Herald* debts…"[262] From this document we also know that, in 1794, he had spent probably six weeks in prison in Dublin having been sued for about £225.[262]

Ireland at this time, inspired by the Americans and the French, was poised to move for political freedom. One of the nationalist newspapers, the *Northern Star*, published by the rebels in Belfast, was widely circulated in the country. This paper "of most treasonable tendency," squawked Heron in a letter of 1797 to the Crown authorities in Dublin Castle,[263] should not escape "instant death."[263, 264] Its "mad owners and editor," he continued "should be arrested."[263, 265] This assured his ailing Waterford enterprise some short-lived government favor and money (paid for publication of Proclamations). But the later withdrawal of this support, and, perhaps, squabbling among the owners, resulted in the collapse of his business later that year[265] and he was once again impecunious. He wrote his last bill to the Government in 1800 from prison.[264] From then on he senesced, dying in Dublin in 1813, at aged 78 with the cause unknown. His passing, which was noted in the *Limerick Chronicle* (Figure 74) for Wednesday, November 3[260] ended a rich, passionate, cantankerous, and often provocative life.

ROBERT JOYCE

With Heron and Simnet gone, New York had certainly been deprived of figures larger than life. Some years later, in 1793, Robert Joyce arrived from Dublin where he had "for seven years carried on business on his own account."[266] This would have put his arrival there in 1786. He may have been an Englishman by birth and have been born circa 1754.[6] He said he had been apprenticed in London[266] but his name is not on the list of London apprentices.[212] He was listed in the directories from 1791 to 1793 at 58 Jervis Street, Dublin.[88-90] While not as strident as his two New York predecessors, there were certainly some signs of grandiosity. One intriguing claim, for example, was that he had been "employed in making timepieces for astronomical observations" (Figure 77). Precision timepieces of this period in Ireland are so rare,[267] and the author is unaware of such instruments by him. A more extravagant assertion was that he made clocks ".... for the principal part of all the public buildings."[266] This would mean that most such clocks would have been constructed while he was there from 1786 until he left in 1793, which is not the case. There are no Robert Joyce turret clocks recorded[6, 268] or known to this author.

Manhattan

In December 1793, he commenced at Beaver Street in New York later moving to 62 Wall Street in 1796[27] by the Tontine Coffee House (Figure 76). Several apparently high-quality numbered watches have survived[6] as well as at least three long case clocks. One, in a mahogany case, with a secondary wood of poplar, made and labeled by Slover and Kortwright is known (Figure 75). Standing 98" in height, the pagoda top sports an inlaid eagle with a striped back and with stars above. The hood door is flanked by fluted columns with brass tops and bases. The trunk door has a round top and there are fluted columns. Concave molding leads to a paneled base. The painted dial has Roman numerals for the hours and there are Arabic numerals at 10-minute intervals. There is a seconds hand below 12. The lightly painted spandrels are in the style of the end of the 18th century. There is a figure on a blue background in the arch surrounded by sprigs.

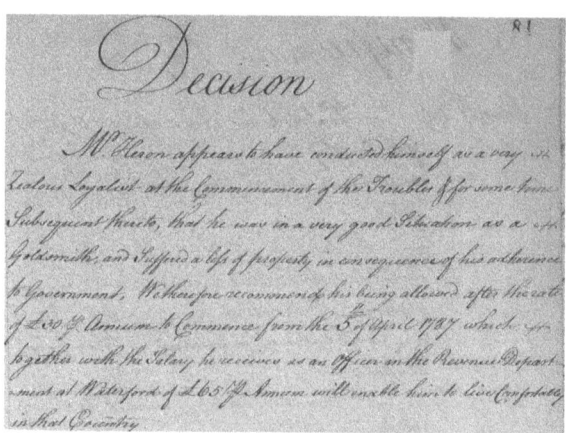

Figure 73. The decision by her Majesty's government to pay Heron £30 per annum in addition to his salary.[259] In the 18th century, £15 to £20 per year was a low wage with about £40 being needed for a family. To be comfortable, £100 per year might suffice and above £500 would have been considered rich.[556] So, despite the relatively meager payment, together with his other income, it might have made the difference between penury and a modest living.

Figure 74. The death notice for Isaac Heron in the Limerick Chronicle for Wednesday, November 3, 1813. Above is that for the sister of Henry Grattan, one of the family of distinguished parliamentarians in Dublin in the 18th and 19th centuries.

Beaver Street Clock

Another, with an almost identical, mahogany case of great elegance (Figure 78) also has a pagoda top with an inlay of flowers and sprigs. The hood door here is also flanked by fluted columns with brass tops and bases and the round topped trunk door is similar in style with fluted columns to the side. There is a graceful elliptical inlay in the door and concave molding leads to a paneled base with another circular inlay pattern. The painted dial has Roman numerals for the hours and there are Arabic numerals at 15 minute intervals. There is a seconds hand below 12. The figure in the arch is virtually identical to the first clock. The label has survived giving an address at 32 Beaver Street (Figure 79).

His notice for August 24, 1798 that he was at 143 Pearl Street [135, 269] was the last. He died a month later, aged 44, "of the prevailing fever."[27, 270] His death notice (Figure 80) gives an idea of the ferocity of the fever epidemics of the 18th and early 19th centuries. Figure 81 shows another surviving long case clock by Robert Joyce.

SAMUEL MARTIN

Samuel Martin was a watch maker in New York at the turn of the 18th and 19th centuries. In 1801, he was at 43 Maiden Lane, and was listed in the city directories intermittently from 1801[271] to 1820[272] at William[273] and Liberty[272] Streets. He may be the same Samuel Martin of Dublin circa 1780–90 who married Mary Dowling in 1791.[6] He is not in Wilson's *Dublin Directory* although others named Martin - George,

Figure 75. A long case clock by Robert Joyce with casework by Slover and Kortwright. Slover was in partnership with Kortwright in 1795 but this lasted only until 1796.[558] Thus, the clock - or at least the case - can be dated not just to the dates of Joyce's presence in New York (1793 until he died in 1798) but more precisely to 1795–96. Photograph courtesy of Bernard and S. Dean Levy, Inc., New York.

Figure 76. Robert Joyce's premises were next to the Tontine Coffee House on Wall Street. The oil on linen by Francis Guy (1760–1820) shows the Coffee House and the colorful but madding hustle of Wall Street in 1797 looking towards the East River.

> ROBERT JOYCE—Watch & Clock-Maker,
> No. 4, Beaver-Street,
> TAKES the liberty of informing his friends and the public, that he has commenced business in this city. Having served his apprenticeship in London, and afterwards wrought with the most eminent in his line there, and in Dublin; and in the latter place for seven years carried on business on his own account, in the course of which he has been employed in making time-pieces for astronomical observations, Airometers for shewing the point of the wind, and the Clocks for the principal part of all the public buildings; so that his experience gives him confidence to assert, that with his strict attention, he will execute every command in his line of business in the best and most satisfactory manner.

Figure 77. Advertisements appeared in The Diary or Loudon's Register, and the New York Daily Gazette from late 1793 to early 1794 for the early period of Robert Joyce in New York.

Thomas and Young - are listed in the last quarter of the 18th century.[82, 84, 88, 92, 94, 102] Samuel was a Mason and was associated with the Erin Lodge in New York.[274] He later changed his line of work to commence the "Tavern and Public business" in the Union Hotel in South Manhattan.[275] The hotel industry did not suit him, however, and he recommenced his old trade in May 1809[276] (Figure 82).

Move to Savannah

In 1818, he moved to Savannah, GA, perhaps to settle the estate of the late Samuel Luke to whom he was next of kin.[71] In December 1818, he had opened his own store there, in Whitaker Street, selling clocks, watches, chains, seals, and silverware[71] and was still there in March 1819 according to *The Savannah Republican*.[71] He may have returned to New York in 1820.[272]

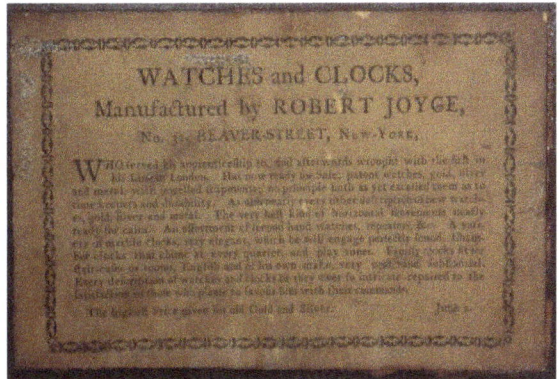

Figure 79. Labels are not commonly found in clocks and this one shows the breadth of his inventory; all kinds of watches as well as musical and chiming clocks.

A handsome, painted dial, tall case clock from the late 18th or early 19th century is known by this maker. The dial has tumbling Arabic numerals for the hours and smaller Arabic numerals at 15 minute intervals (Figures 83 and 84). There is a seconds hand below 12 and a shallow "inverted U" for the date located above the signature, "Saml Martin/New York." The painted arch above shows a patriot surrounded by cannon, spears, a halberd, drums, and flags. In the foreground is an anchor, and one wonders was this perhaps a reference to a naval engagement. The painted spandrels show patriotic American shields surrounded by floral wreaths. The dial can be attributed to the Boston dial firm of Nolen & Curtis.[70] A brass finial sits in the center of the swan neck pediment while turned pillars flank the hood doors. These are echoed by longer turned pillars in the trunk, which flank the door. Below this is a panel and single molding above a plain plinth.

ROBERT McHINCH

Robert McHinch was in Belfast about 1790[5] and emigrated sometime around 1798. He commenced work at Number 92 Water Street New York around January 1799 but moved to Maiden Lane in April of that year.[27] He was gone by 1805.[273] He sold and repaired watches and watch makers tools and materials. He had

Figure 78. The label found inside this clock by Robert Joyce allows a more accurate dating; it is dated June 2 and must have been from 1794 or 1795 since he arrived in December 1793 and left Beaver Street for Wall Street in April 1796. Photographs courtesy of Bernard and S. Dean Levy Inc. New York.

broad retail interests selling Boston Porter[27] and Ulster linen[277] (Figure 85). Verge watches are known from the Ulster Museum.[5]

JAMES ARTHUR

James Arthur was born on February 26, 1842, in Crosscandley, in the county of Derry (Figure 86). When he was young, the family moved to Glasgow and James became interested in horology by making sundials, and restoring and collecting clocks and watches. He was trained by his father as a millwright and as a machinist.[278] In his twenties, he spent seven years in the Glasgow Locomotive Works in Scotland and in 1870–71 he studied mathematics and mechanics under Professor AS Herschel in the Science and Art Department of the Andersonian University in Glasgow. This was the grandson of Sir William Herschel some of whose greatness apparently rubbed off on the young Irishman.

Recent deaths. Messrs Morewood and Ogden.—Mr. Joyce, Watchmaker.—Mr. Merckle. Mr. Doolet, architect, and two fifters.—John M'Kiffon, Esqr.—Mr. Welch.—Mrs. Belvidere.—Mr. G. Brett. —Mr. Mc Tom.—Mr. M. Slidell.—Mr. J. N. Silva.—Mr. Dorling, Printer.—Mr. F. Panton.—Mrs. Dunscumb.—Mr. S. Hopkins.

Burials on Friday	40—33	of the Fever.
Saturday	45—39	
Sunday	46—41	
Monday	48—45	
Tuesday	44—40	
Wednesday	60—58	

Burials in Philadelphia.

20th. Sept.	52 adults	7 children,
22d.	60	8
23d. 24th.	124	22
25th.	74	6

☞ For foreign articles, see the next page.

Figure 80. The death notice for Robert Joyce gives an idea of the ferocity of the fever epidemics of the 18th and early 19th centuries.

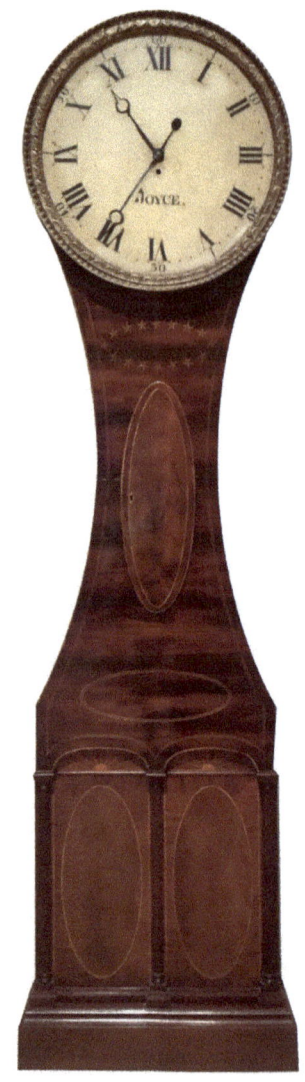

Figure 81. Another clock by Robert Joyce, ca.1795. Being 78" high and 28" wide, the case was made of mahogany and tulip poplar. A very different style of case and with a round dial.

§§§ Samuel Martin informs the public, that on the first day of May next, he will recommence CLOCK AND WATCH MAKING, in all their branches at No. 65 Maiden lane; where he will be happy to receive the commands of his friends. April 5—2w

Figure 82. Samuel Martin was a watch maker in New York at the turn of the 18th and 19th centuries. In 1801, he was at Maiden Lane but made a number of subsequent moves.

America

Arthur came to the United States in 1871 and, in a year, rose to be manager of the steam pump and machine works of Adam Carr in New York. During his seven years there he took out a number of patents but in 1878 he branched off for himself. In 1883, he formed The Arthur Co. Machine Works, which was located at 188-190 Front Street, New York. His firm dealt with the general manufacture and repair of machinery and also the construction of models for inventors.

Figures 83 and 84. A handsome painted arch dial tall case clock by Samuel Martin of New York with detail of dial. Martin moved to Savannah sometime in 1818 where he stayed until 1819 or 1820 after which he disappeared. Images courtesy Paul Foley.

Figure 85. Linen for sale by Robert McHinch from The Daily Advertiser of August 20, 1799, New York.[277]

new york, new jersey, ohio, and west virginia 53

Figure 86. Portrait of James Arthur born in Crosscandley, County Derry on February 26, 1842 and who died in Winsted, CT, on April 27, 1930.

JAMES ARTHUR COLLECTION

He collected widely and donated his magnificent horological collection to New York University, together with a substantial endowment specifying that there should be an annual lecture on "time and its mysteries." Daniel W. Hering, Professor Emeritus of Physics, was appointed curator. The original collection of 1,336 items was enlarged, principally by donation, and by 1932 it contained almost 1,500 items including over 200 clocks, 1,000 watches, and 50 books. Although the collection was left to New York University, the assembly and display of all items was never completed. In 1982, the University decided to divide the collection among the Smithsonian, the Time Museum in Rockford, IL, and the NAWCC National Watch & Clock Museum in Columbia, PA. The books from the Arthur Collection went to the rare books collection of the University, and the records and photographs remained with the University archives.[278, 279]

Clocks

Arthur was exceptionally gifted as a horologist and clock maker, designing and, with his employees, constructing them in his shop. He made many of his own dials and cases. To add to his list of extraordinary gifts, he was a lucid writer and his designs found their way into horological publications such as *The Jewelers' Circular*. His book *Time and Its Measurement*[280] was reprinted from Popular Mechanics in Chicago in 1909 and is now available free to the public on the Internet.

Space precludes an in-depth discussion of all of Arthur's constructions. They have, however, been covered extensively in *The Lure of the Clock*, Professor Hering's detailed discussion of the Arthur Collection, as well as in Arthur's own writings. One example, however, may illustrate the level of his horological skills (Figures 87 and 88). The case is solid oak and stands 85" high. It is a five-minute repeater, which will repeat the time to within five minutes by pulling an attached cord. This cord may be extended and branched off, with bell-pulls placed in various places in a residence so that the clock can be activated to repeat the time including, of course, at night. It strikes the last hour on a bell and a bell of higher tone is struck once for every five minute interval past the hour.

Unusually for a domestic clock, the dial is above its normal position and is no longer covering the mechanism, which is therefore totally visible and readily accessible. It is partially skeletonized with a solid rear plate and the front plate in three pieces. A vertical shaft rises to operate the dial work. In his horological designs Arthur revisited case designs, mechanisms, pendulums, hands, and also dials. For example, this dial is quite small at 9" in diameter but the clock is easy to read as the numerals were cut through the brass dial and appear black from any vantage point. The hands are also distinct and heavy.

The clock has three weight-driven trains with one dedicated to the five minute strike. The clock does not strike each hour unless the cord

Figures 87 and 88. Those with a desire to read a complete technical description of this 5-minute repeater are directed to the March 1905[281] issue of the journal Machinery - now online - where Arthur expounds in detail about his creation. The detail picture from this domestic clock show that the mechanism is readily visible since the dial is above its normal position. The large bell strikes the hour and the smaller five minute intervals.

is pulled and this is likewise the case for the five minute strike. Thus the winding requirements for the trains are minimized.

James Arthur finished his career in 1912 but his horological writing persisted for many years. Some of his articles were almost philosophical in nature such as "Time" and "The Twenty Four Hour Day" published in 1916 and in 1919 respectively well after he retired. He died in Winsted, CT, on April 27, 1930. By an extraordinary coincidence, we shall later hear about the connection between the city of Winsted and another maker from Ulster.

JAMES FARQU(H)AR

James Farqu(h)ar of Newry and Armagh married in 1832[5] and was working in Belfast at 55 High Street (Figure 89) from at least 1835[134] until 1839.[282] He may have been the same maker, then located in Armagh, who married the daughter of the proprietor of the Armagh-Belfast coach in 1832.[5] He went bankrupt then went to New York[48] where his wife died in 1851.[5] One of his watch papers has survived.[135]

Figure 89. "The New Plan of the Town of Belfast," published by James Cleeland in 1819 showing the center of the city and High Street, where James Farquhar worked before he left for New York. High Street was a popular location for many Belfast clock makers including James Chapman, Lee & Son, John Pyper, and the well-known John Knox.

SAMUEL DOWN

Samuel Down was born in Ireland about 1817 and was in New York City from 1834 until the 1870s. He arrived from England and was also a gas meter manufacturer. A clock of his with a porcelain dial is known that dates to 1850.[135] He is not on Irish lists.[129]

H & LJ SHERRARD

H & LJ Sherrard were located in Belfast, but one advertisement refers to the import of American clocks "direct from our house in New York."[48]

NEWBURGH

GEORGE GORDON

George Gordon, watch maker and silversmith from Ireland, was in Newburgh, NY, until 1824.[283] When he arrived there is not clear but he was there in 1808 and was creditor of Mathew Garvey, who had absconded because of indebtedness.[284] He was in Water Street in 1812.[285] As well as a watch maker, he was also the agent for *The Shamrock*, or *Hibernian Chronicle*, a weekly Irish-American newspaper published in New York.[286] There were several contemporary Gordon clock makers in Ireland including Joseph, James, and Thomas in Ballymoney and Dublin. There was another in Ballynahinch, known simply as Gordon, circa 1790–1810 who might even be the same individual.[5]

ALBANY

JAMES LATHAM

James Latham was in Albany in 1795[2, 27] worked "several years for ...gentlemen..... of Great Britain, France and Ireland." He is not mentioned on Irish lists.[129]

Figure 90. Mid-19th century Belvidere where John Nicholl ran his clock business. Published in Barber and Howe's Historical Collections of the State of New Jersey by Tuttle of New York in 1844.

DUNKIRK

THE NELSONS

There were several makers by the name of Nelson in the towns of Dromore and Banbridge, County Down. In Dromore, there were three generations of James Nelsons, the first of whom was working in 1783 and the last of whom emigrated to New Zealand in 1880.[5] Robert Nelson left Banbridge about 1850 and settled in Dunkirk, NY, where he died in 1904 aged 84.[5] His brother Joseph joined him and they became wholesalers of clocks and watches.[287] There was yet another, Samuel, in Banbridge active in 1868[5] who may have been related.[2, 5]

NEW JERSEY

BELVIDERE

JOHN NICHOLL

e have already met Winsted, CT, as the place where James Arthur went to his eternal reward in 1930. So, it is curious indeed that some 50 years later in the same town we discover records of yet another peripatetic Irishman connected with the clock industry. In 1981, the 38-page *History and Travels of an Irish Emigrant* was rescued by a town custodian from the village dump and passed into the hands of a local historian.[288] It documents the life of one John Nicholl, a well-known clock maker with no known connection to Winsted. In fact, he practiced his craft not even in Connecticut but in Belvidere, Warren County, NJ (Figure 90).

History

According to his History he was born in Cullybackey near Ballymena, County Antrim in 1784. It is unclear where he learned his trade. He left Ireland for the first time at age 17 arriving in Staten Island in 1801. This would have been too early for him to have finished a formal apprenticeship although he might have been exposed, or even related to, one of the local clock makers in Ballymena only four miles from Cullybackey. Certainly there were contemporary clock makers in Ballymena around that time including John Creighton, Charles O'Neill, and Robert Welsh to mention a few.[6] He sought, but failed to find, a watch maker's apprenticeship in New York City. He taught in the city and in New York State for several years and then left for Charleston, SC, in 1809 where his sister was located. Returning to Ireland in 1817, he opened a cloth and grocery shop in the village of Ahoghill a few miles south of Cullybackey. On January 12, 1818, it was robbed by William and Alexander Underwood.

Court Proceedings

The court case was reported in the *Belfast Newsletter* later that year[289] (Figure 91). Subsequently, the Underwoods falsely alleged that Mr. Nicholl had broken into the house of a Mr. Charles Underwood and had stolen three spindles of yarn. When it became evident to the judge that this allegation was indeed false, the charges against Mr. Nicholl were dropped. Although acquitted, he left Ireland for the second and last time and returned to the United States via Canada. In 1819, he made a living cleaning clocks and opened a store in Easton, PA. By 1822 he had made his final move to Belvidere, NJ. It has been said that he made his first clock in 1819, but he must at least have had some experience in this area since he had brought oil and tools with him when he returned to America from Ireland in 1818.[288]

Clocks

His clocks were of various types including 8-day timepieces, as well as pillar and scroll clocks. Several long case clocks have also survived, a fine example of which is shown here (Figures 92 and 93). The arch dial is signed "John Nicholl, Belvidere." There is a central sweep second hand and a calendar hand indicating the date below the hours. The hood is adorned with urn finials at the side while the swan necks terminate in gilt paterae. There is an additional central finial of a bird with outstretched wings. The door is flanked by rope columns with gilt plinths and capitals. The rope columns are repeated in both the trunk, with its fan carved door, and in the base with inset panels. There are paw feet.

John Nicholl died in 1861. His dwelling in Belvidere (Figure 94) is on the National Historic Register.

Figure 91. The court cases of the Underwoods and John Nicholl. The Underwoods were found guilty of stealing from John Nicholl and were "transported" - or banished - for seven years. This was usually to Australia or Van Diemen's Land (modern Tasmania).

Figures 92 and 93. A fine example of a long case clock by John Nicholl which is shown here with a detail of the dial. There are hour and minute hands and additional hands for seconds and the date. For those accustomed to a date aperture above six and a seconds indicator below 12, the extra hands make this a very "busy" dial. But these are not uncommon features on American white dial clocks. The date is indicated by the smallest hand on the inside date track. Pictures very kind courtesy of Paul Foley.

Figure 94. The house of John Nicholl located at 316 Front Street, Belvidere, NJ, dating from ca. 1825. The house was extensively renovated about 2006 and is now used as a business premises.

OHIO AND WEST VIRGINIA

CINCINNATI AND AKRON

avid Andrews, born in Ireland circa 1822, was working in Cincinnati as a watch maker and silversmith from circa 1849 until at least 1863.[290]

John Durkin was born in Ireland in 1859 and became chief of police in Akron in 1900. A grandfather clock is extant with his name on the dial.[4]

MINERAL COUNTY

Thomas Fallon was born about 1841 and was in the Piedmont district of Mineral County, West Virginia, from 1868 to circa 1880. He was a silversmith and watch maker.[135]

Chapter Four
Maryland, Kentucky, and Missouri

INTRODUCTION

If asked to mention the cities in America to which their compatriots might have emigrated, most Irish people would surely mention Boston, New York, and Philadelphia. However, the Border States were also important. These were the slave states, including Maryland, Kentucky, and Missouri, that did not secede from the Union to join the Confederacy during the American Civil War. The South—the 11 states that formed the Confederacy in 1861—were also significant destinations for immigrants.[291] In the 18th century, some 250,000 Presbyterians and 100,000 Catholics came to the United States, largely to Pennsylvania and New York, facilitated by the shipping connections required for the linen industry.[291] Many moved south and west from Pennsylvania through Maryland, Virginia, and into the Carolinas along the Great Wagon Road from Philadelphia.[292] Other immigrants moved directly to Charleston, an important port in South Carolina with its own sailing connections with Ireland in the 18th century.

In the South in the 19th and 20th centuries, the descendants of these Protestant immigrants began to refer to themselves as Scotch-Irish to distinguish themselves from the less-fortunate Catholic newcomers. The flow of immigrants in the 18th century became a veritable flood in the 19th century. Between 1815 and 1845 between 800,000 and 1 million people left Ireland, to be followed by nearly 2 million more after the famine of 1847. Many moved to Charleston or Savannah to work on the railroad, to New Orleans to work on the New Basin Canal, or Mobile, AL, for the cotton industry.[291] Life in the Deep South wasn't easy. There were typhus and cholera epidemics in New Orleans in 1847 and 1852, and yellow fever in 1853.[291] Nevertheless, the cotton boom in the 1850s created a shortage of labor and Irish workers could make twice a northern wage on a southern railway.[291] Immigrants quickly assimilated into Southern culture, including acceptance of the slave trade.

MARYLAND

Some of the best-documented Irish clock makers in America are to be found in both Baltimore and Annapolis. In the middle of the 18th century, the former was nothing more than a hamlet of 25 dwellings on the banks of the Patapsco River (Figure 95). However, in the last quarter of the century, it experienced exponential growth, with the population growing to 13,000 by 1790 and doubling to 26,000 a mere 10 years later.[293] Some insight into the magnitude of this growth may be obtained by comparing the populations of the towns from which our tradesmen arrived. The population of Dublin rose from 150,000 in 1750[294] to 182,000 in 1798,[295] Cork from 70,000 in 1750 to 80,000 in 1810,[295] and that of Belfast from 8,500 in 1757 to 20,000 in 1800.[295]

The city was named after Lord Baltimore of the Calvert family, a convert to Catholicism. An Irish connection can be seen in its name, derived from the Gaelic "Baile an Tí Mhóir," meaning

Figure 95. Baltimore in 1752 as seen by Edward Johnson Coale's 1817 reconstruction of the 1752 etching by John Moale of Baltimore. From The Pratt Library via Wikicommons.

the town of the big house, a reference to the Lord's seat in County Longford. Tolerance, as in Philadelphia, was a feature of this new city. As with the other cities above, the trade in labor, that is, people, many as "servants" was heavy in Baltimore. "Within this fortnight," one report from the *Maryland Journal and Baltimore Advertiser* for August 1773 reads, "three thousand five hundred emigrants have arrived from Ireland."[296] This influx of people may have included hundreds, if not thousands, of craftsmen.[297] In the Chesapeake region also there was significant trade with Ireland at this time, particularly for Irish linen. In return, Ireland received wheat. This was of no small importance to the economies of Virginia and Maryland; it has been estimated that, in 1770, about 40% of Baltimore's tonnage of wheat was shipped directly to Ireland.[298]

To this rapidly expanding economy came the Irish craftsmen[299] including seal cutters, cabinet makers, architects, builders, goldsmiths, and silversmiths. Many had spectacular social mobility and financial success in their new environment. For example, the silversmith Christopher Hughes (Figure 96), born in 1744,[46] arrived in the early 1770s. Also a watch and clock maker,[300] he made a fortune in real estate and became an important social figure in the city.[299] He married in 1779 and died—at a ripe age, prosperous, and successful—in Baltimore in 1824.[46]

CHRISTOPHER HUGHES
1774–1824

Figure 96. Christopher Hughes arrived in Baltimore in 1773 and had his own company at the sign of the Cup and Crown on the corner of Market and Gay Streets. According to the Maryland Journal and Baltimore Advertiser for that year he not only dealt in watches but also in silverware, gold rings, seals, and trinkets. Image published in Pleasants and Sill's Maryland Silversmiths 1715-1830.

Not everyone was so lucky. The goldsmith William Hughes, possibly Christopher's brother,[299] was the son of Philip Hughes and apprentice to John Moore in 1758.[31] Free in 1767,[31] he was at Essex Quay from at least 1773.[81, 82, 181, 183, 184, 301] He arrived in Baltimore around 1785 but died in 1791.[299]

BIGGER and CLARKE,
Watch and Clock-Makers from Dublin, at the Houſe of Dr. John Stevenſon, in Market-ſtreet, within ſix doors of Calvert ſtreet, Baltimore,

BEG leave to inform the public, That they execute every branch in the REPEATING, HORIZONTAL, and PLAIN WATCH BUSINESS equal to any in Europe, having ſerved under the inſtruction of the two firſt Watch-Makers in Ireland, Meſſrs. Craige and Clarke, of Dublin, and afterwards done buſineſs under the firſt Workmen in London, which opportunities of improvement, they reſpectfully preſume will admit them as full maſters of their profeſſion. They are furniſhed with a moſt complete ſet of working-tools and engines, collected at great pains and conſiderable expence, the poſſeſſion of which, with a determination to pay the ſtricteſt attention to ſuch commands, as they may be honored with; they hope to meet with the countenance and approbation of an indulgent public.—They have now ready for ſale, a variety of Gold, Silver, and metal Watches, Eight Day Clocks, elegant Gold Hands, beſt Watch Glaſſes, Keys, &c. &c. Alſo, a few elegant ſteel mounted dreſs ſmall Swords, of the firſt faſhion, highly finiſhed; and a few

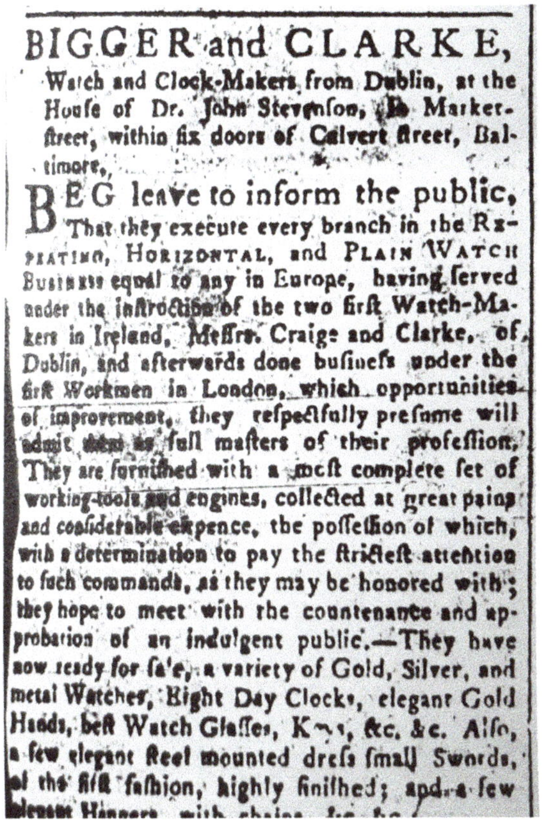

Figure 97. The establishment of Bigger and Clarke's business as noted in The Maryland Gazette November 1783.[303] For Clarke this would be one of several unsuccessful partnerships. Bigger settled on sole proprietorship after their partnership dissolved in 1784.

BALTIMORE

GILBERT BIGGER

Gilbert Bigger was born around 1750 and moved to Maryland from Dublin. The marriage of Mr. Gilbert Bigger, watch maker and goldsmith on Skinner Row, to Miss Lucy Leban of Harold's Cross, is reported for November 30, 1776.[302] Presumably, Lucy died soon after because he married Elizabeth Walsh in St. Brides Church in July 1783.[6]

By November of that year he was in partnership with Ambrose Clarke (see later), another erstwhile Dublin clock maker, at the house of Dr. John Stevenson in Market Street, Baltimore.[303] Clarke had previously been at 17 Dawson Street[82] and was still listed there in 1786,[83] presumably a directory error. They might have been working together in Dublin at Clarke's premises, as Bigger was not listed separately.

Apprentices

They had served under the instruction of "the two first Watchmakers in Ireland, Messrs. Craige and Clarke, of Dublin"[303] (Figures 97 and 98). This is likely a reference to Charles Craig and Christopher Clarke, who were well-established contemporary makers in Fownes' Street.[82] Bigger and Clarke were well equipped with a complete set of "working tools and engines, collected at great pains and considerable expence." and were selling gold, silver, and metal watches as well as 8-day clocks.[303]

In July of the following year his second wife died. One wonders if she had died in childbirth as they had been married a year or so. His partnership with Ambrose Clarke was dissolved in August.[304]

Premises

Bigger continued to trade at the house of Dr. Stevenson but, by November 1784, had moved premises to Holliday Street near the market house. At this time his inventory also includ-

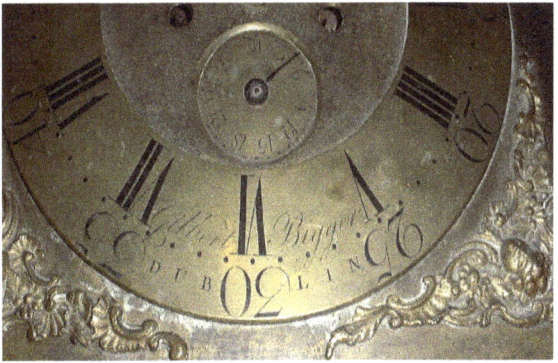

Figure 98. Detail of a surviving Dublin dial by Gilbert Bigger. Born ca. 1750, he would have likely finished his apprenticeship ca. 1770. The dial can thus be dated ca. 1770–83 the year he arrived in Maryland.

Figure 99. Warner & Hanna's Plan of the City and Environs of Baltimore, engraved by Francis Shallus, Philadelphia, 1801, gift of Mr. and Mrs. Arthur J. Gutman, showing the location of the houses of Ambrose Clarke and Gilbert Bigger at upper left and Market Street at lower right. Image very kind courtesy Catherine Rogers Arthur, Director and Curator, Homewood Museum, The Johns Hopkins University.

ed musical clocks, as well as sundry jewelry. He accepted payment by bills of exchange, cash, or tobacco.[305] By May 1785, he had moved again to the corner of Market and Calvert Street[306] and, finally, to 115 Baltimore Street sometime between 1794 and 1796. Here he remained until 1816.[307, 308] His residence was at Biddle Street, leading from Hook's Town Road[309] (Figure 99).

As his stature and local reputation grew, he aided in settling the commercial affairs of others. For example, when Hogan, M'Cutchan & Co.[310] founded by the architect and James Hogan, ceased to trade, the final settlement of accounts was to be discharged through Bigger. This included the sale of a servant man and woman.[310] Along with Standish Barry and Joseph Rice,[311] he provided testimonials for work on the alarm in the cupola of the Baltimore courthouse.[311]

Marriage and Family

In 1791 he remarried, this time to Sally Rice.[312] Business continued successfully in the 1790s with the retail of watches, jewelry, sundials, and "house clocks in mahogany cases" imported from England.[313] Although he imported clocks and watches, he also remained a maker himself and took apprentices. He had sought one in 1784[71] but it is unclear if he had been successful. Two known apprentices were Joseph Barkley (1800)[314] and Wes(t)ley Abbott (1811).[4, 315] Barkley remained in Baltimore, at least until 1824.[135]

His daughter Elizabeth married Captain Pigot Shaw in September 1804.[316] "How happy our lot," the nuptial notice announced, "when by marriage we prove, the envied delights of

Figure 100. A long case clock by Gilbert Bigger.

connubial love..." For others in the Baltimore of the time the lot was less happy; in the next column of the newspaper, 28 interments in one week were noted in the city and precincts of Baltimore, 15 of whom were children and 11 of whom had died of cholera. The 20-year-old daughter would soon have her own curious and coincidental calamity. Like her father, she lost a spouse after a short time; by February 1806 Captain Pigot Shaw was dead.[317]

In the same year, Bigger's premises were burgled and the property of one Mr. Sandell stolen.[318] It is not known if the goods were ever recovered, but the description of the villains, two in number, cannot have helped greatly in their detection: "...one of them stout and tall; the other of a middling stature..."

Clocks

Several of his clocks have survived as well as one of his dials from his Dublin period (Figure 98). One of his mahogany tall case clocks has been admirably described in detail elsewhere[293] and is signed, "Bigger, Baltimore" (Figures 100 and 101). The false plate is marked, "Wilson" and there is a small calendar dial in the arch.[293] with a seconds hand below 12. The dial has Roman numerals for the hours and the minutes are dotted with Arabic numerals at intervals of five. The hands are typical of the late 18th century. The lightly decorated corners are in the earlier, lighter style for painted dials, circa 1790 or so, with floral designs enclosed by a gilt surround. The case has a swan-neck pediment terminating in rosettes. There is a central urn finial and an open frieze. Dentils and concave molding separate the pediment from the upper part of the hood with its inlay of interlacing curved string bands and representations of birds in lighter wood. Turned fluted columns flank the door. Quarter columns are seen in the trunk, the door of which displays a string rectangle as does the plinth. The clock stands on ogee feet and is a fine example of Baltimore craftsmanship from the period when Bigger's business was thriving. As with many Baltimore clocks, this one is tall at some 98½" in height.

Figure 101. Detail of the hood of the long case clock by Gilbert Bigger from his Baltimore period.

Another of his clocks has a moon automation in the arch (Figures 102 and 103). The dial, painted and signed, "G. Bigger, Baltimore," has Roman numerals for the hours with Arabic numerals at intervals of five for minutes. There is a seconds hand below 12. The hands are typical of the early 19th century. The corners are more heavily decorated than one often sees on an American clock and show pastoral ladies in seasonal settings. The arch shows a rolling moon with inner Arabic numerals for the lunar date and outer Roman numerals for the tides. It has a flat top with fluted hood columns, a rectangular door, and ogee feet. There are some features such as the strings of bellflowers and a cross-banded oval which have been attributed

Figure 102. Another long case clock by Gilbert Bigger from his Baltimore period.

Figures 103 and 104. Left: Detail of the long case clock by Gilbert Bigger. Right: Detail of one of his two surviving bracket clocks. Pictures courtesy Stiles Tuttle Colwill and Catherine Rogers Arthur, Director and Curator, Homewood Museum, The Johns Hopkins University. Photography by Will Kirk.

to the work of the cabinet maker Levin Tarr (1772–1821).[293]

Bracket Clocks

Two bracket clocks have also survived.[19] One, however, has not come down to us in its original case, which is some 15½" tall and 10 ¼" wide. The silvered dial, 9¾" tall and 7" wide, has Roman numerals for the hour, has a strike/silent mechanism, and is engraved with swags in the arch and in the corners. It is signed, "Bigger Baltimore" (Figure 104). Other surviving horological artifacts include watch papers (Figure 105).

By the time he had spent more than 30 years in the New World, he had prospered judging by his three-story brick house, his 15,000-square foot summer residence on Biddle Street and an adjoining lot of over 7,000 sq. feet. Bigger

Figure 105. One of two known watch papers for Gilbert Bigger now in the possession of the American Antiquarian Society described in American Watch Papers.[560] The other is in the Maryland Historical Society and was previously illustrated in the Silver in Maryland exhibition in 1983–84.[19] Courtesy American Antiquarian Society.

DR. BAKER's DENTIFRICE and ALBION ESSENCE, a fresh Supply just received by *SPOTSWOOD* and *CLARKE*, at their Store, Market-Street, Corner of Grant's Lane, who have for Sale, Surveying Instruments, made and warranted by *Benjamin Rittenhouse*—They are, as usual, well assorted with a Variety of Books; Stationary Ware; Jewellery; Patent Medicines and Perfumes; best Court Sticking-Plaister; new Music, with a Variety of single Songs, elegantly printed on Royal Paper, for the Purpose of Selection and Binding; Musical Instruments; among which is an excellent Spinet, by Longman and Broderip, of London.—Also, just published, Rosina, a Comic Opera, as performed by the American Company, with universal Applause; the Poor Soldier, with the Words, Songs, Duets, &c. Select Poems, chiefly American; Webster's second Part of his Grammatical Institute; the witty and entertaining Exploits of George Buchanan.—They have also lately received, a neat and elegant Assortment of LONDON GILT BUTTONS.

☞ A. CLARKE, WATCH-MAKER, continues at the Store of *SPOTSWOOD* and *CLARKE*, to follow his own particular Business, in making and repairing all Sorts of CLOCKS and WATCHES. All Orders in the Jewellery Business received and executed in the neatest and most fashionable Manner, and according to any Device.

Baltimore, May 17, 1787.

Figure 106. William Spotswood and Ambrose Clarke had a motley collection of goods for sale ranging from Dr. Baker's Dentifrice to books, watches, and jewelry.

departed this life on Wednesday, November 6, 1816 in his 66th year. His obituary glowed with adulation for he was "excellent ...amiable... benevolent...sincere...cheerful."[319] His property on Calvert and Baltimore Streets was auctioned in November 1817.[320] The final disposition of his estate included the assessment of debts to Edward Sandell[321]and Joseph Barkley.[322]

His will showed that he had a son who was living in Dublin.[323] A William Bigger, possibly related, was at Boot Lane working as a turner from 1780 until 1786[81, 83] and a Hugh Bigger, cabinet maker, is known who died in 1778.[9]

AMBROSE CLARKE

Ambrose Clarke was born in 1757.[4] He was in Baltimore as early as 1777 when, together with John McCabe, he founded the Baltimore Company of Militia.[71] He returned to Dublin perhaps around 1781[6] and was working in Dawson Street until circa 1784.[82] He returned permanently to Baltimore shortly after when he was in partnership with Gilbert Bigger until this was dissolved in August 1784.[304] Clarke left for Philadelphia but returned in October and recommenced business, this time below a printing office of a Mr. Hayes, selling watches and various other items of hardware and sought an apprentice.[71] Several watches were stolen from his premises in December of that year and included watches by the Dublin makers George Parker and Charles Smith as well as two other previously unknown Dublin watch makers, Charles Reynolds and B. Gilbert.[324]

Bibliophile

The location in the printing office is no accident as Clarke was also a bibliophile. He organized a book auction in December 1784[325] and, by1787 had formed another partnership, Spotswood & Clarke, located at Market Street (Figure 106).[326] Presumably, this was with William Spotswood, the bookseller and stationer from Dublin who arrived sometime around 1784[327] and who may have been related to the Dublin cabinet maker George Spotswood.[9] Watches and clocks were sold and repaired alongside

The Light Infantry Company of the 1st Battalion of the 27th Regiment of Maryland Militia, commanded by Col. Swan, is requested to meet at Mr. Grant's Assembly-Room, this evening, precisely at 7 o'clock, on business of the utmost importance.

By Order of the Captain,
AMBROSE CLARKE, Secretary.

Figure 107. From the Baltimore Daily Intelligencer for August 19, 1794.

Departed, this life on Wednesday morning last, Mr. Ambrose Clarke, a native of Ireland, and long a respectable inhabitant of this city, he was sincerely beloved and esteemed by all who knew him.

Figure 108. The obituary of Ambrose Clarke as published in the Baltimore Evening Post, September 8, 1810.

JOHN Mc. CABE,

WATCH and CLOCK-MAKER, in North-Street, Newry, takes this Method of informing his Friends and the Publick, that he continues to make all Sorts of Watches and Clocks equal in Goodness to any now made in London or Dublin, viz. Plain, Repeating, and Horizontal Watches; good plain Weight and Spring Clocks: He likewise makes musical Clocks to play Tunes by either Bells or Organs, so as to play a different Tune every Day in the Week at the Hours of 3, 6, 9, and 12, and a Psalm Tune on Sunday, of which he has now a Clock in Hands as a Specimen, which will be finished in a few Days, and may be then viewed by any Gentlemen who pleases. He returns his sincere Thanks to his Friends and those Gentlemen who were pleased to encourage him and honour him with their Custom. Newry, 10th Feb. 1769.

N. B. A Protestant Apprentice of reputable Parents is wanted by said Mc. Cabe; a Fee will be expected, and no less Term than 7 Years

Figure 109. At the Sign of the Dial in North Street, Newry, County Down in 1767, according to the Belfast Newsletter in May 1767.[340] Although he sought an apprentice for at least seven years, he moved to Dublin in 1769.

books, music, musical instruments as well as patent medicines.[326] In 1789, Clarke proposed a lottery to set up a circulating library.[328] He opened a bookstore in 1791 specializing in legal and other texts.[329] He also had a bookstore with Rice & Co.,[330] but a later book partnership with James Keddie failed.[331] In 1793, he proposed the publication of *The Monthly Mirror,* a magazine for religion, philosophy, and other "interesting and entertaining subjects."[332]

His military interests continued, and a year later he was secretary of the Light Infantry Company of the 1st Battalion of the 27th Regiment of Maryland Militia (Figure 107).[333] By 1810, he had moved into another line of business as an exchange and stockbroker with Thomas Barklie on Lovely Lane[334] but he died in September of that year, "beloved and esteemed by all who knew

John M'Cabe,

WATCH and CLOCK-MAKER,

From DUBLIN, has opened SHOP, at the sign of the DIAL, opposite the COFFEE-HOUSE in MARKET-STREET, BALTIMORE,

WHERE he carries on said branches in an extensive manner, and having conducted business for many of the most capital artists in London, Dublin, and Liverpool, he can, under the testimony of their approbation of his abilities, and fixed determination to pay the strictest attention to business, assure the public that he is enabled to execute and furnish them with watches and clocks of the following kinds, equal, if not superior, in elegance of workmanship and accuracy of construction, to any imported, and upon seasonable terms, viz. plain, repeating, horizontal, stop, or seconds watches; musical clocks, to go either by springs or weights; astronomical, chime, quarter, and plain ditto adjusted with balance, common, or compound pendulums; also turret, or steeple clocks, constructed to endure for a long continuance of time: Any of which, ladies and gentlemen may be furnished with, and no money be expected until the test of proof shall confirm their intrinsic value. He likewise makes spring clocks for mariners, with Sun's motion in the arch of the dial, which will keep time on a principle, he believes, superior to any hitherto practised; as a proof whereof, he will suffer them to be tried two or three voyages at Sea before he requires payment.—He also makes the electrical aparatus, and air pumps; and repairs orreries, reflecting and solar telescopes, land and sea compasses &c.

Baltimore February 24, 1774.

Figure 110. John McCabe opened at the Sign of the Dial opposite the Coffee House in Market Street, Baltimore in 1774. From The Maryland Journal and the Baltimore Advertiser from February 24 to March 3, 1774.

him (Figure 108)."[335] Despite his various commercial endeavors, he was not listed in many of the contemporary Baltimore directories.[307, 309, 336–339]

JOHN McCABE

John McCabe was the brother of the distinguished London maker James, and of Thomas, the noted revolutionary. There was another brother, William, of whom we shall hear more later.

John was the third son of Patrick McCabe of Lurgan and was born between 1740 and 1748. If he started in business in Newry around 1767[340] his birth date would likely have been 1745 or 1746. He moved to Dublin in 1769.[341] He was

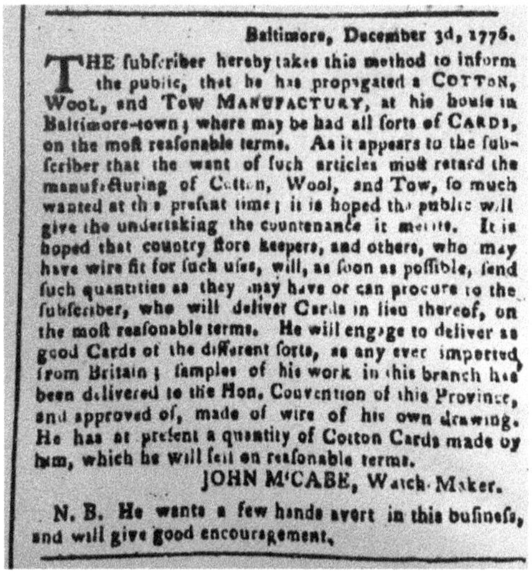

Baltimore, December 3d, 1776.

THE ſubſcriber hereby takes this method to inform the public, that he has propagated a COTTON, WOOL, and TOW MANUFACTURY, at his houſe in Baltimore-town; where may be had all ſorts of CARDS, on the moſt reaſonable terms. As it appears to the ſubſcriber that the want of ſuch articles muſt retard the manufacturing of Cotton, Wool, and Tow, ſo much wanted at the preſent time; it is hoped the public will give the undertaking the countenance it merits. It is hoped that country ſtore keepers, and others, who may have wire fit for ſuch uſes, will, as ſoon as poſſible, ſend ſuch quantities as they may have or can procure to the ſubſcriber, who will deliver Cards in lieu thereof, on the moſt reaſonable terms. He will engage to deliver as good Cards of the different ſorts, as any ever imported from Britain; ſamples of his work in this branch has been delivered to the Hon. Convention of this Province, and approved of, made of wire of his own drawing. He has at preſent a quantity of Cotton Cards made by him, which he will ſell on reaſonable terms.

JOHN M'CABE, Watch-Maker.

N. B. He wants a few hands avert in this buſineſs, and will give good encouragement.

Figure 111. John McCabe's mechanical talents extended to the manufacture of cards for the cotton, wool, and tow industries. From Dunlap's Maryland Gazette; or, the Baltimore General Advertiser on December 3, 1776.[344]

skilled in making not only cylinder, repeating, and stop watches but also musical clocks playing "by either bells or organs"[342] (Figure 109). His stay in Ulster was relatively short as he moved to Dublin, Liverpool, and London and then on to America. He may not have worked independently in Dublin as he was not in the city directories.[101, 181]

The Maryland Journal and the Baltimore Advertiser of 1774[343] places him at the Sign of the Dial in Market Street noting that he had conducted business for "many of the most capital artists" in London, Dublin, and Liverpool (Figure 110).

A Versatile Craftsman

He could also construct turret or steeple clocks. His spring clocks for mariners with a principle for keeping time "superior to any hitherto practiced" suggests that he may have worked with a marine clock manufacturer in Liverpool or London but the principle is unknown. He had clearly been exposed to more than clocks in his travels as he also repaired telescopes and compasses.[343]

In 1776, he constructed a cotton, wool, and tow factory at his house, which was still functioning shortly before he died (Figure 111).[344]

Militia

In 1777, he was one of "... the Subscribers, being desirous to pay due Obedience to the ...Congress... and being Convinced that it is a duty ... to Qualify ... for the Defence thereof, have assembled ... Ourselves into a Company to be called ... the Baltimore Artificers Company of Militia ..."[71]

He was joined by, among others, Ambrose Clarke, the Dublin clock maker in Baltimore, and John Lynch, possibly the long-lived clock maker discussed below. Judging from the other signatories' names, Ryan, McCray, Maloney, Lanahan, Flanerey, Byrne and O'Leary, there was no shortage of Irish volunteers.[345] Unfortunately, McCabe died in the Revolution on July 17, 1778.[4, 127] His administrator was Phebe M'Cabe, perhaps a wife or daughter (Figure 112).[346] The Baltimore census records a John McCabe in 1791,[347] possibly his son.[348]

RANDALL CASHELL

Randall Cashell, goldsmith and lapidary, was at 23 North Second St, Philadelphia in 1807[349] where he was listed as a goldsmith and jeweler. By 1811, he was at 87 South Second Street.[74] He moved to Baltimore later that year[350] and in 1812, was in Georgetown in a partnership as Cashell & Lagary (Figure 113).[351]

A year later he was on F Street, Washington, DC.[352] Here the wandering, and apparently hapless, Cashell tried his hand at another venture. In 1813, one Ezra Corkings had obtained a patent to turn cider into wine (Figure 114). Sadly, the details of this fascinating process have not survived as most American patents prior to 1836 were destroyed by a great fire in December of that year.[353] Cashell purchased the rights and offered them for resale in Washington, Virginia, the Carolinas, and Georgia.

Profit could not have been great as, by June 1814, he ended up insolvent.[354] After his release, he was in Fredericktown, MD, cleaning and repairing firearms.[355] Four years later, he had moved to Winchester, VA,[356] and was there in 1819.[357] According to the *Winchester Gazette* for 1818 he had worked in Ireland[356] and indeed he appears with Daniel Egan on Dublin silverware hallmarked for the year 1816.[31] Like Ambrose Clarke he may have returned to Ireland and then back to America permanently.

ALL perfons indebted to the eftate of John M Cabe, late of Baltimore, deceafed, either by bond, note, or book accouut, are defired to make immediate payment; and thofe who have any demands againft faid eftate, are defired to bring in their accounts, legally proved, that they may be adjufted, by

PHEBE M CABE, Adminiftratrix.

Baltimore, July 15, 1778.

Figure 112. Following his death in the American Revolution, Phebe McCabe was left to settle the affairs of John McCabe.

NEW MANUFACTORY.

CASHELL & LAGARY,
(LATE FROM EUROPE,)

Inform the Ladies and Gentlemen and the public in General, that they have commenced in Georgetown, Columbia, four doors above the Union Bank, the Watch-Making, Jewelry and Lapidary business, in all their various branches. R Cashell being regularly brought up in London, and Augustus Lagary in Switzerland—they engage to make, and also to repair in the best manner every kind of Watches and Time Pieces, at present in use; Diamonds and Pearls set, and old Pearls strung, &c. in the newest style now used in England and France.

N B. Particular attention will be paid to bespoke Watches in the making, and every article in the Jewelry, &c. &c. Watches and words etc. newly Gilt to look equal to Gold and last longer than any ever done in America.

December 3—

Figure 113. The partnership of Cashell and Lagary did not last long—just a year later Cashell found himself in Washington.

PATENT NOTICE.

EZRA B. CORKINGS having obtained from the Secretary of State of the United States, a patent right to make Wine from Cider (it is made in a manner both cheap and expeditious, and well worth the attention of shopkeepers in general) any person wishing to buy a right for a part or the whole of the district of Columbia, will please apply to R. CASHELL, watch-maker, F street, city of Washington, he having purchased the right of the same, and is the only person to be treated with on the subject from the 8th day of October, 1813.

N B Any person wishing to buy for a part or the whole of the states of Virginia, North and South Carolina, Georgia, &c will please direct a letter, post paid, to R. Cashell, and they shall meet due attention.

October 12—3t

Figure 114. Randall Cashell's advertisement for his ill-fated patent to convert cider into wine. From the Daily National Intelligencer, Washington, DC on October 18, 1813.

JOHN LYNCH

John Lynch, silversmith, watch, and clock maker, was born in 1763 and was in Baltimore for over 50 years.[323] He worked on Boundary Street in 1796 and Howard Street in 1801 before moving to Franklin Street. His name was in the city directories until 1842.[358] His clock-making business included the repair and cleaning of watches, the making of 8-day clocks, and also the maintenance of "clocks of all kinds." His yearly maintenance rate in 1796 was 15 shillings for 8-day clocks and 35 shillings for musical clocks.[359] By 1810, in the new currency, the annual fee would be two dollars. He would also maintain, but not wind, clocks "in the country" but by 1801 had ceased to offer this as part of his service.[360]

He sought journeymen in 1810,[361] 1815,[362] and again in 1820.[363] He hired at least one apprentice, John Spalding, in 1801.[71] However Spalding lasted only four years, running away in 1805 with an apprentice blacksmith, Mathias Baker.[364] In addition to his watch and clock enterprise, Lynch made and sold a considerable amount of silver, which has been well

To John Lynch,

Clock and Watch-Maker, Howard-st.

SIR,

I HAVE observed your little, low-cunning advertisement, in Mr. Pechin's paper of yesterday, concerning negro NATHAN. Why not tell the public how I got Nathan in my possession, and then the public can judge whether I have a right to keep him in possession or not. This I hope you will do in to-morrow's paper, or I shall be under the necessity of doing it myself. I expect you will state the matter correctly, as you well know that I have the best of witnesses to prove how I got said Nathan, namely, Mr. Thomas Wedderstrand.

A. G. HAMMOND.

June 25.   6t†

Ten dollars reward,

WILL be given to any person who will apprehend and secure, so that the subscriber gets him again, negro NATHAN, formerly the property of Mrs. Susan Cannon, and now owned by John Lynch. Said negro is between thirteen and fourteen years of age, and from undoubted information, is now in the possession of A. G. Hammond, resident in York-street, Old-Town.—Whoever will take him up, and deliver him to the subscriber, his lawful owner, shall receive the above reward.

JOHN LYNCH.

☞ All masters of vessels and others are forbidden to harbor, secrete, or carry off said negro fellow, as they will positively be punished with the utmost severity of the law.

June 24.   6t

Figure 117, above. The Lynch white dial clock now at Hampton National Historic Site, Towson, MD. The turned pillars to the hood and quarter columns in the trunk are later Federal period features.

Figures 115 and 116, left. Another altercation in a newspaper involving clock makers. Although this time it was not between two competitors vying for custom, it may nonetheless be even more disturbing since the exchange concerned a slave "Negro Nathan."

Figure 118. Detail of the arch of the Lynch white dial clock showing the battle on February 24, 1813, between the USS Hornet under Captain James Lawrence in which the British vessel HMS Peacock was destroyed.

described.[365] He was also a gilder, jeweler,[366] and sword dealer.[367]

We do not know when he first arrived in Baltimore. While many Irish craftsmen who had recently immigrated were quick to advertise their origin, Lynch made no such claim. His name is certainly suggestive and he used a harp on his silverware[299, 365] but he may have been second generation. There were several individuals of this name in Dublin in 1780–86 but none a clock maker.[81-83, 184] His name is not on the apprentice, freemen or quarter brother lists for Dublin, but there was a Robert Lynch, clock maker, in Limerick circa 1750.[6] In the 1780s, there were Lynch goldsmiths in Limerick including Robert, Arthur, and James, and a Farrell Lynch in County Meath.[31] An undated Thomas Lynch, Cork is also known.[7]

An Argument about a Slave

If public argument in the newspaper was acceptable in New York and New Hampshire, Maryland was no different. Lynch and a certain AG Hammond exchanged verbal blows in the *Democratic Republican* in late June 1802 concerning the matter of "Negro Nathan," Lynch's slave[368, 369] (Figures 115 and 116). A $10 reward was offered by Lynch for Nathan's return. Hammond's reply, calling it a "little, low-cunning advertisement," was swift. Lynch later responded that "nothing was more repugnant ... than a controversy in a newspaper ... with a man of dubious character..." The outcome for Nathan, valued at $215, is unclear.

Clocks

One of Lynch's white dial long case clocks, from 1815–20[19] has a 13" dial with Roman hour numerals and Arabic minute numerals (Figures 117 and 118). There is a seconds hand below 12 and a shallow "inverted U" for the date located above the signature. The arch shows a naval engagement in the War of 1812 against the British. The spandrels show shields, a not uncommon motif on clocks of this patriotic period in America. The colors of painted dials of this period showed shades of red, green, yellow, and blue.[17] The case is tall at 105". It is decorated with turned finials, and is a typical Baltimore style of inlaid decoration. There are four turned hood pillars and quarter columns in the trunk flank the rectangular door with double molding above the plinth. The four-pillared movement has a rack and snail striking on a bell (Figures 119 and 120).

Another mahogany clock stands almost 98" high with a broken arch, a pagoda top, three carved wooden finials, a trunk with a wide

Figures 119 and 120. The movement of the Lynch clock with rack and snail striking on a bell. The 2mm thick single sheet dial lacking a false plate can possibly be attributed to the Boston dial firm of Nolen & Curtis.

door, and a plinth with a raised panel. The painted dial has hands circa 1790, Arabic numerals for both hours and minutes, and lightly painted floral spandrels.[29]

A third clock measuring 96" in height is now in the possession of the Maryland Historical Society. The dial has Roman numerals for the hours and Arabic numerals marking the five-minute intervals. There are fruits and flowers adorning both the corners and the arch.[29]

John Lynch died on January 15, 1848 and was survived by two sons and two daughters.[323]

He bequeathed his commercial property to his son Benjamin. The name John Lynch reappeared in the 1853–54 directory at the same address.[370] Perhaps this was an attempt to restart the business with the reputation already established by his father. Whatever the case, neither of the names Benjamin or John appear in the directories for 1855 to 1857[371, 372] and this appears to have definitively marked the end of Lynch and his watch and clock enterprise.

Figure 121. Multi-talented, James Stewart, watch and clock maker, engraver in copper, gilder and seal maker arrived in Baltimore some time in 1792. The location of his workshop suggests he would have been in direct competition with Gilbert Bigger, who was only a stone's throw away.[373]

Figure 122. The notice in The Federal Gazette & Baltimore Daily Advertiser for February 22, 1798, that James Stewart of the New Inn, Fell's Point had ceased his watch-making business.

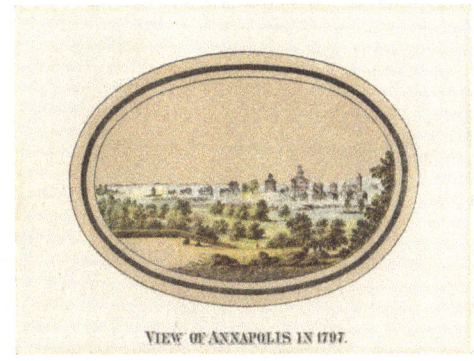

Figure 123. Annapolis, MD, ca. 1797. From the New York Public Library's Digital Library via Wikicommons.

Figure 124. The announcement by the maker from Cork, Ireland, William Knapp that business had commenced in Annapolis, MD.

JAMES STEWART

James Stewart arrived from Dublin sometime around July 1792[373] (Figure 121). He was not listed in the Dublin directories for the years before this.[82-84] A watch and clock maker, he was also an engraver, seal cutter, and gilder and had worked in both London and Dublin.[373] He imported preordered watches from both those

maryland, kentucky, and missouri 75

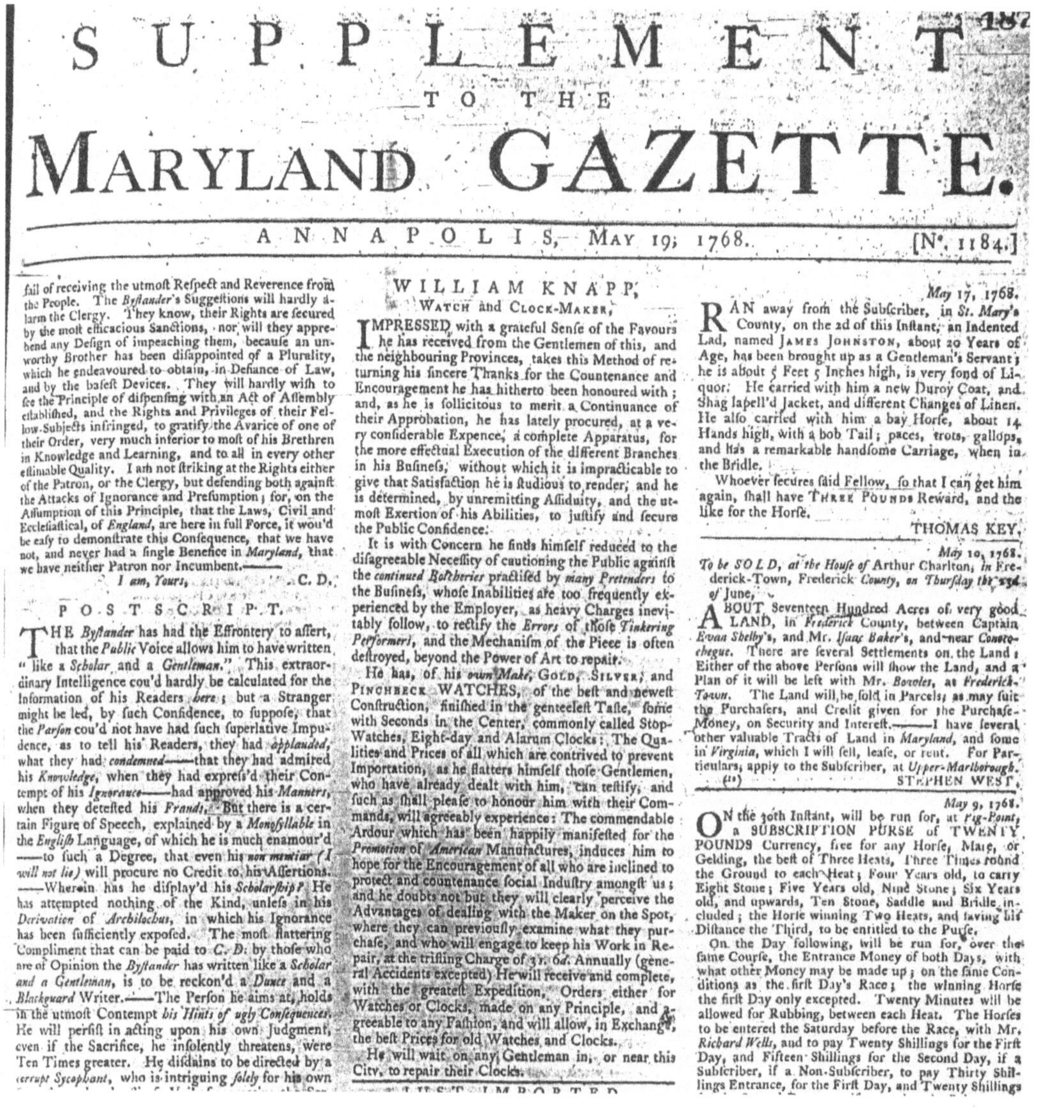

187

SUPPLEMENT TO THE MARYLAND GAZETTE.

ANNAPOLIS, MAY 19, 1768. [N°. 1184.]

fail of receiving the utmost Respect and Reverence from the People. The *Bystander*'s Suggestions will hardly alarm the Clergy. They know, their Rights are secured by the most efficacious Sanctions, nor will they apprehend any Design of impeaching them, because an unworthy Brother has been disappointed of a Plurality, which he endeavoured to obtain, in Defiance of Law, and by the basest Devices. They will hardly wish to see the Principle of dispensing with an Act of Assembly established, and the Rights and Privileges of their Fellow-Subjects infringed, to gratify the Avarice of one of their Order, very much inferior to most of his Brethren in Knowledge and Learning, and to all in every other estimable Quality. I am not striking at the Rights either of the Patron, or the Clergy, but defending both against the Attacks of Ignorance and Presumption; for, on the Assumption of this Principle, that the Laws, Civil and Ecclesiastical, of *England*, are here in full Force, it wou'd be easy to demonstrate this Consequence, that we have not, and never had a single Benefice in *Maryland*, that we have neither Patron nor Incumbent.——

I am, Yours, C. D.

POSTSCRIPT.

THE *Bystander* has had the Effrontery to assert, that the *Public* Voice allows him to have written "like a *Scholar* and a *Gentleman*." This extraordinary Intelligence cou'd hardly be calculated for the Information of his Readers *here*; but a Stranger might be led, by such Confidence, to suppose, that the *Parson* cou'd not have had such superlative Impudence, as to tell his Readers, they had *applauded*, what they had *condemned*——that they had admired his *Knowledge*, when they had express'd their Contempt of his *Ignorance*——had approved his *Manners*, when they detested his *Frauds*. But there is a certain Figure of Speech, explained by a *Monosyllable* in the *English* Language, of which he is much enamour'd ——to such a Degree, that even his *non mentiar (I will not lie)* will procure no Credit to his Assertions. ——Wherein has he display'd his *Scholarship*? He has attempted nothing of the Kind, unless in his *Derivation* of *Archilochus*, in which his Ignorance has been sufficiently exposed. The most flattering Compliment that can be paid to *C. D.* by those who are of Opinion the *Bystander* has written like a *Scholar and a Gentleman*, is to be reckon'd a *Dunce* and a *Blackguard* Writer.——The Person he aims at, holds in the utmost Contempt *his Hints of ugly Consequences*. He will persist in acting upon his own Judgment, even if the Sacrifice, he insolently threatens, were Ten Times greater. He disdains to be directed by a *corrupt Sycophant*, who is intriguing *solely* for his own

WILLIAM KNAPP,
WATCH and CLOCK-MAKER,

IMPRESSED with a grateful Sense of the Favours he has received from the Gentlemen of this, and the neighbouring Provinces, takes this Method of returning his sincere Thanks for the Countenance and Encouragement he has hitherto been honoured with; and, as he is sollicitous to merit a Continuance of their Approbation, he has lately procured, at a very considerable Expence, a complete Apparatus, for the more effectual Execution of the different Branches in his Business, without which it is impracticable to give that Satisfaction he is studious to render; and he is determined, by unremitting Assiduity, and the utmost Exertion of his Abilities, to justify and secure the Public Confidence.

It is with Concern he finds himself reduced to the disagreeable Necessity of cautioning the Public against the *continued Botcheries* practised by *many Pretenders* to the Business, whose Inabilities are too frequently experienced by the Employer, as heavy Charges inevitably follow, to rectify the *Errors* of those *Tinkering Performers*, and the Mechanism of the Piece is often destroyed, beyond the Power of Art to repair.

He has, of his *own Make*, GOLD, SILVER, and PINCHBECK WATCHES, of the best and newest Construction, finished in the genteelest Taste, some with Seconds in the Center, commonly called Stop-Watches, Eight-day and Alarum Clocks: The Qualities and Prices of all which are contrived to prevent Importation, as he flatters himself those Gentlemen, who have already dealt with him, can testify, and such as shall please to honour him with their Commands, will agreeably experience: The commendable Ardour which has been happily manifested for the *Promotion* of *American* Manufactures, induces him to hope for the Encouragement of all who are inclined to protect and countenance social Industry amongst us; and he doubts not but they will clearly perceive the Advantages of dealing with the Maker on the Spot, where they can previously examine what they purchase, and who will engage to keep his Work in Repair, at the trifling Charge of 3*s.* 6*d.* Annually (general Accidents excepted) He will receive and complete, with the greatest Expedition, Orders either for Watches or Clocks, made on any Principle, and agreeable to any Fashion, and will allow, in Exchange, the best Prices for old Watches and Clocks.

He will wait on any Gentleman in, or near this City, to repair their Clocks.

May 17, 1768.

RAN away from the Subscriber, in *St. Mary's* County, on the 2d of this Instant, an Indented Lad, named JAMES JOHNSTON, about 20 Years of Age, has been brought up as a Gentleman's Servant; he is about 5 Feet 5 Inches high, is very fond of Liquor. He carried with him a new Duroy Coat, and Shag lapell'd Jacket, and different Changes of Linen. He also carried with him a bay Horse, about 14 Hands high, with a bob Tail; paces, trots, gallops, and has a remarkable handsome Carriage, when in the Bridle.

Whoever secures said Fellow, so that I can get him again, shall have THREE POUNDS Reward, and the like for the Horse.

THOMAS KEY.

May 10, 1768.

To be SOLD, at the House of Arthur Charlton, *in* Frederick-Town, Frederick *County, on Thursday the* 23d *of* June,

ABOUT Seventeen Hundred Acres of very good LAND, in *Frederick* County, between Captain *Evan Shelby*'s, and Mr. *Isaac Baker*'s, and near *Conococheague*. There are several Settlements on the Land: Either of the above Persons will show the Land, and a Plan of it will be left with Mr. *Bowles*, at *Frederick-Town*. The Land will be sold in Parcels, as may suit the Purchasers, and Credit given for the Purchase-Money, on Security and Interest.——I have several other valuable Tracts of Land in *Maryland*, and some in *Virginia*, which I will sell, lease, or rent. For Particulars, apply to the Subscriber, at *Upper-Marlborough*.

(tf) STEPHEN WEST.

May 9, 1768.

ON the 30th Instant, will be run for, at *Pig-Point*, a SUBSCRIPTION PURSE of TWENTY POUNDS Currency, free for any Horse, Mare, or Gelding, the best of Three Heats, Three Times round the Ground to each Heat; Four Years old, to carry Eight Stone; Five Years old, Nine Stone; Six Years old, and upwards, Ten Stone, Saddle and Bridle included; the Horse winning Two Heats, and saving his Distance the Third, to be entitled to the Purse.

On the Day following, will be run for, over the same Course, the Entrance Money of both Days, with what other Money may be made up; on the same Conditions as the first Day's Race; the winning Horse the first Day only excepted. Twenty Minutes will be allowed for Rubbing, between each Heat. The Horses to be entered the Saturday before the Race, with Mr. *Richard Wells*, and to pay Twenty Shillings for the First Day, and Fifteen Shillings for the Second Day, if a Subscriber, if a Non-Subscriber, to pay Thirty Shillings Entrance, for the First Day, and Twenty Shillings

Figure 125. In this notice, published shortly before his death, William Knapp spoke of his new equipment and his extensive inventory of various types of clocks and watches. Like his curmudgeonly compatriot, Isaac Heron of New Jersey and New York, he could not pass on the opportunity to swipe at his competitors. From the Maryland Gazette, May 19, 1768.

cities selected by his brother who was "on the spot."[330] Precisely which spot—London, Dublin, or even both— is unclear but the brother, it seems, was a "perfect master of the business,"[71] suggesting he may himself have been a watch maker or at least in an allied trade.

One G. Stewart, a dial painter, engraver, and watch case maker, is known from Belfast from 1780 to 1820[5] and a John Stewart of Belfast is also known from 1785 to 1827.[6]

In February 1793, Stewart and King sought two apprentices in the *Baltimore Daily Repository*.[374] Unlike previous notices, mathematical instruments were mentioned. A William King,

Figure 126. Portrait of William Knapp ca. 1759. According to the description of the distinguished art historian J. Hall Pleasants, Knapp has powdered brown hair and blue eyes. He wears a blue coat with a collar and white satin waistcoat.[379] The artist of this fine portrait is unknown but the work has been attributed to the 18th century British School. Illustration kind courtesy of the Frick Art Reference Gallery.

mathematical instrument maker, is known from Dublin for 1767[6] but not for later years,[81, 82, 84, 181, 183, 184] and perhaps he, or a relative, had migrated and formed a partnership with Stewart.

The orphaned Patrick Roach was taken as apprentice in 1794 to learn the "art and mistry of a mathymatical Instrument maker"[375] but the young man left after two and a half years to become a mariner.[376] Another apprentice was taken in 1796 to be a brass founder.[71]

A Tavern Keeper?

What became of Stewart is unclear as his name is not in the later Baltimore directories.[307, 309, 336-339] However, *The Federal Gazette & Baltimore Daily Advertiser* for February 22, 1798,[377] noted that James Stewart of the New Inn, Fell's Point "...*having declined all other business ... will be constantly supplied with the best wines...*" (Figure 122). Perhaps, following the examples of Samuel Martin in New York and Robert Egan in North Carolina, he had abandoned the watch maker's workbench and wished to permanently embrace the more colorful world of the tavern keeper.

The marriage of a James Stewart to Harriet Bankson in 1809 is also recorded.[378] The author is unaware of any items by this maker.

ANNAPOLIS

WILLIAM KNAPP

William Knapp, born circa 1735 in Cork,[379] opened premises in Annapolis, MD,[380] (Figure 124) as a mender, rather than maker, of watches. It is said that the family records indicated that he was the son of Edwin recte Edmond[381] Knapp, Alderman of Cork.[379] Alternatively, he may have been the son of John Knapp, the early 18th-century Cork clock maker.[37] He had received instruction from the "most Eminent in London and Dublin," but did not mention the city of Cork where he had been apprenticed to the well-known Cork maker, James Aicken. In 1759, he married Frances Cudmore[37] and together they had six children.[379] He opened his own premises in 1760 "at the sign of the dial in Broad Lane."[37] At this time, Cork was a major Atlantic port and arguably the most cosmopolitan town in Ireland, with extensive trade links to many European countries.[382] Despite this financially buoyant time, he left his native town and had begun work in Annapolis by March 1764.[380] Later that year, he had taken an assistant and was also making his own watches. He moved some time around January 1766,[27] and tried to expand his catchment area into the Baltimore district.[27]

Figures 127 and 128. A rare survivor. A watch by William Knapp now in the Maryland Historical Society.[19] *The outer case, by a curious coincidence, contains a watch paper by William McParlin, another Irish immigrant clock maker.*

Berating His Competitors

Like many of his contemporaries, he had a low opinion of his competitors. Passing scathing comment on "the unskilful and injudicious" work of "pretenders" to the watch-making business, he undertook, at "a very moderate expence" to keep the watches he repaired in order for 10 years except if damaged by accident "such as a Fall…" or by the "Breaking of a Main Spring."[383] He continued his trope again in 1768 (Figure 125) when he described other clock makers as "tinkering performers" and their work as "butcheries," remarks that may have been directed at Abraham Claude and William Faris, the father of Charles Faris, whom we will meet later.[384] He hoped watches of his own make would profit from the "ardour…for the Promotion of American Manufactures" and, for the "trifling sum" of three shillings and six pence annually he would keep his work in repair.[385]

Knapp's fortunes varied. In April 1769, for reasons which were unclear, he mortgaged his property. This included his mahogany and walnut furniture, beds and featherbedding, chintz, silverware, and, not surprisingly, an assortment of clock and watch tools. A salient feature of his "property" included his servants, three men and two women. A "negro boy" was also part of the

Death

Knapp died around 1769; the notice for Burrage's return was signed in that year by Frances,[386] not William, and the mortgage of his property was also in the same year.[71] He is said to have died at sea while on business in 1767[387] but this must be erroneous because he was still advertising in 1768.[385] It has also been suggested that ill health brought about a voyage to the West Indies. At this time, these islands were deemed favorable for climatic treatment of consumption or tuberculosis,[388] which certainly could have been the cause of his demise.

Frances later married William Whetcroft (see later), another goldsmith/watch maker from Cork in 1769[15] or 1770.[387] Although he was romantically described as "an old lover" of hers who had "come from Ireland to seek her hand on hearing of her husband's death,"[387] Whetcroft had, in fact, already been in Annapolis since at least 1766.[389]

A watch from Knapp's atelier has survived and is now in the Maryland Historical Society.[19] The dial has features of the second half of the 18th century with beetle and poker hands and Roman hour and Arabic minute numerals. The name Knapp is below 12 (Figures 127 and 128). The case has English hallmarks.

Figure 129. Silver point and watercolor on vellum bust-length profile of William McParlin, Annapolis, 1807, by Swiss-French émigré artist David Boudon. Dimensions: height 2¾" and width 2¼". Boudon came to America ca. 1795. Like many artisans, this miniaturist moved often. He arrived in Charleston but also worked in New York, Savannah, Philadelphia, Baltimore, and the Federal City (Washington).[397]

inventory who, if one can believe it, had been named "Cork." One of the adult servants, an Englishman by the name of John Burrage, was a clock maker by trade. The notion of being mortgaged may not have greatly appealed to him as a notice placed in *The Maryland Gazette* for July 1769 says that he absconded. A £5 reward was offered for his return to Knapp's wife Frances Knapp.[386] Burrage is recorded in 1769 as a clock maker in Baltimore.[2]

> **WILLIAM M'PARLIN,**
> **CLOCK AND WATCH-MAKER,**
> RESPECTFULLY informs the citizens of Annapolis, and its vicinity, that he has commenced BUSINESS at the shop lately kept by WILLIAM FARIS, in West-street, where clocks and watches of every description may be repaired in the most approved manner, and on the most moderate terms, also gold and silver work made, sold, and repaired; engraving, such as cyphers, seals, &c. neatly executed, and he assures those who please to honour him with their commands, that the utmost of his abilities shall be exerted to give general satisfaction.
> N. B. Old gold and silver bought as usual.
> August 22, 1804.

Figure 130. McParlin wasted no time in taking over of the business of William Faris: only a week after his death this notice appeared in the Maryland Gazette for August 23, 1804.[392]

Figure 131. Thomas McParlin, son of William, is buried in Arlington Cemetery. Breveted Brigadier General, November 26, 1866, for meritorious service at New Orleans where cholera and yellow fever prevailed, he died January 28, 1897.[561]

WILLIAM McPARLIN

William McParlin (Figure 129) or McFarland was born in Loughbrickland, County Down circa 1780[390] and, with his two brothers, left home to seek his fortune in America. He was apprenticed to Charles Faris, who had brought him from Baltimore to Annapolis, in 1799.[391] Affectionately known as "Billee" in the Faris household where he lived, he was naturalized in 1806.[384] Charles Faris died of yellow fever in September 1800 and the apprenticeship of Billee then fell to Charles's father, William Faris.

Billee's duties in the Faris household were not only those related to his apprenticeship, but

Figures 132 and 133. The bracket clock signed, "William McParlin, Annapolis." The silvered brass dial has Roman numerals and strike silent mechanism in the arch. The clock strikes on a bell and has an undecorated back plate. Pictures very kind courtesy Paul Foley.

80 passing time across the water

also included painting, and, in particular, assisting the aging Faris with gardening. The young apprentice was also musically talented, and was able to read and transcribe music.[391]

Diary

William Faris's diary is a fascinating insight into contemporary Annapolis and the various Irish connections there. It sheds much light on the odd, and assuredly infuriating, quirks in the personality of the young Irishman, William McParlin.[391] One evening he left home, taking his clothes with him. Not returning in a timely fashion, Faris, accompanied by one Mr. Pitt, went in search of the roving blade and found him in a "saussey" condition. This may have meant that he was drunk—he was certainly known to be a toper and to disappear for days at a time. The following morning, Faris asked where were the clothes he had removed from the house. Young McParlin replied that he didn't know. Faris threatened to take the "cow skin" down and give him a "sevear whiping," a threat that had the desired effect as the clothes were promptly brought back home. Although he promised Faris, "...never to do the like again..," some months later, he arrived home "tipsey" and he carelessly took a watch apart. Later that day, Faris noticed the watch was gone, and McParlin said he had thrown it over the fence into a neighbor's garden! It was returned to Faris the next day apparently having been hidden all the time.

Independent Business

William Faris died on August 15, 1804.[390, 391] Despite his eccentric foibles, and his inebriate leanings, McParlin had finished his apprenticeship and the Faris's business at West Street was taken over by him instantly (Figure 130).[392]

His success, which was considerable, was not immediate, as five years after he had taken over Faris's business, he was calling for the immediate payment of debts which were of

Figure 134. Half-length portrait on canvas, 36"x 27¼" of William Whetcroft by Charles Willson Peale.[365] Possibly painted at Baltimore in 1791 as the costume is of that period. Peale's list of 1770–75 work contains an entry for a possible "head size" portrait.[46] Picture courtesy Yale Art Gallery.

"serious importance" and stated those unpaid would be passed to an officer for immediate collection.[393]

By 1811, his business had improved substantially and included gold seals, chains, keys, pearl and topaz breast pins, combs, buttons, spoons, tea tongs, and, almost by the way, "a few watches."[394]

Raffish if not rakish, he finally settled, marrying Cassandra Hilleary Beall Woodward (1800–65) in 1816[395] with whom he had six children.[390] His son Thomas (Figure 131) became an army physician and had the distinction of fraternizing with then Colonel Robert E. Lee and treating Kit Carson's daughter.[390]

By 1819, William rose to be town commissioner.[396] He took an apprentice, Montmorency Price, in 1820.[71] He died in 1850.[365]

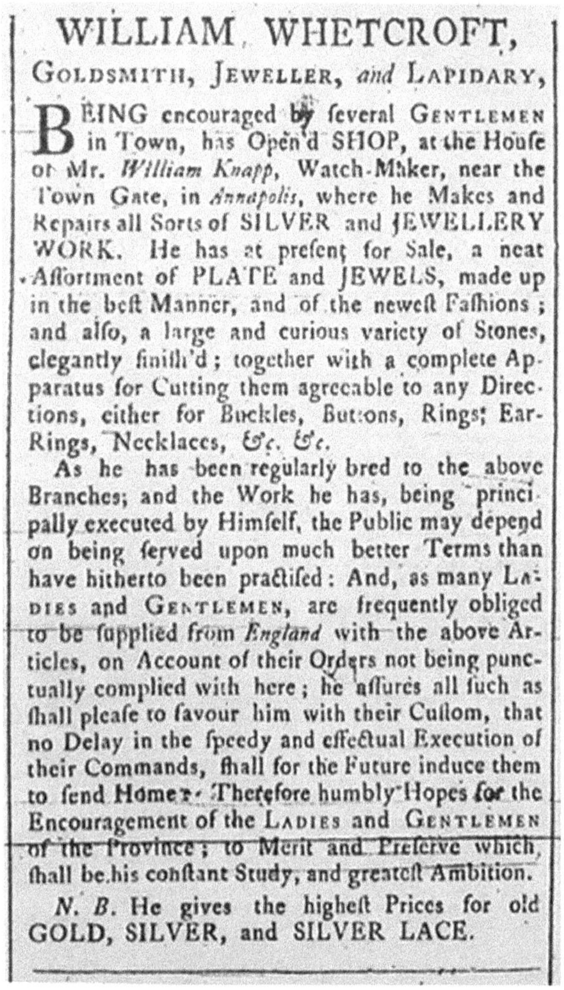

WILLIAM WHETCROFT,

GOLDSMITH, JEWELLER, *and* LAPIDARY,

BEING encouraged by ſeveral GENTLEMEN in Town, has Open'd SHOP, at the Houſe of Mr. *William Knapp*, Watch-Maker, near the Town Gate, in *Annapolis*, where he Makes and Repairs all Sorts of SILVER and JEWELLERY WORK. He has at preſent for Sale, a neat Aſſortment of PLATE and JEWELS, made up in the beſt Manner, and of the neweſt Faſhions; and alſo, a large and curious variety of Stones, elegantly finiſh'd; together with a complete Apparatus for Cutting them agreeable to any Directions, either for Buckles, Buttons, Rings; Ear-Rings, Necklaces, &c. &c.

As he has been regularly bred to the above Branches; and the Work he has, being principally executed by Himſelf, the Public may depend on being ſerved upon much better Terms than have hitherto been practiſed: And, as many LADIES and GENTLEMEN, are frequently obliged to be ſupplied from *England* with the above Articles, on Account of their Orders not being punctually complied with here; he aſſures all ſuch as ſhall pleaſe to favour him with their Cuſtom, that no Delay in the ſpeedy and effectual Execution of their Commands, ſhall for the Future induce them to ſend Home: Therefore humbly Hopes for the Encouragement of the LADIES and GENTLEMEN of the Province; to Merit and Preſerve which, ſhall be his conſtant Study, and greateſt Ambition.

N. B. He gives the higheſt Prices for old GOLD, SILVER, and SILVER LACE.

Figure 135. William Whetcroft began work in Annapolis, MD, working from the house of his Irish compatriot William Knapp, also of Cork.

Clocks

A surviving bracket clock (see Figures 132 and 133) is signed, "William McParlin, Annapolis." An elegant piece, it has a silvered brass dial with Roman numerals and a strike silent arch mechanism. Some silver work has also survived as well as the watch paper illustrated earlier in the Knapp watch.[397]

WILLIAM WHETCROFT

William Whetcroft (Figure 134) worked as a silversmith in Cork in 1759.[31] When he left Ireland is unknown, but by 1766 he had started as a goldsmith, jeweler, and lapidary in Annapolis, in the house of William Knapp (Figure 135), also previously of Cork.[389] A year later he opened a shop on Gay Street, Baltimore, which he operated at the same time as the Annapolis enterprise.[398] Several other members of the Whetcroft family also moved to Baltimore.[391]

Unfortunately, Knapp died in the late 1760s. By the end of 1769, Whetcroft had purchased all his servants and had acquired "all the materials.. for ...watch and clock making."[399] He married widow Knapp in 1769 or 1770, and they had eight children together.[379]

Social Setting

The social mixing of the Irish expatriate community was often mentioned in William Faris's diary.[391] Faris was not only a clock maker but an avid gardener as was his friend Upton Scott, the Irish physician to Governor Horatio Sharpe, and the founder and first President of the Medical and Chirurgical Faculty of Maryland.[391]

Another friend was John O'Donnell, the captain of the first ship to bring goods directly from China after the American Revolution.[391] The Whetcroft family were also friends of Faris and lived across West Street from him from 1776 until 1798.[391]

Whetcroft's thriving business expanded with importation of materials and also workmen.[399] The firm of Wallace, Davidson & Johnson were the middle men for the importation of goods for Whetcroft and others in Annapolis including the cabinet makers Shaw & Chisolm.[400] This may be the same as Matthew Shaw, the Dublin joiner and cabinet maker.[9]

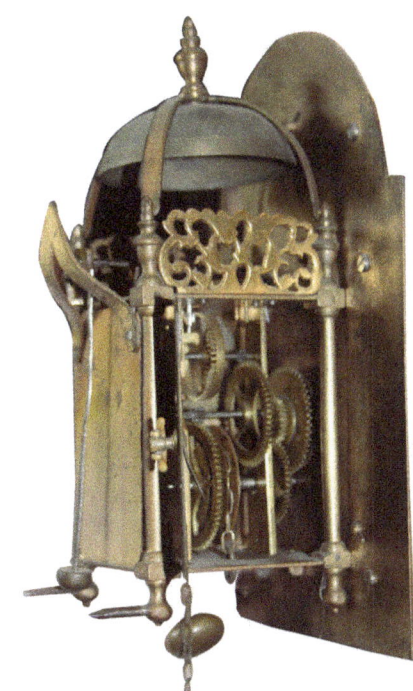

Figures 136–139. Although little is known of his horological work one clock has survived and it is doubly unusual. American lantern clocks are rare and such clocks by Irish makers even more so. It is a timepiece alarm. Unlike other lantern clocks which were housed in wooden cases, this type was made to be displayed as the side fret work and doors would suggest.[416] The brass dial has applied spandrels with a floral or wreath pattern, black Roman hour numerals, and Arabic numbers at five-minute intervals. The arch contains a boss flanked by applied floral spandrels and is signed, "Wm Whitcroft/Annapoles" (sic). Four knopped brass pillars support a single train movement which is regulated by a crown-wheel escapement. The clock alarms on a bell being set by a centrally placed disc on the dial. Pictures very kind courtesy Ed and Virginia LaFond.

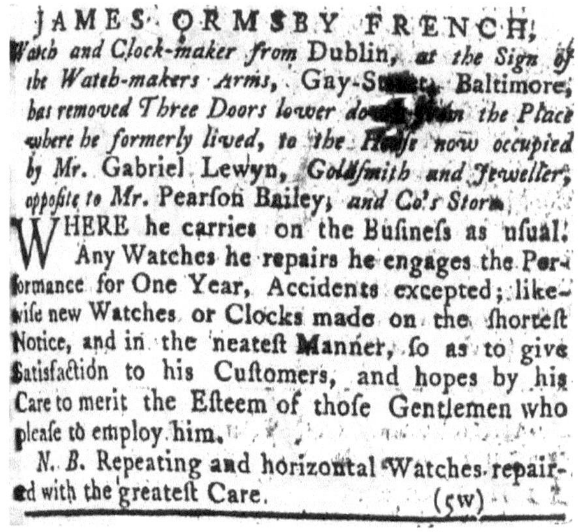

Figure 140. An earlier arrival in Baltimore, French traded alone at first but later with Abraham Claude. Claude was diversifying into the sale of glass, household goods, and Caribbean imports. Their partnership was a separate enterprise but located under the same roof. Claude died ca. 1800.[27]

Figure 141. A description of the complex clock by John Finney from The New-England Courant, for the dates of Monday, November 6–13, 1721 in Boston, Massachusetts.

Business and Integration

In a short time, Whetcroft joined in the habits of the Colonies; in 1769, he had for sale a "…young, active negro boy about 13 or 14 years of age, who has had the SmallPox…the time of a servant man, a clock and watchmaker by trade…with a complete set of Clock and watch tools…" and indentured servants.[401]

By 1773, he had 24-hour and 8-day clocks, as well as watches in gold, silver, and fish skin cases. He kept clocks in order and wound them weekly for an annual fee of 15 shillings.[402] His impressive inventory included coffee and teapots, waiters, tankards, punch ladles, silver work, settings for miniature pictures, bracelets with diamonds, lockets, and other expensive and desirable luxuries fit for the prospering town of Annapolis. His enterprise expanded to include flour, wine and Caribbean rum,[71] wig powder, hairpins,[403] cloth of different types, salt-making pans,[404] nailrods, and sheetiron.[405] Not one to miss an opportunity, he moved into the gun supply business just before the American Revolution. The Maryland Council of Safety promised him payment for importation "of workmen, and …good substantial proved Muskets, three and a half feet long in the barrel, and of three quarters of an inch in the bore."[406] He also continued his trade in people. He had first announced the sale of servants in 1769[399] and this continued at least until 1775.[402] This was no small trade as, in the latter year, he had the following for sale:

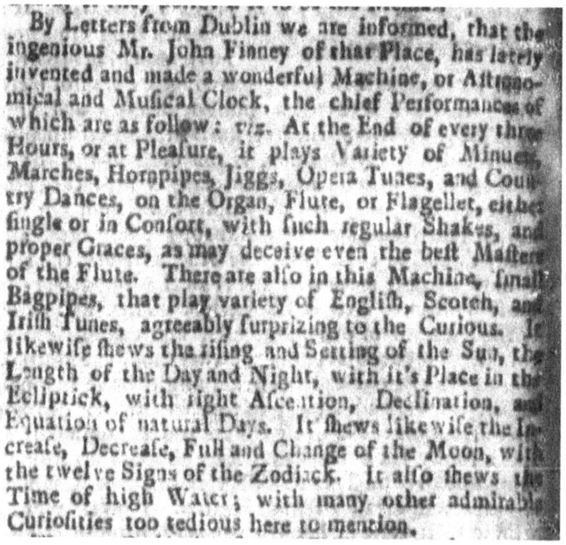

> …a number of healthy four, five, six and seven year servants…carpenters, joiners, cabinetmakers…" and many other types of tradesmen as well as "…a great number of both English and Irish farmers…[402]

One can assume that not all those in Whetcroft's charge were happy as several ran away.[407] Another was set free, provided that his father prevented him from becoming "…either expensive or troublesome!"[71]

By 1775, he was postmaster of Annapolis[408] and became assimilated into old Southern culture, having presented his nephew, Burton Whetcroft, with a nine-year old slave named Cass.[71]

84 passing time across the water

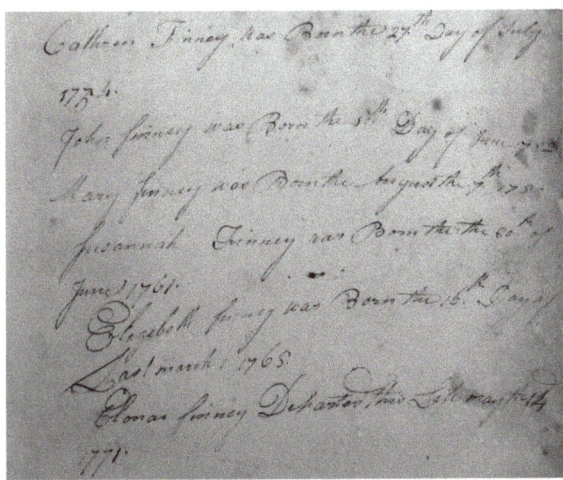

Figure 142. From the Register of St Mary Anne's Parish Church in Charlestown, MD, for 1727–99. Not in chronological order, the births of several individuals of the name Finney are recorded including Cathren - sic - (1754?), John (1752), Mary (1750), Susannah (1761) and Elizabeth (1765). Elonar (recte Eleanor?) departed this life in 1771.

Figures 143 and 144. A long case clock by John Finney with an earlier dial, with cherub spandrels, smaller Arabic minute numbers, and half-hour and half-quarter marks. The hood style, and the long tombstone door with lenticel are also earlier features.

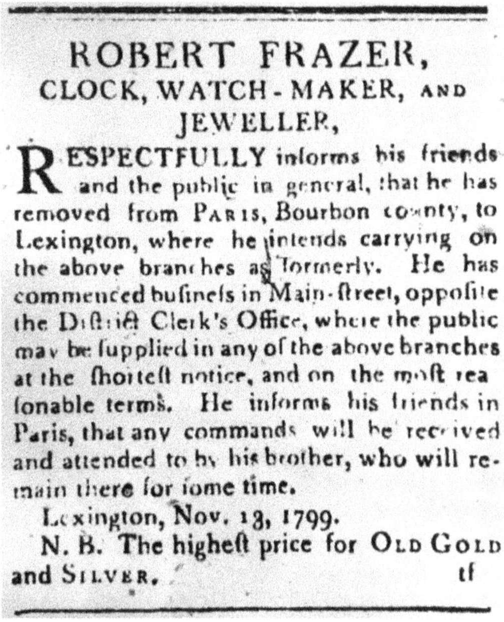

> **ROBERT FRAZER,**
> CLOCK, WATCH-MAKER, AND JEWELLER,
>
> RESPECTFULLY informs his friends and the public in general, that he has removed from PARIS, Bourbon county, to Lexington, where he intends carrying on the above branches as formerly. He has commenced business in Main-street, opposite the District Clerk's Office, where the public may be supplied in any of the above branches at the shortest notice, and on the most reasonable terms. He informs his friends in Paris, that any commands will be received and attended to by his brother, who will remain there for some time.
> Lexington, Nov. 13, 1799.
> N. B. The highest price for OLD GOLD and SILVER. tf

Figure 145. Robert Frazer moved from Paris, KY, sometime around November 13, 1799. His brother Alexander would join him later in Lexington.[425]

Diversification

In May 1777, he announced that his mill for the manufacture of nailrods, sheet iron, and hooping was open and a year later he intended "...to sell a great variety of materials for the clock, watch and jeweling business..." at Elk Ridge Landing.[409] He must have commanded great local confidence as money for this project, £600, had been advanced interest-free to him for the setting up of the mill.[410] By early 1780, he wished to sell a quarter or a half of the mill to one who would undertake the management[411] and, by September, he and his associate, Alexander McFadon, announced that the mill was in complete order having apparently been idle for the previous two years.[71]

McFadon died by 1784 and the mill became a thorn in Whetcroft's side, even involving the courts and landing at least one of the protagonists in the debtors' jail.[71] Whetcroft had other commercial travails that also became public knowledge in the local Maryland newspapers in 1795.[71]

Despite this, he flourished and, in 1795, acquired 600 acres of land in Fairfax County, Virginia.[15] By 1797 he had thousands of acres in Virginia that he would "exchange for property in the Federal City" (Washington).[412]

In July 1791, his 20-year-old daughter Letitia married Josias King. According to a contemporary letter, the wedding was "very merry...and ... in ten days there were five Balls..."[391] *The Baltimore Telegraphe and Daily Advertiser* published a eulogy in August 1799[413] after his death at 62 years old; he was a man of "probity, philanthropy and swavity of manners..." He left a son, also William, and five daughters,[414] and debts despite his wealth. One of these was owed since 1779 to John Lampe, a fellow watch and clock maker, who had moved to Baltimore from Annapolis in 1780.[391] His son later had to clear these debts by the sale of, inter alia, "a negro man" part of Whetcroft's "personal property."[415] Clearing his debts went on for years and they were still being settled in 1805.[71]

Clocks and Artifacts

Although little is known of his horological work one clock has survived and is illustrated and described in Figures 136 to 139.[416] Some of his silverware including a tankard, a coffee pot, and a snuff box have also survived.[71]

Whetcroft was a veritable microcosm of the New World, achieving more than he ever could have on his native soil. The lower echelons of urban Georgian Ireland he left behind had no such life of portraits and balls for their daughters' weddings. For many, their squalor was stark; just a stone's throw from the address of one of our émigré clock makers, "we may find from ten to sixteen persons, of all ages and sexes, in a room not fifteen feet square, stretched on a wad of ... straw, swarming with vermin and without any covering save ... wretched rags..."[417] The rest of the description of these people is too graphic to include in a work on the genteel subject of clocks. Suffice it to say that in this, and other, parts of Ireland, poverty was rife.[382]

JAMES ORMSBY FRENCH

James Ormsby French, a watch and clock maker and repairer, from Dublin, was at the Sign of the Watchmakers Arms, Gay Street in May 1771.[418] He was later in partnership with Abraham Claude in Annapolis from 1783 to 1785 (Figure 140).[4, 419]

Other Frenches in Dublin at this time[98] include Robert, Calfrey's son, apprenticed to clock maker John Ebbe in 1766 or 1773.[31] William French, Paulgry's son, was apprenticed in 1761, and is mentioned as a quarter brother in 1767 and again in 1784.[31] A James Moore French is known from Belfast.[6]

Clocks and watches are known by James Ormsby French,[420] and the Maryland Historical Society has signed silverware.[15]

THOMAS M'CROW

Another maker, Thomas M'Crow, apparently from Dublin, was in Annapolis in 1767.[300]

CHARLESTOWN

JOHN FINNEY

John Finney was at the Sign of the Ship in Temple Bar, Dublin in 1720.[6] He may be the same as John Fenny who was Free of the Goldsmiths Company in 1723 and was listed as a quarter brother in 1737–38.[31] He was quite the genius. Indeed, while still in Dublin, his fame had already wafted to America on Atlantic breezes. In November 1721, *The New England Courant*, informed by letters from Dublin,[421] publicized the "wonderful machine or astronomical and musical clock" that Mr. John Finney had lately invented (Figure 141). It reported that the clock played:

[A] variety of minuets, marches, hornpipes, jiggs…on the organ, flute or flagellet…There are also in this machine small bagpipes, that play (a) variety of English, Scotch and Irish tunes, agreeably surprising to the curious. It likewise shows the rising and setting of the sun, the length of the day and night… its place in the eclipstick…the change of the moon, with…the time of high water; with many other admirable curiosities… Heavens above! Although seeming inordinately complex, such clocks were well-known in the 18th century, one maker trying to be more ostentatious than the next.[422]

Maryland

Finney appeared in 1749 as a Justice of the Peace in relation to the apprenticeship of Benjamin Chandlee in Delaware, a relative of John Chandlee, of Wilmington, DE,[135] perhaps?

Figure 146. This posthumous portrait of Robert Frazer painted by his nephew Oliver around 1841.[21] Oliver was born February 1808 and, in the opinion of the historian George Washington Ranck, was "greatly gifted in conversation, well read in the best art and other literature, and his taste was exceedingly delicate and correct."[427] Oliver died in April 1854.

Figure 147. A James Frazer of Comber white dial clock with a cottage in the arch.[559] He was a relative of the Kentucky Frazer brothers, who also came from Comber, County Down.

smaller Arabic minute numbers, and half hour and half-quarter marks. There is some dial engraving, but it is restrained and elegant and is not as profuse as on other early Dublin dials where it occupies the whole center. Concave molding separates the hood from the trunk with its long tombstone door with lenticel and further molding leads to the plinth with an applied panel. This style is characteristic of early Dublin clock-making. Other examples are known by the early Dublin makers Pat Smith, William Marshall, and John Crampton.[424] The cases are often made of walnut since they frequently date from the first quarter of the 18th century and thus antedate the introduction of mahogany into Ireland, which occurred about 1730.

KENTUCKY AND MISSOURI

LEXINGTON

THE FRAZER (OR FRASER) BROTHERS

Alexander Frazer was in Comber, County Down from 1760[5] to 1790[2, 6] where he is known as a maker of brass dial clocks.[5] He moved to Philadelphia circa 1795 with his brother Robert and, around 1799, arrived in Paris, KY.[21] Late in 1799, Robert Frazer moved to Lexington, KY, (see Figure 145) leaving his brother in Paris[425, 426] but, by August 1803, Alexander had joined him.[21] Alexander concentrated mainly on clocks and watches while Robert focused on silversmithing.[21] Indeed, Robert's name is not

In 1754, he was in Maryland in the hamlet of Charlestown. He shared commercial life with a printer, a cabinet maker, and a blacksmith.[423] After February 7, 1754, when he "made and mended all sorts of clocks and watches, in the best and cheapest manner," we hear no more of him. Other Finneys, mentioned in the records of the local church, possibly family members, may explain why he chose this small town to settle in (Figure 142).

Two of his clocks from his Dublin days have survived and one is illustrated here (Figures 143 and 144). The stylistic features suggest an early date. Two urn finials sit atop the clock. The carving above the caddy top echoes that above the door of the hood, which is flanked by ebonized columns supporting gilt Corinthian capitals. The dial is an earlier one with cherub spandrels,

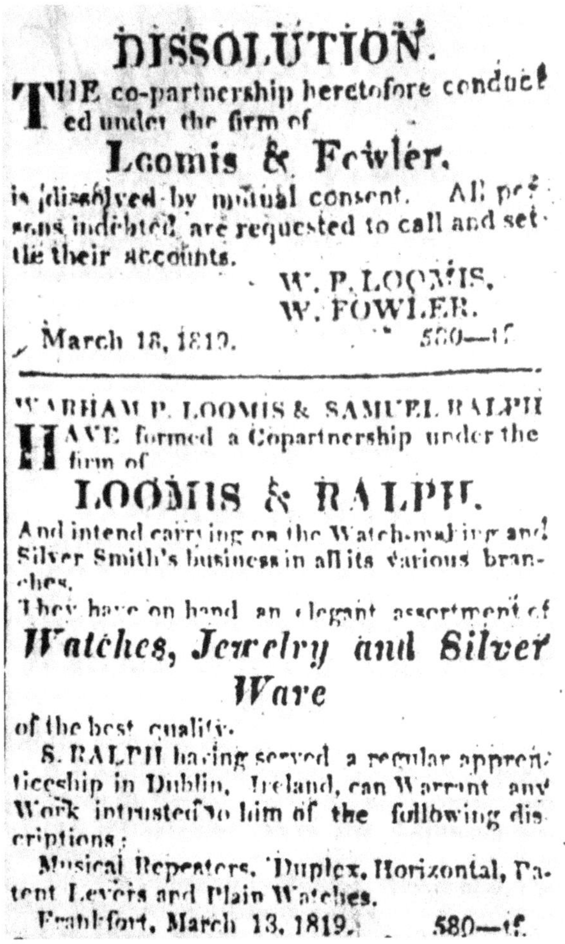

DISSOLUTION.

THE co-partnership heretofore conducted under the firm of

Loomis & Fowler,

is dissolved by mutual consent. All persons indebted are requested to call and settle their accounts.

W. P. LOOMIS,
W. FOWLER.

March 18, 1819. 580—tf.

WARHAM P. LOOMIS & SAMUEL RALPH

HAVE formed a Copartnership under the firm of

LOOMIS & RALPH.

And intend carrying on the Watch-making and Silver Smith's business in all its various branches.

They have on hand an elegant assortment of

Watches, Jewelry and Silver Ware

of the best quality.

S. RALPH having served a regular apprenticeship in Dublin, Ireland, can Warrant any Work intrusted to him of the following discriptions:

Musical Repeaters, Duplex, Horizontal, Patent Levers and Plain Watches.

Frankfort, March 13, 1819. 580—tf.

Figure 148. Samuel Ralph formed a partnership with Worham P. Loomis in Frankfort, KY, in 1819. Curiously, this advertisement is directly below another, announcing the dissolution of the partnership of Loomis and Fowler. WP Loomis was still there in 1838.[135] From the Argus of Western America March 19, 1819.[429]

listed as a clock or watch maker in Ireland.[129] In 1804, Alexander took John Wooldridge as his apprentice, at 19 years old, surely a late starter. The apprenticeship lasted only two years as noted in *Kentucky Order Book 1803-1809* although he was working as a silversmith in Frankfort, KY, in 1819.[21] From the same source it is known that he took another apprentice, 12-year-old George Shivery.

Alexander married Nancy Oliver in 1804 and had two sons. James died young and Oliver studied as a painter in America and Europe becoming one of Kentucky's best known portraitists (Figure 146).[427] Alexander Frazer died on November 7, 1810, and his death notice appeared in the *Kentucky Gazette* for November 13.[428] His house was reoccupied by a Mr. Bowlin, boot and hoe manufacturer, and his effects were sold on December 26, 1810.[428]

Nephew

Robert Frazer continued in business. He and Alexander had been joined by a nephew, Robert Frazer, Jr., and another nephew and niece, Mary and Robert Russell, from Ireland in about 1800.[21] Although Robert Senior never married, he undertook to look after Alexander's son as well as that of his other younger relatives after Alexander's death.

He was a successful businessman, had interests in railroads and property, and also helped to found the Fayette Lunatic Asylum.[427] On his death in 1851 he left a large library. In his will, he mentioned an uncle John in Belfast, possibly John Frazer mentioned in the Belfast directory for 1852, a mechanic on North Queen Street.[132] He also mentioned his deceased brother James Frazer (worked circa 1790–1810[5]), probably the well-documented maker of Comber, County Down, from where Alexander and his brother had originally emigrated (Figure 147).

Robert Junior

With the death of his uncle, Robert Junior continued the business. He married in 1831 but both his children died before the age of five.[21] The census of 1860 records various others with the name Frazer in Lexington who had been born in Ireland, including William Frazer, watch maker, age 18.[21] Other makers of this name are known in Ireland including David of Longford[6] and William, of Drogheda, circa 1770.[6]

FRANKFORT

SAMUEL RALPH

Samuel Ralph was in Frankfort, KY, in 1819. He had been apprenticed in Dublin[429] although it is not clear when or to whom.[31] He is not known as a maker in Ireland[129] but a Patrick Ralph was in Dame Street, Dublin in 1842[430] and later may have moved to Castlebar, County Mayo in the western province of Connacht.[431, 432]

Samuel Ralph's partnership with Warham Loomis was advertised in 1819,[429] but was dissolved a year later (Figure 148).[433] Also by 1820, he had worked in this business in Ireland and/or the United States for 14 years.[434] Assuming this period began just after he had completed his training, he would have completed his apprenticeship circa 1806 and would have been born circa 1785.

COVINGTON

Another previously undocumented individual, Peter Haunt, a watch maker from Ireland, is known from Covington, KY, from the census of 1850. He was married to Catherine and had two children, Thomas H. and Mary.[21]

HICKMAN COUNTY

Moses Campbell, born circa 1822, immigrated to Kentucky from Ireland and was found in Hickman County in 1850.[4] There were various makers with the name Campbell in the north of Ireland between 1780 and 1858.[5] Daniel Ruttle was born in Ireland circa 1823 and was in Kentucky circa 1859 working with Henry Terlau.[4]

MISSOURI

One R. Frazer is known from Jackson, MO, from 1821. It is unclear if this was Robert Frazer, Jr., who may possibly have left Kentucky and returned.[21]

Chapter Five
Virginia, North Carolina, and South Carolina

VIRGINIA

RICHMOND

Charles Purcell, Jr. was born in 1790[135] and was in Richmond from about 1812 until 1824.[16] He was the son of the Limerick watch maker John Purcell[71] who worked circa 1787[6] and who died in 1813.[31]

John Purcell had a brother, Charles Purcell, Sr., a silversmith who had settled in Richmond before 1790 (Figure 149).[435] He was a prosperous man of property but with calamities of his own including a fire on November 12, 1798 in which, according to the *Alexandria Advertiser*, he lost nearly everything.[436] Good business acumen ensured a recovery; at his death in 1815, he bequeathed $15,000 to his Limerick nephew Charles.[71] Today, this would be over a quarter of a million dollars—avuncular generosity indeed. In 1816, Charles Junior came to Richmond to collect his inheritance.[435, 437]

Figure 149. Richmond, VA, became home to the Purcells of Limerick, William McCabe, and others. This image, from Henry Bowe's Historical Collection of Virginia, published in 1849, shows the Capitol, City Hall, and the Governor's House in the center.

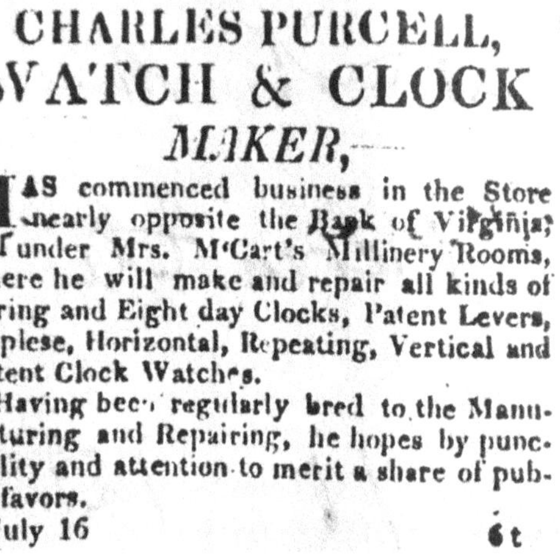

> **CHARLES PURCELL,**
> **WATCH & CLOCK**
> **MAKER,**
>
> HAS commenced business in the Store nearly opposite the Bank of Virginia, and under Mrs. M'Cart's Millinery Rooms, where he will make and repair all kinds of Spring and Eight day Clocks, Patent Levers, Duplese, Horizontal, Repeating, Vertical and Patent Clock Watches.
>
> Having been regularly bred to the Manufacturing and Repairing, he hopes by punctuality and attention to merit a share of public favors.
>
> July 16   6 t

Figure 150. Charles Purcell came from a well-documented family of watch makers in Limerick and began business in Richmond in 1817 according to the Virginia Patriot for July.[439]

Alimony Suit

Charles Senior had a skeleton in his cupboard exposed by the bizarre suit for alimony by Mrs. Ann Purcell nee Hazleton. She and Charles Senior had become estranged, leaving her penniless and relying on charity. In the Court of Chancery, Richmond, in the fall term of 1809, she said she had married Charles Senior on April 10, 1786. They had met, she said, in the autumn of the previous year in Philadelphia and were allegedly wed by a clergyman of the Swedish congregation. Charles Senior fought her claim for alimony, stating she was never his wife although conceding they had cohabited for many years. Perhaps attempting to slur her character or to appear generous — or both — he said he met a young lady from Ireland in 1797, one Ann Church, who was the illegitimate daughter of Ann Purcell. He had educated the younger Ann and had even given her a house. The court nonetheless found in favor of the plaintiff, Mrs. — if this is the correct title — Purcell awarding her $300 to "restore her the comforts of bed and board."[438] After this, we hear no more about her.

Clock Repair Business

Charles Junior stayed in Richmond and started business in 1817 (Figure 150).[439] He was at East Street in 1819.[71] He had declared his intention to become a citizen in August 1817 and took the oath in 1820.[71] He married Sarah Brouggy[435] but died in 1824,[71] leaving five children (John, Charles, William, Anna Maria, and James).[440] He was not as shrewd as his uncle; the value of his inventory was only a few hundred dollars.[71] Legal proceedings concerning his estate persisted until late 1825.[440]

Charles Junior was also acquainted with William Lamb (see below). They must have been close, as Lamb left Purcell's children large amounts of property when he died in 1827.[71]

Parenthetically, Charles Junior's brother, John, remained in Limerick. He was in Patrick Street from 1821[441] to 1824,[442] Henry Street in 1846,[431] and Denmark Street in 1856.[432] A James Purcell is also known from Limerick for 1809.[443]

A Charles Purcell, jeweler, was in Cork in 1787.[31] Could this be Charles Purcell Sr., who first went to Cork and thence to Richmond? None of his work is known to the author.

WILLIAM LAMB

William Lamb, a native of Ireland, was a clock maker in Richmond, VA, in 1803.[444] He was living on Cary's Street in 1810 and became a United States citizen in 1811.[71] In 1812, he married Mary Ryan, the widow of William Ryan, and, "in consideration of the love she has for William Lamb" she conveyed her estate to him.[71] There are many records of land dealings for Lamb for the ensuing years[71] but few concerning clocks and watches. He may have lost interest in that business, finding greater opportunities for his considerable talent in real estate. He died around February 1827 bequeathing his property to his wife, including a black slave woman Amie who had been "appraised" at $300. The good news was that after the death of his wife Mary, Amie was to be emancipated

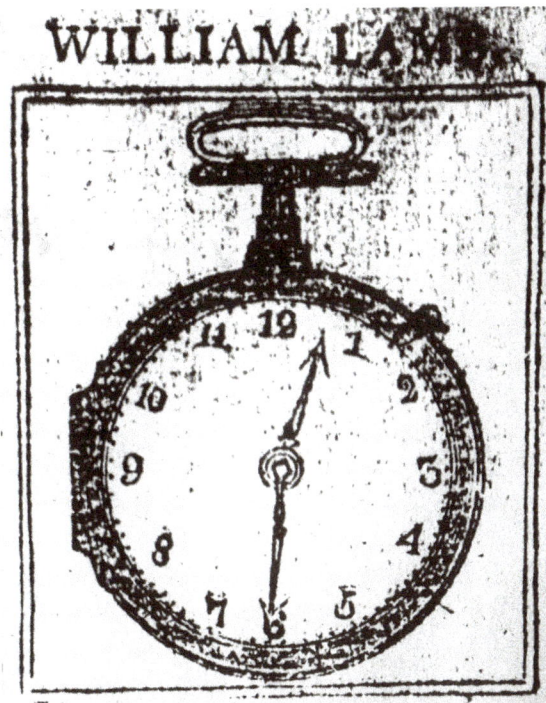

Figure 151. William Lamb notice in the Virginia Argus for November 1803 that "no exertions of his shall be wanting to deserve their future approbation."[444]

and given $100. He had done exceptionally well in business. He left several houses to various individuals as well as 10,000 acres to a Joseph Hagan and a further amount to Bernard Hagan and Charles Purcell's children. Hagan may have been a friend from the old country but does not appear to have been a clock maker. None of his artifacts are known to the author.

Figure 152. The first notice to appear for William McCabe appeared in Richmond in 1804 in The Enquirer.[448]

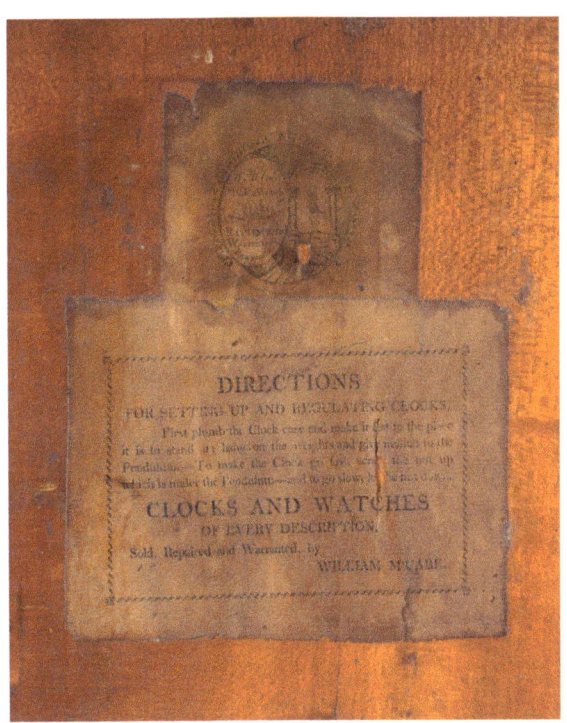

Figure 153. Two labels on the back of the clock door. The upper Masonic label reads "the silent breast and secret heart preserves the mistery of the art." The lower gives directions for setting up the clock. Picture courtesy Gary Sullivan Antiques.

virginia, north carolina, and south carolina 93

Figures 154 and 155. One of several clocks with the name of William McCabe, although he may not have made it himself. The dial is likely from Boston and the case also from Massachusetts. Another is in the Colonial Williamsburg Foundation where works and case are all of Massachusetts manufacture.[348] Picture courtesy Gary Sullivan Antiques.

WILLIAM McCABE

The clock maker William McCabe was active in Richmond in the late 18th and early 19th centuries. His origins are obscure although he may be from one of the distinguished families of clock makers originating in Lurgan, County Armagh. This family began with Patrick McCabe who was born circa 1708 and died in 1782.[445] The most famous of his sons was the youngest, James, who emigrated to London, England founding the House of McCabe. The eldest, Thomas, remained in Ireland and had revolutionary leanings. We have already met another son, John, who came to Baltimore in 1774. He predeceased his father, dying in 1778 around 30

94 passing time across the water

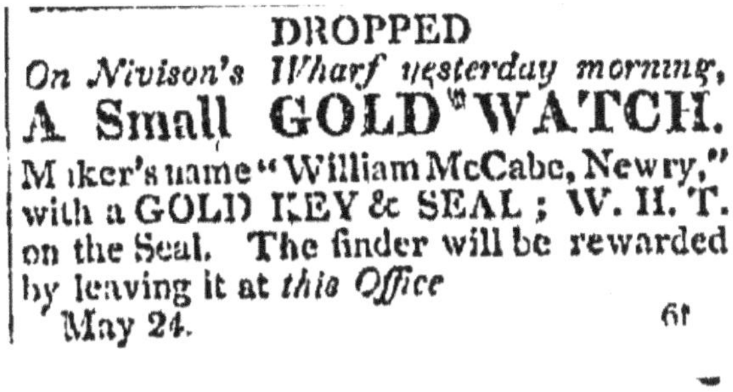

> DROPPED
> On *Nivison's Wharf* yesterday morning,
> A Small GOLD WATCH.
> Maker's name "William McCabe, Newry,"
> with a GOLD KEY & SEAL ; W. H. T.
> on the Seal. The finder will be rewarded
> by leaving it at *this Office*
> May 24.   6t

Figure 156. A notice for a lost watch in The American Beacon and Norfolk & Portsmouth Daily Advertiser for May 24, 1820.[565] The watch made by William McCabe of Newry. Did William McCabe of Richmond or a family member go to the coast and lose an heirloom or was this a pure coincidence?

years old, perhaps in the Revolutionary War. The last of the four clock-making sons was William (whom we shall call William I) born in 1740 or 1741 and who died in 1785.[341] William I's son, William II, was probably born around 1770.

The Mysterious Mr. McCabe

A clock-making William McCabe was in Richmond, VA, from 1804, or perhaps as early as 1790[4] to 1820 (Figure 152).[16] As the following account demonstrates, who he was and when he came is a little more mysterious.

William II remained in Ulster until 1800[341] or 1805.[5] It is said he moved to London where he worked until 1824.[341] Certainly, there is a William McCabe there whose dates would fit.[2,8] But, like his brother John, he might have gone to America and have had a coincidental, and not uncommon, namesake in London.

John McCabe, who died in Baltimore, is said to have had two sons, John and William (who we shall call William III and who is said to have migrated to Richmond).[348] There was, indeed, a John McCabe in Baltimore in 1790 noted in the U.S. Census there, but no William– at least until 1820. To frustrate our enquiries, the early census for Richmond was destroyed in the War of 1812.

In trying to research this further, any morsel of information would certainly have helped. So,

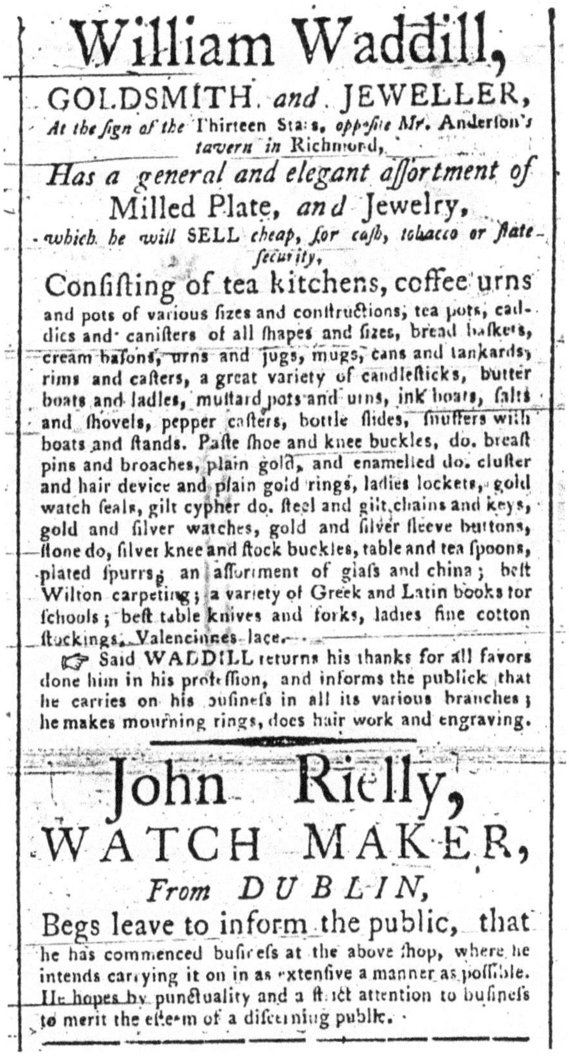

> **William Waddill,**
> GOLDSMITH and JEWELLER,
> At the sign of the Thirteen Stars, opposite Mr. Anderson's tavern in Richmond,
> Has a general and elegant assortment of Milled Plate, and Jewelry,
> which he will SELL cheap, for cash, tobacco or plate security,
> Consisting of tea kitchens, coffee urns and pots of various sizes and constructions, tea pots, caddies and canisters of all shapes and sizes, bread baskets, cream basons, urns and jugs, mugs, cans and tankards, rims and casters, a great variety of candlesticks, butter boats and ladles, mustard pots and urns, ink hoats, salts and shovels, pepper casters, bottle slides, snuffers with boats and stands. Paste shoe and knee buckles, do. breast pins and broaches, plain gold, and enamelled do. cluster and hair device and plain gold rings, ladies lockets, gold watch seals, gilt cypher do. steel and gilt chains and keys, gold and silver watches, gold and silver sleeve buttons, stone do, silver knee and stock buckles, table and tea spoons, plated spurs, an assortment of glass and china ; best Wilton carpeting ; a variety of Greek and Latin books for schools ; best table knives and forks, ladies fine cotton stockings. Valenciennes lace.
> ☞ Said WADDILL returns his thanks for all favors done him in his profession, and informs the publick that he carries on his business in all its various branches ; he makes mourning rings, does hair work and engraving.

> **John Rielly,**
> WATCH MAKER,
> From DUBLIN,
> Begs leave to inform the public, that he has commenced business at the above shop, where he intends carrying it on in as extensive a manner as possible. He hopes by punctuality and a strict attention to business to merit the esteem of a discerning public.

Figure 157. There were two advertisements for John Reilly, lately arrived from Dublin, one for April 23, 1785,[457] and this from the Virginia Gazette and Independent Chronicler, with a misspelling, for May 21, 1785.[458]

from a faded and stained old label in one of his clocks, we learned our clock-making William McCabe was a Richmond Mason (Figure 153). Naturally, this led to the records of the Library of the Grand Lodge of Virginia in Richmond. There, indeed, we find a William McCabe, his family name spelled variously as M'Cay, M'Cabe, or McCabe. He appears first on the rosters of Richmond Lodge No. 10 in 1801, served

Figure 158. Alexandria, VA, in the early 19th century showing detail of a slave ship at the waterfront. From a broadside published by the American Anti-Slavery Society. Original caption of the image: "View of a section of Alexandria, with a slave ship receiving her cargo of slaves."[563]

as senior warden in 1804, master in 1807, and grand senior deacon for the Grand Lodge of Virginia in 1807–09. He withdrew from Richmond Lodge No. 10 on June 6, 1820. Notably, his name does not appear on the deceased roster in the 1823 Grand Lodge of Virginia Proceedings (see below).

Now for the bad news. The *History and By-Laws of Richmond Royal Arch Chapter No. 3 A. F. & A. M.*[446] states that the William McCabe, who was master in 1807 and on the Roster of High Priests from September 1812 to July 1813,[446] had already been a member of Chapter No. 10 in Lynchburg, VA, since 1785. Clearly, as William II was only about 15 in 1785, this must be another William. If he was an adult member of Lynchburg in 1785, he might have been born in 1765 and unlikely to be the son of John of Baltimore, as the latter would only have been 17 years old. Let us call him William IV.

Shockoe Cemetery

One of the headstones in Shockoe Cemetery in Richmond is of particular interest to us; that of — yes — William McCabe. Born circa 1778, he died in 1823 at only 45 years old.[447] It has been suggested that this is the grave of William McCabe III of Baltimore.[348] He cannot be the Mason above as the latter was born before 1778, and there is no William McCabe in the 1823

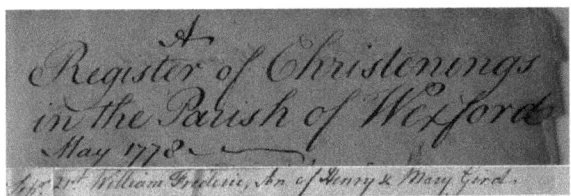

Figure 159. The baptismal record of William Gird at St. Iberius Church in Wexford. His was a large family and there were another nine siblings. Source Representative Church Body Library; Image Copyright National Archives of Ireland.

William F. Gird,
CLOCK and WATCH-MAKER, King-street, near Mott's Tavern,
HAS JUST RECEIVED,
A handsome assortment of English Watches:
AND HAS ON HAND,
A few good Clocks, with or without cases; table and tea-spoons; sugar-tongs: gold and gilt ear-rings; gold and gilt finger-rings; gold and gilt breast-pins; silver thimbles; gold mounted combs; chains; seals; keys—and a variety of other articles in the jewellery line—which will be sold on moderate terms.
November 15. co3t
N. B. A JOURNEYMAN Watch-Maker wanted.

Figure 160. Gird imported many watches from abroad and included work by some distinguished makers[564] including Pierre Gregson, an Englishman fl. 1778–90, who made high-end watches and was clock maker to the King of France.[8]

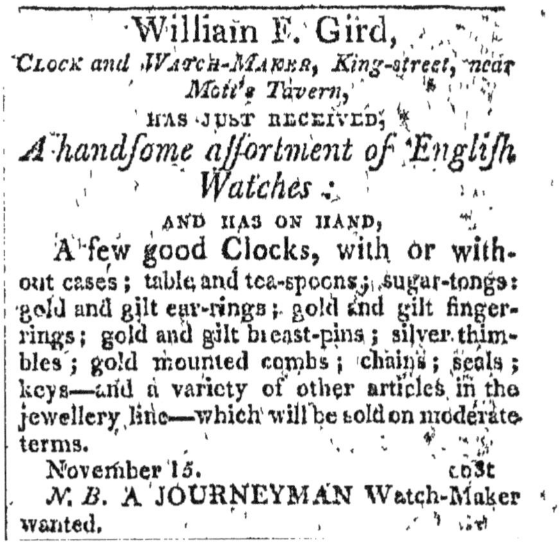

deceased roster. Thus, there were at least two individuals by the name of William McCabe in Richmond in the early 19th century. So, let us call him William V.

To this author it would be a remarkable—but not impossible—coincidence to have two clock makers named William McCabe in Richmond at the same time, but the Mason records suggest only one individual. Conceivably, the William McCabe originally from Lynchburg was older than surmised here, and could have been the father of William V. The latter might not even have been a clock maker at all. If William V was the same as William III it is odd that the dates do not correspond with those of the Mason clock maker since our clocks have the Masonic label. To make matters more complex, other makers called William McCabe, were in Baltimore circa 1770[4] and Washington County, MD, in 1801.[4]

McCabe Commences Business

Surrounded by this dense fog of history, we can say for sure that a clock-making William McCabe started business in 1804 opposite the house of Captain Richardson.[448] He formed a partnership with a Mr. Walker in 1805[449] that was dissolved shortly thereafter.[16, 435] His name appeared over the years in the *Richmond Enquirer* and elsewhere, and he sought apprentices and journeymen.[450-452] Illnesses in 1814[453] and 1816 almost forced his retirement,[454] but part of his right thumb was amputated and he could work again.[455] He also had military interests. "The company met under the command of Captain William McCabe on Saturday last," stated the *Virginia Argus* in April 1813 (he had been commissioned captain on March 16, 1810[16]), "and were taken to an elevated and pleasant situation on Adams' Hill." McCabe had made a prize medal for shooting, which was "of tasty workmanship."[435]

Clocks

Several of his clocks have survived. One is a colorful painted dial clock with filled-in spandrels (Figures 154 and 155). Roman numerals indicate hours while Arabic numerals indicate minutes. The dial is unsigned but the case is similar to the other two mentioned here. This clock is of interest because of the label, which suggested that McCabe was a Mason. The fine Roxbury case might have been produced for export to the South by the Willard brothers of Massachusetts who had a formidable commercial machine for clock production in the late 18th and early 19th centuries.

A painted arch dial long case clock with gilded scroll spandrels and rolling moon automation is in the Colonial Williamsburg Online Collection. It is an 8-day, weight driven, with anchor escapement and rack and snail striking on a bell. There are three brass ball finials and pierced Roxbury-style fretwork atop the hood. The trunk has fluted quarter columns and a rectangular door with molded edges. Applied molding forms a square in the base and there are French feet. "Sold, Repaired and Warranted" by William McCabe, it may not even have been made by him. A similar clock from the Valentine Museum, Richmond, VA, was illustrated by James Gibbs in *Dixie Clockmakers*.[384]

It is hoped that the identities of the various individuals called William McCabe will be clarified by future studies. Unless, of course, another shows up to complicate matters even further (Figure 156).

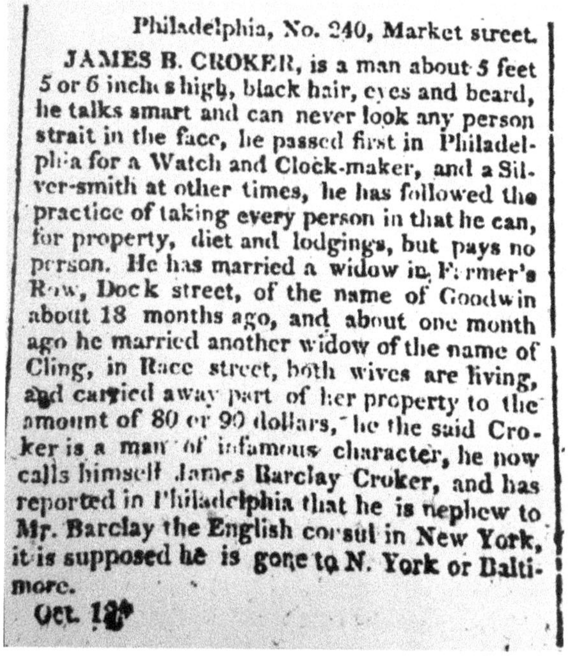

Philadelphia, No. 240, Market street.

JAMES B. CROKER, is a man about 5 feet 5 or 6 inches high, black hair, eyes and beard, he talks smart and can never look any person strait in the face, he passed first in Philadelphia for a Watch and Clock-maker, and a Silver-smith at other times, he has followed the practice of taking every person in that he can, for property, diet and lodgings, but pays no person. He has married a widow in Farmer's Row, Dock street, of the name of Goodwin about 18 months ago, and about one month ago he married another widow of the name of Cling, in Race street, both wives are living, and carried away part of her property to the amount of 80 or 90 dollars, he the said Croker is a man of infamous character, he now calls himself James Barclay Croker, and has reported in Philadelphia that he is nephew to Mr. Barclay the English consul in New York, it is supposed he is gone to N. York or Baltimore.

Oct. 12

Figure 162. The peccadilloes of James Croker exposed in The Baltimore Whig on October 12, 1811, after he had married two widows and absconded with property worth $80 or $90.[469]

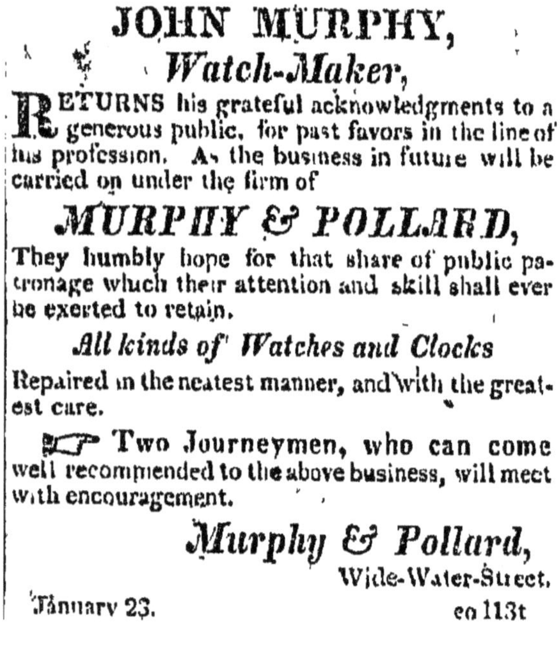

JOHN MURPHY,

Watch-Maker,

RETURNS his grateful acknowledgments to a generous public, for past favors in the line of his profession. As the business in future will be carried on under the firm of

MURPHY & POLLARD,

They humbly hope for that share of public patronage which their attention and skill shall ever be exerted to retain.

All kinds of Watches and Clocks

Repaired in the neatest manner, and with the greatest care.

☞ Two Journeymen, who can come well recommended to the above business, will meet with encouragement.

Murphy & Pollard,

Wide-Water-Street.

January 23. eo 113t

Figure 161. The 1818 partnership with Lewis Pollard announced in January in the American Beacon and Commercial Diary.[466] *The business continued until 1820.*[4] *The author knows of no clocks or watches by Murphy.*

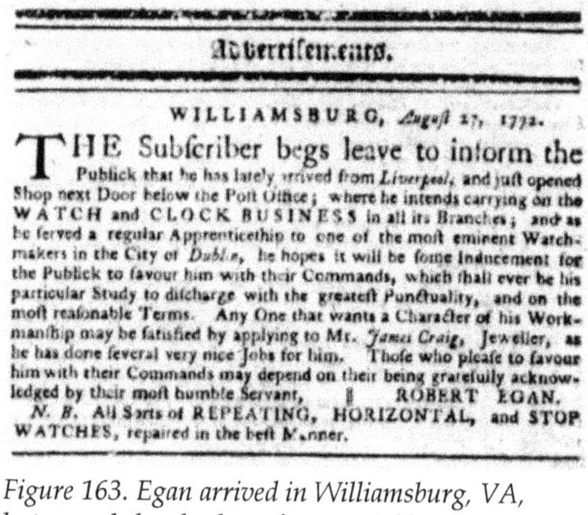

Advertisements.

WILLIAMSBURG, *August* 27, 1772.

THE Subfcriber begs leave to inform the Publick that he has lately arrived from *Liverpool*, and juft opened Shop next Door below the Poft Office; where he intends carrying on the WATCH and CLOCK BUSINESS in all its Branches; and as he ferved a regular Apprenticefhip to one of the moft eminent Watchmakers in the City of *Dublin*, he hopes it will be fome Inducement for the Publick to favour him with their Commands, which fhall ever be his particular Study to difcharge with the greateft Punctuality, and on the moft reafonable Terms. Any One that wants a Character of his Workmanfhip may be fatisfied by applying to Mr. *James Craig*, Jeweller, as he has done feveral very nice Jobs for him. Thofe who pleafe to favour him with their Commands may depend on their being gratefully acknowledged by their moft humble Servant, ROBERT EGAN.

N. B. All Sorts of REPEATING, HORIZONTAL, and STOP WATCHES, repaired in the beft Manner.

Figure 163. Egan arrived in Williamsburg, VA, but moved shortly thereafter to neighboring North Carolina.

ALEXANDRIA

WILLIAM GIRD

William F. Gird was at King Street near to the Washington Tavern in Alexandria, VA, (Figure 158) from at least 1798[459] until 1807 when he took United States citizenship.[71] He was born in Ireland in 1778 into Henry Hatton Gird and Mary Hind's large family and christened William Fredric Gird in St. Iberius Church in Wexford (Figure 159). A letter from 1792 states that "Willie" was apprenticed to his cousin's father and that he was "making good." This cousin was Margaret Maria Lahee, whose mother was the sister to Willie's father, Henry Gird, Sr.[460] The Wexford clock maker Samuel Lahee was working between 1765 and 1788 and it is likely he was master to William. It is said that the family left Ireland in the late 1790s for Philadelphia. William's father was a barber. It was said that he was wealthy enough to charter a ship to America. He must have cut a lot of hair.

Henry Gird, Jr. became the proprietor of the *Columbian Mirror* in Alexandria and William Gird commenced business as a clock and watch maker in the same premises on the corner of Cameron and Fairfax Streets (Figure 160).[459] With "assiduity and attention," he also dealt in jewelry and had a broad inventory of silverware also.[461] He prospered, seeking a journeyman in 1806.[462] What became of him after 1807 is unclear.

The author has not seen any of his clocks or watches, and there are none in the Alexandria museum.

An extensive family history of the Gird family and their development can be found at tinyurl.com/yjc5873n.

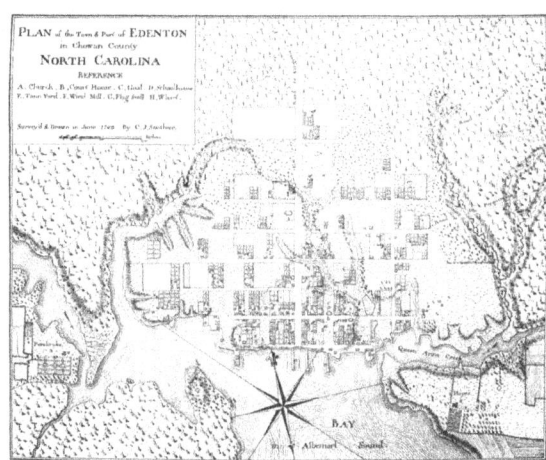

Figure 164. A plan of the Town and Port of Edenton in Chowan County, North Carolina dated 1769 and drawn by C. J. Sauthier. Egan arrived in the town some 10 years after the completion of this map.

JOHN REILLY

The name Reilly or Reily is recorded in the Dublin watch-making trade from 1738 to 1786[7] and is on the List of quarter brothers of the Dublin Goldsmiths Company for the years 1749-50 and 1771-72.[31]

John Reily was at 17 Crampton Court from 1762[96] to 1784.[82] This was a favored location for watch makers in the late 18th and early 19th centuries.[456] He had moved to nearby Capel Street by 1786[83] but was gone in a year.[84] This may be the same John Reilly, who moved to Richmond, VA, and worked at the premises of William Waddill at the Sign of the Thirteen Stars in 1785 (Figure 157).[457,458] The discrepant dates might be an error in the directory, as with Ambrose Clarke of Baltimore. It is unclear if he was a maker, repairer, or retailer. In 1785, he was appointed clerk of the market, but was removed in 1786.[71]

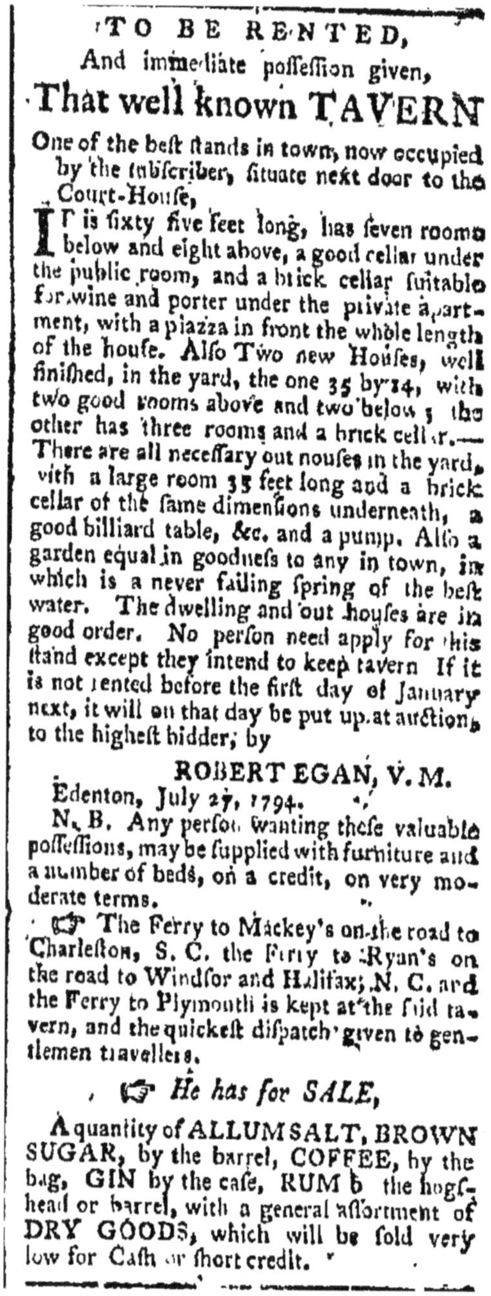

TO BE RENTED,

And immediate poſſeſſion given,

That well known TAVERN

One of the beſt ſtands in town, now occupied by the ſubſcriber, ſituate next door to the Court-Houſe,

IT is ſixty five feet long, has ſeven rooms below and eight above, a good cellar under the public room, and a brick cellar ſuitable for wine and porter under the private apartment, with a piazza in front the whole length of the houſe. Alſo Two new Houſes, well finiſhed, in the yard, the one 35 by 24, with two good rooms above and two below; the other has three rooms and a brick cellar.—There are all neceſſary out houſes in the yard, with a large room 35 feet long and a brick cellar of the ſame dimenſions underneath, a good billiard table, &c. and a pump. Alſo a garden equal in goodneſs to any in town, in which is a never failing ſpring of the beſt water. The dwelling and out houſes are in good order. No perſon need apply for this ſtand except they intend to keep tavern. If it is not rented before the firſt day of January next, it will on that day be put up at auction, to the higheſt bidder, by

ROBERT EGAN, V. M.

Edenton, July 27, 1794.

N. B. Any perſon wanting theſe valuable poſſeſſions, may be ſupplied with furniture and a number of beds, on a credit, on very moderate terms.

☞ The Ferry to Mackey's on the road to Charleſton, S. C. the Ferry to Ryan's on the road to Windſor and Halifax, N. C. and the Ferry to Plymouth is kept at the ſaid tavern, and the quickeſt diſpatch given to gentlemen travellers.

☞ *He has for SALE,*

A quantity of ALLUM SALT, BROWN SUGAR, by the barrel, COFFEE, by the bag, GIN by the caſe, RUM by the hogſhead or barrel, with a general aſſortment of DRY GOODS, which will be ſold very low for Caſh or ſhort credit.

Figure 165. Robert Egan's tavern and two houses up for rent as advertised in the Virginia Chronicle, & General Advertiser for July 31, 1794.[562] He also ran ferry services across the Albemarle Sound – see the Town Plan for 1769 – a great convenience for those traveling further south in North Carolina.

NORFOLK

JOHN MURPHY

John Murphy and his wife Mary are known from Norfolk, VA, in 1795 when they may have been in Church Street.[71] A maker by that name, likely the same person, was at 16 Fen Church Street[71] in 1801. He was at 8 Wide Water Street when watch seals were returned to his shop by a black man.[463] In 1806, he was at 16 Water Street[71] and sought journeymen in 1809[464] and in 1811.[465] In 1816, he was a trustee of the Methodist Church,[71] and was in partnership with Lewis Pollard a few years later (Figure 161[466]).

PETERSBURG

JAMES BARCLAY CROKER

James Barclay Croker manufactured and repaired watches of all types[467] and also set miniature paintings.[467] "Late of London and Dublin,"[467] he may have been apprenticed in the British capital.[3] He was a law-breaker, who first appeared in New York in 1805; from there word was sent to Southern newspapers alleging him to be a swindler. The public were warned to be vigilant as he may have gone to Virginia.[468] He went north, however, as a J.B. Croker, clock maker, watch maker, and jeweler appears at 14 Marlboro Street, Boston, in 1807.[3] In 1808, he was indeed in Virginia, on Sycamore Street in Petersburg, VA, manufacturing and repairing watches.[467] His bigamous practices were publicized in *The Baltimore Whig* in 1811 (Figure 162) in which it was alleged that he had married the widows Goodwin and Cling and absconded with the property of one.[469]

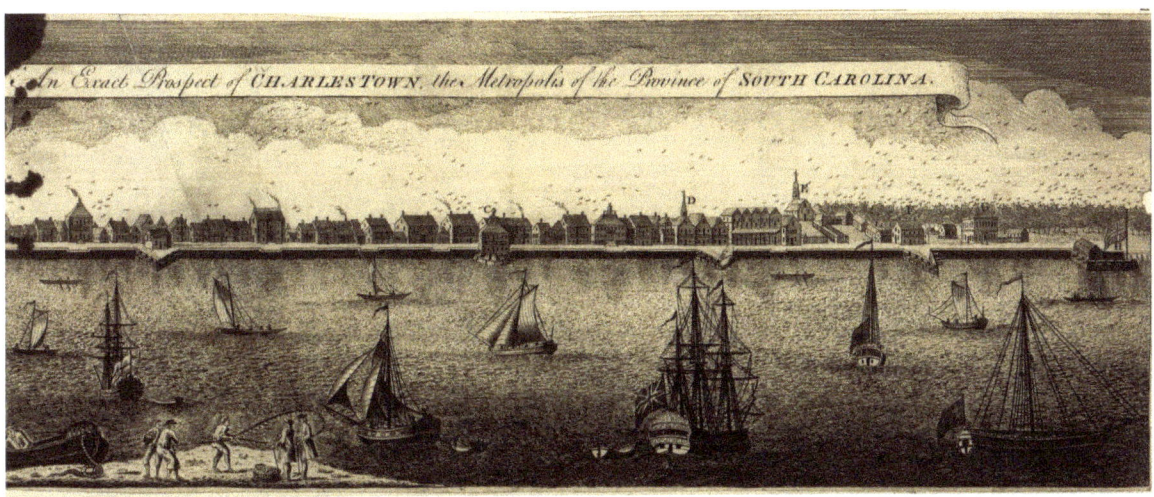

Figure 166. A mid-18th-century panoramic view of Charleston waterfront and quays which would have been the view seen by the immigrants as they arrived in the Province of South Carolina. The Province of Carolina had been divided in two in 1729 and the States were formed about 60 years later. This view of Charlestown was published in the London Magazine in 1762.

NORTH CAROLINA

EDENTON

ROBERT EGAN

Robert Egan arrived in Williamsburg, VA, via Liverpool in 1772 (Figure 163).[470] He may have collaborated with James Craig, a local jeweler, who spoke of the "eminent hand" he had taken on.[471] It is unclear to whom he was apprenticed but it was "one of the most eminent watchmakers in Dublin,"[470] although Egan's name is not on the Dublin apprentice list.[31]

He was a repairer and maker of repeating, horizontal, and stop watches. He stayed in Williamsburg for some time. A Robert Egan, watch maker and presumably the same, ap-

JOHN NARNEY,

WATCH-MAKER, lately arrived from *Dublin*,

Makes and *cleans*,

(In the houſe lately poſſeſſed by Mr. *Boone*, between Capt. *Colcock*'s and Mrs. *Clifford*'s,

At the ſouth end of the *Bay*, in *Charles Town*,)

ALL ſorts of repeating and plain WATCHES, in the beſt and faithfuleſt manner.

As the ſaid *Narney* was *regularly bred* to the watch-making buſineſs, and followed it ſeveral years in the city of *Dublin* with credit and reputation, and is thoroughly ſorted with all the materials belonging to it: Gentlemen and Ladies may depend on having their watches mended, regulated, and put in the very beſt order they are capable of.

N.B. He has ſeveral watches, made by him in *Dublin*, to be diſpoſed of, which he will engage their performance to be as good as any made in *London* or elſewhere.

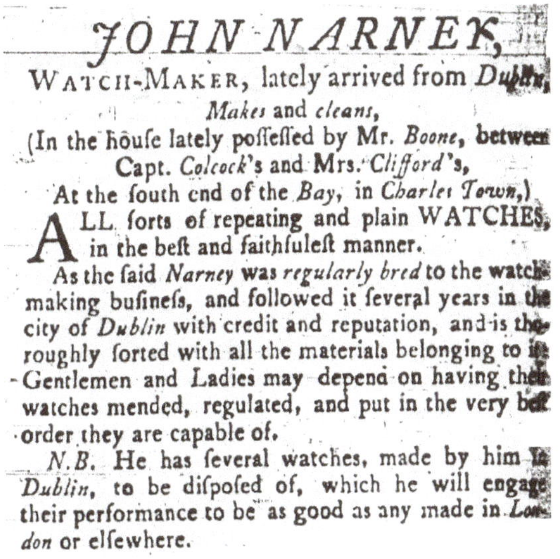

Figure 167. Narney was one of the earlier arrivals to the Province of South Carolina establishing himself there in 1753. From the South Carolina Gazette for September 24,1753.[477]

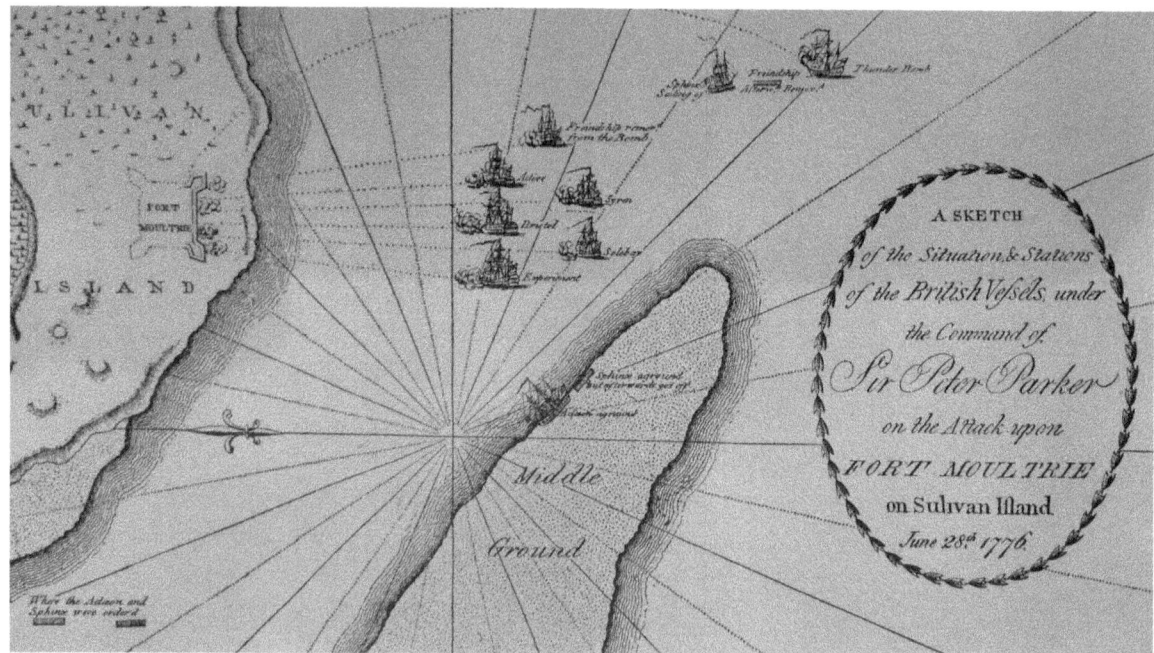

Figure 168. On June 28, 1776, about five years after Narney left, Fort Moultrie, on nearby Sullivan's Island, Charleston, was attacked by the British. The island is named after Florence O'Sullivan the Irish soldier of fortune, surveyor, and early colonist. An intriguing account of some of his endeavors and contributions to the history of South Carolina can be found in Captain Florence O'Sullivan and the Origins of Carolina.[566] In the assault, the British were repulsed.

pears in the 1779 deed records of Edenton,[71] a small coastal town about 100 miles south in the neighboring state of North Carolina (Figure 164). Shortly after his arrival, he purchased what became known as the Coffield House on East King Street.[472] In 1788, he was still in Edenton in the watch repair and sale business and had also taken over a tavern from one Captain Kock.[27, 71] He later moved near to the courthouse and started another tavern while continuing as a watch maker.[473]

By 1794, he had become a general merchant selling tobacco, sugar, rigging, fancy clothing, real estate, and slaves.[474] He also had supplies of coffee, gin by the case, and rum by the barrel. Later that year he rented his tavern[474] and left North Carolina for New York, returning in December 1795[475] to his various business ventures that now included a ferry across the scenic Albemarle Sound (Figure 165).

His wife, Sarah, died in January 1796 at the age of 46 after a lingering illness.[71] *The State Gazette of North Carolina* for October 27 of that year records the passing of Egan himself in New York.[476] None of his watches or clocks are known to the author.

FAYETTEVILLE

CHARLES CONOLLY SMITH

Charles Conolly Smith arrived from London and was in Fayetteville from 1841 to 1857 as an Irish silversmith and worked as a manufacturing jeweler and watch repairman.[4]

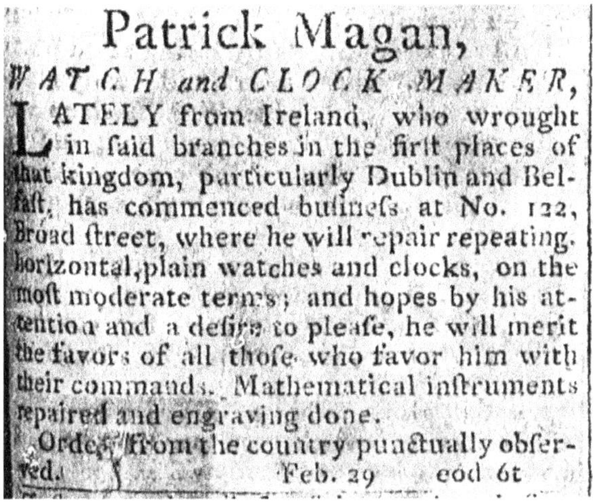

Figure 169. Fresh off the boat. Patrick Magan's advertisement appeared on page 3 of the February 29, 1792, edition of Charleston's City Gazette and Daily Advertiser.

SOUTH CAROLINA

CHARLESTON

(Figure 166)

JOHN NARNEY

Figure 170. A white dial mahogany long case clock and the only specimen known from Patrick Magann's atelier. The case may have been imported from Massachusetts to South Carolina. Now in The Mabel Brady Garvan Collection of Yale University. Picture kind courtesy Yale University.

John Narney came to Charleston, SC, around 1753 (Figure 167).[477] Located at the South End of the Bay, he made, mended, and cleaned watches. He had spent "several years in Dublin with credit and reputation,"[477] and is mentioned, as John Nearny, on the quarter brother list in Dublin for 1744.[31]

The *Dublin Gazette* for August 15–18, 1767, reported that his wife had died at Gilltown, County Kildare but that he was then in South Carolina.[478] A Teresa and William Narney arrived in Charleston shortly before September 1767 on the *Britannia* from Newry.[479] Teresa was then 33 years old. William's age was not stated but, as his name was linked to a survey for a land bounty, he was presumably an adult. They may have been relatives, children perhaps, of John and left after the death of their mother.

Charleston was another seaboard city with a quickly growing economy. Indeed, by 1770, with a population of over 10,000, it would grow to be the fourth largest in the colonies after Philadelphia, New York, and Boston.[480] A verge silver pair case watch circa 1745 is known, and the case is probably by William Currie.[481]

Narney had left for a time as the *South Caro-*

Figures 171 and 172. Detail of the Magann dial. The 6" x 4½" brass, 8-day movement has smooth drums and has rack and snail striking on a bell. Between the brass movement, sitting on the wooden seat board, and the dial is the false plate. This is signed, "Ashwin & Co." of England. The false plate and dial came from the dial maker and permitted correct positioning of the dial to fit a movement made by another craftsman. Since Ashwin may have died in 1791[518] the date of the clock may be refined further to ca.1770–91.

lina Gazette for December 19, 1761, reported that he had returned to the city and was carrying on business as usual.[482] He made at least one other trip to London in June 1769.[483]

Land Dealings

Like others, he was notable for his land dealings. In 1756, he purchased 500 acres of land for "£1,000 current money of the Province."[484] He had made purchases of 350 acres in 1758, 450 acres in 1764, and a further 300 acres in 1768.[485] The value of land from his first purchase had risen from £2 an acre to £6.25 an acre, but the 1764 purchase was for £600 or £1.3 an acre. By now, he had a handsome plantation and in January of 1772, he sold 1,600 acres for "£10,000." This consisted of 300 acres suitable

Figure 173. From the City Gazette and Daily Advertiser for February 4, 1790. Published in Charleston, SC.[501]

104 passing time across the water

for rice planting, a house, barns, carts, wagons, and 200 head of cattle. By this time, Narney had also acquired 85 "choice slaves."

He stated his intention to leave the province in 1772.[486] Perhaps he could see the Colonies were on the threshold of the Revolution; the Boston Tea Party would occur in 1773 and war would follow. Hostilities would come to Charleston and the British would make a failed attempt to take Fort Moultrie on nearby Sullivan's Island (Figure 168). The sale of his goods was carried out around January 1772[486] and the *South Carolina Gazette and Country Journal* of May 21, 1772, noted his embarkation for England a few days before,[487] final destination unknown.

Narney was in Dublin in 1744[31] and possibly again in 1771[7] although the reference for the latter date is not clear. If the dates refer to the same person, then he certainly had an interesting life in the interim. His name does not appear in the Dublin directories as a watch maker for 1772-1784.[81, 82, 181, 183, 184, 301]

Note Gibbs[384] and Palmer[126] both refer to a Joseph Narney but the first advertisement placed in the *South Carolina Gazette* may have been an error he is subsequently referred to as John.[71]

PATRICK MAGANN (MAGAN, McGANN)

Patrick Magann, born around 1745, opened for business at 122 Broad Street in Charleston, SC, in February 1792 (Figure 169).[488] He was versed in several skills including clock- and watch-making, mathematical instrument work, engraving, and was also a silversmith.[22, 488] Why he left Belfast is unclear as the city was then thriving; the population had risen from 8,500 in 1757 to about 20,000 in 1800[295] largely due to the booming linen and cotton industries. He "had wrought in watch and clock making in...Dublin and Belfast."[488] The Dublin reference may mean that he had been apprenticed there although he is not on the usual apprentice lists.[31, 212, 213] His contemporaries in Belfast in the early 1790s would have included Thomas Bagnall, Robert Neill, and the well-known Job Rider.

He was initially successful in Charleston, working first on Broad Street but later moving to East Bay until 1824.[489, 490] A short time after his arrival, he formed a partnership with Joseph Latham[71] and had contact with other Ulstermen who were in to Charleston. Indeed, he was one of the executors of the will of Robert Johnston, gardener, formerly of Greenwill Street, Newtownards, County Down.[491]

Barsheba Cattle

He was also executor to Barsheba Cattle.[71] She was a "free colored person" with shares in banking organizations and with at least two slaves, a "wench Nanny" and a "negro man slave Bob." An extraordinary aspect of her will was not that Bob would be sold, nor that Magann would get half the proceeds, but that the other half would go to her "daughter Jane Rebecca McGann."[492] Officially frowned upon, miscegenation was quite prevalent in the 18th century and the mulatto population grew steadily.[493]

Clock

The clock in Figures 170-172 has already been well described in *The American Clock*.[494] The 13"x18" arched, painted iron dial has a subsidiary second hand dial below XII. Above VI is the name, "Patk Magann, Charleston" and an arched date aperture. Hours are in Roman numerals. Minutes are indicated by dots and there are Arabic numbers at five-minute intervals in keeping with a date between 1770 and 1800. The floral designs in the corners are typical of these earlier dials. The hands have been replaced.[494] The mahogany case with architectural top is 99" high.[494]

Magann was at 24 Queen Street in 1829[495, 496] but died in Charleston Poor House on April 21, 1834, when he was 90 years old.[497]

Figures 174–177. John McKee, his wife Mary (nee Alexander Hayden), and daughters Julia Felicia and Mary Ellen. The adults have plain backgrounds while the children have background scenes. A cravat with pin and sideburns suggest a well-to-do and fashion-conscious Mr. McKee and were early 19th-century features. Mrs. McKee's high-waisted dress is seen ca. 1790-1800. Mary Ellen (1822–1906) the elder daughter sits by a fruit basket in a dress with ruffled pantaloons. Julia, born 1828, died aged seven and carries a doll. Descriptions from the Museum of Early Southern Decorative Arts, North Carolina.

Figures 178-180. Not surprisingly, most McKee clocks have features of dates from 1808 to 1830 and are signed for "Chester S.C." A movement is shown here with a conventional layout and rack striking system for the period. Pictures courtesy of the Museum of Early Southern Decorative Arts.

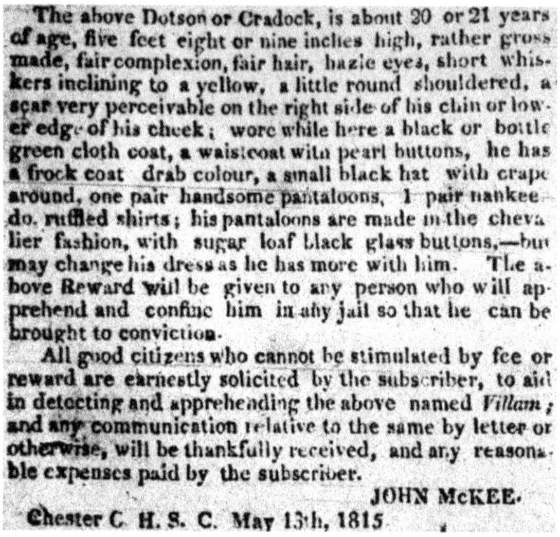
The above Dotson or Cradock, is about 20 or 21 years of age, five feet eight or nine inches high, rather gross made, fair complexion, fair hair, hazle eyes, short whiskers inclining to a yellow, a little round shouldered, a scar very perceivable on the right side of his chin or lower edge of his cheek; wore while here a black or bottle green cloth coat, a waistcoat with pearl buttons, he has a frock coat drab colour, a small black hat with crape around, one pair handsome pantaloons, 1 pair nankee do. ruffled shirts; his pantaloons are made in the chevalier fashion, with sugar loaf black glass buttons,—but may change his dress as he has more with him. The above Reward will be given to any person who will apprehend and confine him in any jail so that he can be brought to conviction.

All good citizens who cannot be stimulated by fee or reward are earnestly solicited by the subscriber, to aid in detecting and apprehending the above named *Villain*; and any communication relative to the same by letter or otherwise, will be thankfully received, and any reasonable expenses paid by the subscriber.

JOHN McKEE.

Chester C. H. S. C. May 13th, 1815

Figure 181. A reward of $200 was offered by McKee in The Star of Raleigh, NC, for helping convict the thief of McKee's horse, saddle, one gold watch, and four silver watches. The description of the villain, Elijah Dotson, speaks to the attention to detail which was part of McKee's personality. It stands in stark – if not laughable – contrast to Gilbert Bigger's earlier description of his own thieves. This particular robber was subsequently apprehended.

ALFRED BROWN

A watch maker, Alfred Brown was located at 236 King Street in 1849 and 1852.[498, 499] He was not listed in the Charleston directory for 1855,[500] the year he became a citizen.[384] According to the United States Federal Census he was 28 years old in 1850 and had been born in Ireland. He is not listed there.[129]

JOSEPH LATHAM

Joseph Latham was in Charleston in 1790 and, with David Clark, had a clock-making business at 125 Broad Street (Figure 173).[501] Neither was described as being from Ireland. The partnership did not last, however, and two years later "Magan and Latham...lately from Ireland" were just a couple of doors away in competition with Clark.[71] Magann was from Belfast, but Latham's origin is unclear.[129]

In February of that year, he married Martha Rolain[71] and they had at least one son, Gilbert.[71] Latham died in August 1806 aged 55. His obituary in the *Charleston Courier* on August 11 spoke of a lingering illness and of the lack of need for "panegyrick" for "a good man."[502] By that year, Gilbert had moved to New York City, where Joseph's brother John had also moved to make sails.[71] Latham made no fortune in America; after he died, his estate was valued at $418.75. He also had a small wooden house at 318 Water Street, New York.[71]

ALEXANDER BOYD

This maker was at 13 Broad Street in 1819[503] but had moved to Number 5 by 1822[504] and had gone by 1824.[490] An Alexander Boyd is known from Belfast for 1814[2, 6]

CHESTER

JOHN MCKEE

John McKee was born in Rathfriland, County Down on November 4, 1787, the son of Andrew and Jane McKee.[384] Clock makers with the name McKee are also known from the towns of Richhill, Lurgan, and Portaferry. This history of the family is based on a typed manuscript written by descendants and now in the possession of the Museum of Early Southern Decorative Arts (MESDA), Winston-Salem, NC.

The McKee family came to Ireland from Scotland in 1692. Andrew, John's father, left Ireland for South Carolina with one of his sons in the 1790s. About seven or eight years later he was joined by John McKee, two brothers, and a sister. The date of arrival was probably June 18, 1798.[505] His father died in May 1800. In 1808, John's elder brother, also Andrew, died. Andrew had sold his watch-making equipment on April 22 of that year to John for $54. He moved from Rocky Creek to Chester Court House, now

Figures 182 and 183. Two John McKee watch papers. One, very crude, with what appears to be a child holding a watch on a chain with a ship, an eagle, and a serpent below. Inscribed "Jno. McKee Watch & Clock MAKER Chester South-Carolina." The second, somewhat more polished, shows Father Time with the obligatory scythe and carrying what could possibly a chalice. Inscribed "Clocks made and watches carefully repaired. Most kinds of jewellery (sic) work. J McKee Chester So. Carolina." Pictures very kind courtesy of the American Antiquarian Society.

simply Chester, SC, and became a naturalized American citizen in 1809.[506] The "family watch-making tools" suggest that he may have learned his trade at home perhaps from his brother or father.

Marriage and Daughters

John McKee married Mary Hayden in 1818 and had at least two daughters[71] (Figures 174–177). Prosperous, he became one of the Commissioners appointed by the State to aid and to advise the civil and military engineers in the construction of the new Court House for Chester County.[507] His success in America contrasted with the abject poverty that he had left behind, reflected by the poignant letters from his mother and sister.

"I am much surprised," his mother wrote from Rathfriland on February 23, 1806, "that you never think of your old mother and sister. I reared you tenderly, and did everything that was in my power for you all…"

His sister, who had remained in Ireland, wrote that "our mother is very poorly off" but she herself was "…thank God, young and strong…We have a long and sore winter…I am almost afraid of it before it comes."

These letters must have touched him, because both his mother and sister arrived in South Carolina about 1818. His mother died some years later and is buried in Rocky Creek, SC.[71]

In his very successful business he made clocks either with or without cases,[508] the latter for export to other places in America and that could be fitted with a case by local cabinet makers.[384] Cases of various types of wood including mahogany, cherry, birch, and walnut were also available if required. He dealt in watches, jewelry, and even pistols.[509]

Several clocks have survived. One researcher knows of 16, as well as items of silverware including spoons and a sugar tongs.[71] Like most Ulster (and American) clocks of the period they are painted arch dial clocks. Of 13 clocks in the MESDA records most have automations, nine with rolling moons and three rocking ships (Figures 178–180). Where date apertures are apparent they are usually above the six. Most have subsidiary seconds dials below 12 although one example has both central seconds and date hands popular with Americans. Both Arabic and Roman hour numbering is seen. In either case, minute numbering is most often indicated at the quarter hour, rather than at each five-minute interval. The hands are typical for the early 19th century. All the dials are signed, "(Jn or John) McKee Chester (SC)," and one is numbered 19. The spandrels are lightly painted with floral or shell designs and solid spandrels are unusual.

Precise dating of the surviving clocks is difficult but all were presumably made after 1808 when McKee moved to Chester from Rocky Creek.[71] The dials and hands suggest dates before 1830 for all the clocks seen by this writer. Notices in the *Catawba Journal* of Charlotte, NC, indicate he was still in business until 1827.[71] For details of a thief who stole from McKee see Figure 181 and for two watch papers see Figures 182 and 183.

South Carolina and the Civil War

The réclame of John McKee was not, however, horological but historical. On December 24, 1860, together with another 170 individuals, he, one of the "People of South Carolina," declared that "the Union heretofore existing between this State and the other States of North America, is dissolved, and that the State of South Carolina has resumed her position among the nations of the world, as a separate and independent State; with full power to levy war, conclude peace, contract alliances, establish commerce, and to do all other acts and things which independent States may of right do." This, the Ordinance of Secession of South Carolina in 1860, proclaimed in Charleston, would usher in the American Civil War (Figure 184).

If John McKee and South Carolina reserved the right to make war, they surely got a bloody one. John McKee died on May 1, 1871,[71] having witnessed the failure of his effort at independence for Confederate America.

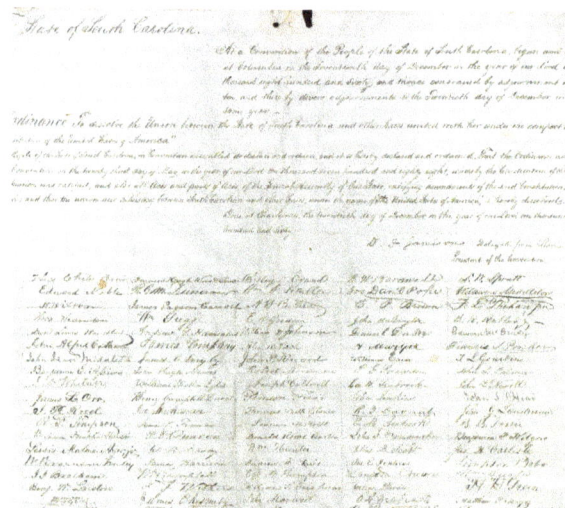

Figure 184. The 1860 Ordinance of Secession of South Carolina. The signature of John McKee is second from the bottom on the left column.

The final paragraph reads:

We the People of the State of South Carolina ... declare ... the Constitution of the United States ... and also all Acts ... of the said Constitution, are hereby repealed; and the union ... between South Carolina and ... "The United States of America," is hereby dissolved.
Done at Charleston, the twentieth day of December in the year of our Lord one thousand eight hundred and sixty.

GEORGETOWN

Little is known about Francis Elliott, except that he was a watch maker from Ireland who died in Georgetown, SC, in 1811.[4,71] His death notice spoke of his disconsolate widow and his infant son. Francis Elliott was not listed in Ireland,[129] although there were contemporary clock makers with this family name in Counties Cork and Down.

OTHER MAKERS ELSEWHERE IN AMERICA

Edward Gilliam advertised in the *Nashville Republican and State Gazette* of Tennessee on September 18, 1834 that he was "Lately from Ireland"[20] but is not mentioned in the usual sources.[129] John McCullough went to Rodney, MS, from Newry, County Down where he died aged 28 in 1837.[5] Robert Sherwood was apprenticed in Londonderry, moved to Sacramento, CA, and became a partner in Messrs. Barrett & Sherwood.

Michael Kelly was a watch maker born circa 1821 and was working in Bonnersville, ND, circa 1880.[135] James Chapman was a watch maker in Belfast at 64 High Street in 1843 until at least 1858 and is also noted as a jeweler and chronometer maker.[510-13] James Chapman was the son of William who was born circa 1790 and moved from Dublin.[2] He died in 1836 and his wife, JuliaAnn, took over the business with James until 1858.[2] James moved to America, location unknown, around that time.[135] Certainly, he was no longer listed in Belfast in 1861 when Benjamin Chapman, also a watch maker, is found at Number 64. This address, adjacent to the premises of John Lowry, the watch and chronometer maker, was listed as vacant in 1863[514] when Benjamin was at Rosemary Street. JuliaAnn died in 1876 in Holywood, County Down.[5] A Joseph Chapman was in Essex Quay, Dublin from 1840[515] to 1860.[516]

John N. McCartney, at 48 Market Street, Armagh in 1843[510] moved to 6 Donegall Place, Belfast.[512] He sold out to James Neill and went to the United States circa 1853, location unknown.[5]

Chapter Six
Miscellaneous and Summary

e have seen details of the lives of some of the clock and watch makers known to have come from Ireland together with some examples of their work. There may, of course, have been many more. Other possible candidates are listed in Appendix 1.

What was the influence and legacy of this group of clock makers? If any is to be noted it must surely be in the entrepôts of Philadelphia or Baltimore, where large numbers of craftsmen came together. The sporadic arrival of clock makers from Ireland to the United States as well as their thin distribution precluded the survival of pure regional styles from the Old World. In the Northern cities of Boston and New York, and those in the South such as Charleston, the numbers of Irish craftsmen were particularly scant and collaboration with other ethnic groups may have been essential for survival. So, in the melting pot of Philadelphia, Laurence Birnie of Templepatrick collaborated with Pennsylvania-German Jacob Godshalk and the Welsh-sounding Griffith Owen. One might expect that, in this rapidly changing environment with its constant influx of immigrants, specific ethnic influences might be slight and ephemeral. Despite the emergence of identifiable local American styles in the late 18th and early 19th centuries in Pennsylvania, Baltimore, Roxbury, and elsewhere, some immigrant influences can still be found.

A clock is a composite construction requiring the input of multiple craftsmen; the most important of whom are the clock maker, the cabinet maker, and the dial maker. While the clock maker may be the one whose name is associated most obviously with the clock, in general this individual is responsible for the least visible part, the movement, which in most 18th-century tall case clocks, is hidden behind the dial. Thus, the cases and the dials lend themselves most readily to study, and scholars are only occasionally lucky enough to be able to scrutinize clock mechanisms in any great detail.

Cases

In general, studies of the contribution of Irish cabinet makers to the development of the furniture of America are still sparse despite the craft connection between Philadelphia and Dublin having certainly begun early. The joiner George Miller, for example, was elected to the Common Council of the City of Dublin in 1729.[9] Curiously, though still on the Dublin Council in 1732, he is listed in John Watson's *Gentleman and Citizen's Almanack* as being in Philadelphia for that year.[517] He worked from 1716 to 1731 in Dublin[9] and was to be found on Chestnut Street, Philadelphia in 1737.[13]

Decorative characteristics of Irish furniture in this century have been summarized by the late Desmond Fitzgerald and James Peill in their sumptuously illustrated and magnificently scholarly work *Irish Furniture*. Carving on tables, chests, chairs, and other domestic furniture "...has low relief foliated detail...often centered on grotesque lions' masks...and scallop shells. The shell motif...is particularly common on chairs, settees and tables."[9] This description perfectly fits the base of the pediment of many a mid- to late 18th-century Dublin cases.[518-521] Standing around 90" in height, such clocks may sport scrolls or "swan-necks" above. The ends of the cornices are decorated with carved

113

flowerheads and the break in the pediment may be occupied by a shell or an eagle. The trunk is relatively narrow, often with a long door possessing a characteristically round top, and terminates on a base usually some 20" in height. Interestingly, primordial swan-neck decorations can be seen in late 17th-century London clocks,[422, 522] one even with a shell[518] so beloved of the Irish carvers three quarters of a century later.

PENNSYLVANIA

The style of the prominent swan-necks and thin trunks may have traveled from Dublin to Philadelphia[148] but other Pennsylvania clocks have these features with swan-neck pediments, elaborately carved terminal rosettes, and floral scroll work on the pediment. One in particular, (Figure 185) housing a clock by Rudy Stoner of Lancaster,[150] has a raised carved shell in the tympanum which the author described as "a very unusual device."

Another feature that recalls a Dublin style in some of these clocks is the relatively long tombstone trunk door. Decorative woodwork patterns of Philadelphia and Dublin may be derived from, or related to, Rococo ceiling plaster work from the latter city in the mid-18th century.[523, 524] This type of design seems to have found its way on to at least one Philadelphia high chest[523] and is reminiscent of the clocks in the Lancaster Chippendale style of Thomas Burrowes, among others, illustrated in *Clock makers of Lancaster County and their Clocks 1750-1850*.[150]

The Dublin case described above was not the only type at this time. A much different design, housing a clock by Thomas Sanderson is also known (Figures 186 and 187). The most striking aspects are the proportions. While the clock is still approximately 90" tall, the hood and the trunk are almost the same height lending a huge weight to the top. This apparent bulk is further compounded by the densely heavy pediment. Here, a combination of tall flambeau finials, erect swan-necks, and a massive centrally placed shell-like carving create a hugely overbearing effect recalling the pediment of the clock

Figure 185. The clock by Rudy Stoner of Lancaster with a raised shell in the hood a common motif on Irish pieces – see Irish Furniture by Fitzgerald and Peill for many examples.

Figures 186 and 187. Thomas Sanderson of Dublin, with its hood of heavy proportions due to the dense pediment, flambeau finials, erect swan-necks, and the large central carving of a shell.

by Edward Duffield of Philadelphia illustrated by John Robey in *The Longcase Clock*.[518] Thomas Sanderson died in 1752.

CABINET MAKERS

Of the individual cabinet makers themselves we know relatively little as their names are often lost. The Museum of Early Southern Decorative Arts has records of several, however, and other sources mention more of likely Irish origin.[9, 13, 71, 157, 300, 525-528] In other cases, a name, such as William Kennedy of the Anthony Hay shop in Williamsburg, VA, might suggest such a birthplace.[157, 529]

There are some with specific clock connections. Joseph Barry, who was born around March 27, 1757,[530] and who died in 1838, was a well-known cabinet maker who worked in Philadelphia and Savannah.[525, 531] He was said to have been born in Dublin and trained in London.[135, 525, 531] His large repertoire included

Figure 188. Long case clock made in 1750 by George Glinn of Boston, MA, housing the clock of Thomas Hughes of London. Courtesy of the Art Institute of Chicago, Alyce and Edwin DeCosta and Walter E Heller Foundation, and Harold Stuart Endowment.

clock cases.[135] Theophilus Jones was a freeman of Dublin as a joiner in 1763[9] and was at 33 Mary Street in Dublin from 1773 until 1778.[180, 181, 183, 184, 301] He had left by 1780[81] for Charleston, later moving to Wilmington, DE. His first wife died within weeks and he himself died circa 1783, in St. Kitt's, West Indies, at sea on the ship *Liberty* about 42 years of age.[532] Whether he made any clock cases is unknown, but his son George Jones became a well-known clock maker.[135]

John Lemon was a cabinet maker who was originally from Ballyhalbert, County Down,[533] and arrived in Salem on the ship *Eliza* on August 8, 1795. With Charles Lemon, he advertised in the *Salem Gazette* on November 15, 1796, that "they make all kinds of cabinet work ... Salem, Court Street." John also worked in Malden and Andover, MA. He died in 1855.[70, 533] He was active in Boston from 1822–30 although he had also been in Salem, Beverly, and Charlestown. In 1802 he became a naturalized citizen having resided in Salem since 1795.[3] He is known to have made clock cases[206] and a bill of sale from the latter year for a case for a lyre clock has survived.[135] William Lemon, an upholsterer, is known from Belfast in 1793 and also advertised his "geese feathers and trimings for beds."[9]

BALTIMORE

An influence on Baltimore furniture by Irish makers has also been inferred from similarities in style between sofas and sideboards from both places.[299] Although Fitzgerald and Peill note only one Irish cabinet maker as having emigrated, James McCormick, one other, unnamed, had also been brought over by the doomed firm of Hogan, M'Cutchan & Co.[299] McCormick had been in Dublin in 1779 and was in Baltimore in 1786 where he made cabinet work "in all its branches....on the most reasonable terms" on the west side of Calvert Street, between Baltimore and the court house.[527] He later moved to Alexandria, Norfolk, and Petersburg.[9] On the register of cabinet makers for Maryland, compiled by Henry Berkley,[527] are the names of several others in Baltimore including John Dougherty (1796-

1808)[527] perhaps the same individual who was in Coleraine in 1787-88.[9] Whether they can be tied to clocks will require further investigation.

On other parts of the eastern American coast Irish influences have also been found on furniture. Thus, we find trifid, paneled, and slipper feet, common on Irish furniture, but rare in America unless Irish immigrants were present,[9, 298] on furniture of the lower Rappahannock River basin of Virginia.[298] This may be another area of fruitful study.

Some of the makers above may have made clock cases but associating a specific maker with a surviving clock is still unusual.[293] This makes the case (Figure 188) housing the movement by the London clock maker Thomas Hughes now in the Art Institute of Chicago all the more interesting.[534] It was made in Boston in 1750 by one George Glinn, possibly of Irish origin. The name Glinn is not at all rare in Ireland and, indeed, there were two other cabinet makers with this name, John and Bernard,[9] in Marlborough Street, Dublin later in the 18th century who could even have been related. The prominent pilasters, supporting pedestals, and claw feet lend a most unusual appearance to the plinth but it certainly does not look like a regular Dublin clock, the long tombstone trunk door notwithstanding. Of Glinn, or where he learned his craft, we know little.

SOME IRISH CABINET MAKERS IN AMERICA

A detailed study of Irish cabinet makers in America is well beyond the scope of this study. Some have already been noted and more are listed in Appendices 2 and 3. In this work, comparison of lists and sources on both sides of the Atlantic served well in yielding a number of migrant clock and watch makers. The temptation to try a similar, albeit preliminary, approach to the cabinet makers was too great to resist. Thus, names of cabinet makers in the Irish newspapers to 1800,[9] in the almanacs and directories for Dublin to 1800,[535] and in 18th-century Cork and Limerick directories[106, 536, 537] were cross-referenced with *Prime's Gleanings*,[13, 528] *Berkley's Baltimore list*,[527] Hornor's list in *Philadelphia Furniture*,[530] and the *Longcase Clock*.[518] The overlap between sources was indeed small but at least yielded George Miller, James McCormick, and John Dougherty and, possibly, a Mr. Freeman.[9, 518] This trawl may have been thin for many reasons not the least being that furniture makers commonly do not sign their creations while clock makers do. But at least it is a start. Hopefully, the combination of electronic sources from around the Atlantic seaboard including directories, newspapers, genealogical records, and passenger lists combined with powerful search engines will replace the gargantuan task of comparing one printed source with the next.

DIALS

The dial is often signed with the clock maker's name although it may in fact have been made by a specialist dial maker and engraved by another craftsman. Those involved in these crafts may not always be readily identified although some important work has already been done in this area.[518, 538] We know that at least two of our makers were also engravers, Patrick Magann and James Stewart, and we also know that the former imported, or at least used, one dial that had made its way from England to Charleston. Recently, a possible influence on Philadelphia painted dials from Belfast has been pointed out.[539] Many such dials from circa 1816 to 1845 appear similar and show features found in Ulster clocks of the same period. In addition, many dials from Philadelphia have been attributed to William Jones, who may have learned his craft from one James Harden who had worked in Belfast from 1806 and arrived in Philadelphia in 1816. Little is known of either Harden or Jones except that they were dial makers and worked together for a time. They also both died young; Harden suddenly aged 41 in 1823 and Jones of apoplexy at only 45 years old. The Belfast advertisement of 1806 for the partnership of Harden and Ryding stated they were from Birmingham,[539] certainly an important place for the contemporary British painted dial industry, and perhaps that is where Harden himself had been trained.

MOVEMENTS

Of clock movements and mechanisms made by Irish makers in America little is known although the late Edward LaFond has pointed out similarities and differences between Pennsylvania German and English clocks.[19] Unfortunately, the researcher in this field is hampered by the widespread and thin distribution of artefacts of Irish makers and the difficulty of obtaining movements for examination and study. Some distinguished horologists[422, 518, 519] have described features of Irish movements that are broadly similar to British examples but there is still only a small amount of literature in that area.[520, 521, 540, 541]

AN UNUSUAL CLOCK

One unusual find in the course of this work was an American musical clock with an Irish connection. Most early American makers of musical clocks were not of Irish origin[542] but we have met some including John McCabe, Gilbert Bigger, James Latham, and John McLean who made, repaired, and/or sold such clocks. One clock, by George Long (fl. 1796–1803) of Hanover, PA, is of particular interest however because of its repertoire of eight tunes. These include "Pady (sic) Whack," "Irishvalteer" (possibly the Irish Volunteers), "Fish's Hornpipe," "Washwoman," "Trip to Bath," "Nagls (sic) hornpipe," and "Free from Envy." "Fish's Hornpipe" and "Washwoman," are probably The "Fisherman's hornpipe" and "The Irish Washerwoman." The lyrics of the Irish Volunteers are patriotic in content. The "Melody of Paddy" Whack recalls that of the "Old Orange Flute," a song still widely sung in folk circles in Ireland. The musical content of this clock may have been selected to reflect the taste, political or esthetic, of the maker or purchaser. George Long was not known in Ireland, although a Leonard Long was in Dublin at Mountrath Street and Ormond Quay from 1786[6] until 1800.[103] The clock did not play these tunes on bells but on a "music box attachment" driven by a "very heavy weight."[543] Other tunes heard on many of these clocks include the polka "The Rakes of Marlow (Mallow)" and the jig, "Merrily Dance the Quaker (Merrily Kiss the Quakers Wife)."[542] Even today, many of these tunes are commonly played by those interested in Irish music — both in Ireland and North America — another area which has seen a rich cross-fertilization between these two Atlantic seaboard cultures over the generations.

SUMMARY

The makers of clocks and watches who traveled from Ireland were as motley as their reasons for leaving, ranging from politics to religion, to commerce and adventure. Whatever the motive in so doing, they certainly availed themselves of "the culture of opportunity that life in the new land promised."[544] The story of the marks they left on the artifacts of their host country is still unfolding. It is hoped that this work will have helped to focus attention on their contributions and stimulate further studies in this and allied fields.

APPENDIX 1
NAMES OF CLOCK MAKERS WITH POSSIBLE CONNECTIONS TO IRELAND

PENNSYLVANIA

ALLENTOWN

Thomas Murphy was at Allentown in the late 1830s and was registered in a list of clock makers in Lehigh and Northampton Counties compiled from tax records in the court houses in Pennsylvania.[571] He may have been the same Thomas Murphy who was born in 1809 in Dublin[6] and who was in Lancaster in 1851.[2] His relationship, if any, to John Murphy is unknown. cf. also John Murphy, Norfolk, VA.

A Phillip Reily is known from Washington County circa 1805–14,[135] cf. Phillip Reilly Dublin early 19th century.[180]

Thomas Wells, Washington, PA, 1796–1802,[135] cf. T. Wells, Ballinahinch circa 1800[6] – see also Robert Wells below.

PHILADELPHIA

William Bailey, Philadelphia 1816–40,[135] and William Bailey, Portaferry 1790.[6]

Alfred Bennett, Philadelphia circa 1837–47,[135] and A. Bennett, Dublin 1830.[6]

George Bowers, Philadelphia circa 1850,[135] and George Bowers, Kilrush 1824.[442]

James Cherry, Philadelphia circa 1849,[135] and James Cherry, Banbridge, County Down 1843.[510]

James Coleman, Philadelphia circa 1833,[135] and James Coleman, Belfast.[6]

John Coleman, Philadelphia circa 1848,[135] and John Coleman, Cork 1844.[6]

The records of the New 11th Pennsylvania Regiment show that Robert Hadlock, watch maker born in Ireland, enlisted in 1779.[14] He was born in 1746. A William Hadlock is known from Dublin in 1727 and also in Cork.[6]

Kinkead may have connections with others of this name in Strabane, County Tyrone,[569] including Christopher Kinkead, circa 1770, who signed a petition to the Earl of Abercorn in June 1768,[6] and John Kinkead who, had been given "one guinea to further the roads ....." according to the agent for the Abercorn estate in August 1750.[570]

James Murphy is listed in Philadelphia from 1828–46[162] and may have moved there from Boston as a watch maker and jeweler with this name is in the Boston directories for 1803–06[126] and advertised in the *New England Palladium*.[162] There are several makers with the name of Murphy but no James in the usual Irish sources.[5-7]

The records of the Winterthur Museum note a John Reily of Philadelphia whose will was proved in 1766 and who may be related to the above Reily, and a John Reilly, general merchant, was in Philadelphia in 1751 (Accessible. com).

William Sinclair Philadelphia circa 1837[135] and William Sinclair, 164 Capel Street, Dublin 1818–21.[196-198, 568]

MASSACHUSETTS

BOSTON

Joseph Bell, Boston circa 1852–61,[135] and Joseph Bell, Coleraine 1824.[6]

John McClure, clock and watch maker, died in Boston in 1829. It is unclear if he was from Ireland, although the 1823 Boston tax records say he was an alien.[135, 206] He is not a documented maker[129] but a Joseph McClure[6] or McClurg[2] is known from Coleraine for 1795.

William McKay was born in Ireland in 1812 and appears as a watch maker in Boston in 1832. He was in partnerships with others until 1855.[3] His early age in Boston suggest that he may not have had an independent trade and he is not on lists from Ireland.[129]

John Mears was in Roxbury in 1761,[3] and Josias Mears, Dublin circa 1760.[420]

James Murphy, was born circa 1774 and died in Boston in 1827.[3] A James Murphy is also listed in Philadelphia from 1828–46.[162] The Boston Murphy was first a watch maker and jeweler[169] in Marlboro Street, then a watch maker,[170, 171] then a shopkeeper,[172-175] and lastly a dry goods merchant.[176-178] James Murphy advertised in the *New England Palladium* 1804-1807.[162] He is not mentioned in the usual sources.[129]

NEW YORK

Alexander Baker, New York circa 1854,[135] and Alexander Baker, Newry and Dublin 1846.[5, 6]

John Leatham from Waterford is known from circa 1780,[7] and James Latham is known from Albany in 1795.[2]

A watch paper survives from 1831 for a John Martin of 184 and 288 Spring Street, New York City.[126] cf. John Martin, Comber circa 1790–1810.[2] Joseph Molyneux NY, circa 1819–50,[135] and Joseph Molineaux Skinner Row, Dublin 1804–13.[187, 194]

Robert Montgomery "from Europe" in NY 1783–86 and died 1787.[135] cf. Robert Montgomery Ballyrogan, Lisburn, and Belfast.[6]

MARYLAND

Lavallin Barry's name is not on the list of Dublin goldsmiths but those of Spranger (1736) and William (1761) are. A watch maker from Cork of 1824 by the name of Joseph[37] and two jewelers from Cork, Robert (Kinsale, 1784) and John (Bandon, 1784), are also known and may be related.

John Davis, Dublin 1738,[572] and John Davis, Annapolis, circa 1730s, who died 1743.[135]

A John Lynch is also known from Kent County, Maryland, in 1793.[27]

Thomas McConnell, Baltimore 1815[17] and Dublin 1770.[7]

Reilly, Riley etc. Other watch makers of this name are known including one in Philadelphia circa 1785–1814 (or 1785–1818 per Cutten[435]) and a J.C. Reiley & Co. from Louisville, KY, 1816–18.[71] A John Riley was taken as an apprentice to Elie Bentley of Frederick County, Maryland in 1782 at age 17 and was a clock maker in Libertytown in 1790.[17, 71]

Samuel Spratt, Maryland before 1831.[17] See Samuel Spratt family of Saintfield and Ardmillan in Counties Armagh and Down 1750–1880s.[6]

James Stewart, Baltimore from 1792, (see G. Stewart watch case maker, from 1780 to 1820[5]) and John Stewart, 1785–1827 of Belfast.[6] Later clock makers of the name Stewart are also known in Dublin in the mid-19th century.[573-575]

Eugene Sullivan, Baltimore, 1850,[17] and William F. Sullivan, 1860–90, Clonakilty, County Cork.[6]

KENTUCKY

Henry Jenkins, watch maker and silversmith, was born about 1820 and worked in Cincinnati from about 1842. In 1863, he formed a partnership by the name of Jenkins & Hatch that lasted until 1874. He lived in neighboring Kentucky from 1856 until his death from malaria in 1877.[21] Jenkins clock makers in Ireland include Newth (Cork and Bandon circa 1763–87), William (Bandon 1824) and Thomas (Ballymacarrett circa 1835).

Hugh McConaghy was in Danville, Boyle County in 1870. In the census of 1870, his youngest child was registered as a Kentucky native indicating that he had moved from there in about 1865.[21] He is not on lists or directories for Ireland.[129]

VIRGINIA

William Cooke, VA, circa 1826–30,[135] and William Cooke, Dublin, 1813.[6]

Joseph Barrington, Dumfries, VA, 1792,[135] and Barringtons of Dublin and Limerick.[6]

A John B. Murphy was also in Norfolk in the early 1830s and later moved to Augusta, GA,[435, 576] and a JH Murphy is known from Clarksburg, WV, 1851–54.[16]

Andrew Robinson, Portsmouth, VA, 1835–46.[135] cf. Andrew Robinson, Galway 1820–24.[6]

Robert Wells, Winchester, VA, circa 1787–1813,[135] and Robert Wells, Ballinahinch 1775–83.[6]

NORTH CAROLINA

Other makers were noted who may have come from Ireland to North Carolina include James Pool, who was in Washington, NC, in 1846,[384] and a James Poole is noted in Dublin at 82 Dame Street from 1800–06.[103-105, 186-189] cf. John C Stedman, Raleigh 1819–33 and Henry Stedman in Dublin 1792; J. Barrington, Virginia:[4] Salisbury NC, 1792[27], Isaac Barrington Dublin 1805–30,[188, 574] and Isaac Jr. 1831–1832, and Benjamin Barrington, Limerick 1693–1733.[7]

SOUTH CAROLINA

John Dease, watch maker, was at 13 State Street, Charleston in 1831[496] and had moved to 88 East Bay by 1835.[577] A John Dease was active in Youghal in 1820.[37]

William Evans was listed as a watch maker in the Charleston directories beginning in at 155 King Street in 1816,[578] later moving to 153 and 299 in 1822.[503, 504] This may have been the same William Evans in Charleston from 1814 to 1822 from Bermuda.[4] He was not listed in the Charleston directories for 1829 or 1831[496, 579] and presumably was gone. A William Evans was active in Dublin in 1802[6] although no clock makers of this name are listed in the Dublin directories for around this time.[102-104, 185-187] A verge escapement watch with an enameled panel and another dated 1802 are known.[7]

John or Joseph Massey was in Charleston in 1736[135] and John Massey is known from Cork in 1733.[6]

Alexander Robinson was in Charleston, SC, in 1822, and Ballyclare and Larne in the late 18th century.[6]

NEW MEXICO

James Booth was born about 1832 and was in Santa Fe, NM, in about 1880.[135] He might have been related to the well-known Booth family of Dublin.[6]

OHIO

John Walsh, Delphos, OH, 1880.[135] cf. John Walsh, Limerick, 1858.[6]

TENNESSEE

There are a number of Irish craftsmen in Tennessee mentioned by Caldwell including the silversmiths Robert Donahoe of Knoxville, 1860, and John Hinklin, Robertson County (circa 1847).[20] A James Simpson, born "near Belfast" in 1797 and who died in 1821, may be related to Simpsons of Irvinestown, Derry, or Armagh. Thomas Gowdey of Nashville was born in Castlewellan, County Down, in 1795 and died 1863 but there are no recorded makers of this name in Ireland. Both were silversmiths and formed partnerships with others and became watch and clock repairers and/or makers.[20]

VERMONT

Richard Fitzgerald was in Burlington in 1830 and was a retailer and repairer of watches and clocks.[234] His name has not previously been recorded in Ireland[129] although a William Bolster Fitzgerald, watch and clock maker from Newcastle in the county of Limerick, is known from 1824,[442] as well as an Edward Fitzgerald from High Street, Dublin for 1849.[567]

DESTINATION UNKNOWN

Though John McCalmont, a grandson of a Scottish Covenanter minister who fled persecution in Scotland, was apprenticed in Armagh, he ran away to America in 1766 and "joined the revolutionary army."[48]

Appendix 2
Cabinet Makers in Baltimore of Irish Origin or Possibly So
(Those from the MESDA Records, Reference 71, Were Originally from Ireland)

Coyle, David, 1819 [527]

Dermont, Henry, 1775, indentured servant; carpenter, cabinet maker.[71]

Dougherty, John, (1796–1808)[527] cf. John Dougherty Coleraine in 1787–89 and Christopher Dougherty, Dublin (fl.1784- at least 1800).[82, 103]

Doyle, John, 1813, died age circa 25 years [71]

The Finley— also Finlay and Findlay— brothers, John and Hugh, said to be of Irish origin,[299, 583] were in Baltimore circa 1799 until at least 1810 and made a wide variety of furniture including chairs, sofas, seats, and tables.[527] Perhaps they were related to Christopher Finlay, the cabinet maker and auctioneer in Abbey Street, Dublin from 1784 to 1790.[82, 87]

The Foleys, John (1799–1800)[527] and Timothy (1807–31)[527, 580-582]; Kennedy, possibly Samuel, in partnership with Brown in 1795.[527]

Harris, William, Cork, 1773–80,[9] and William Harris, Baltimore, 1795.[528]

Lee, John, 1819, date is desertion U.S. Army, age 23.[71]

McCabe, Thomas, 1796.[527]

McFadden, Mr., 1795.[527]

McSweeney, Paul. It is unclear if Paul Sweeney[527] is the same as Paul McSweeney. Paul McSweeney was apprenticed in America in 1798 and is said to have been active from 1802 until after 1820[527] but he is not in Keenan's Directory for Baltimore for 1822-23.[580] A Paul McSweeny, grocer and liquor dealer, was at the corner of Eutaw and Bottle Alley.[580]

Phalon, Timothy (sic), 1774, indentured cabinet maker/joiner.[300]

Sedley, Francis, 1774, indentured cabinet maker/joiner.[300]

Raley[299] also deemed other names to be Irish such as Berry, Jenkins, and Patterson. While not originally of Irish origin, as we have seen, one would not be at all surprised to see such names attached to Irish craftsmen with British forebears.

Appendix 3
Dates of Some Irish Cabinet Makers from Locations Other than Baltimore[9, 71, 157, 300, 525, 526]

NAME	DATE	LOCATION	NOTES
Charles Bush	1737	Wilmington, DE	Cabinetmaker
James Calder	1809-1822	Charleston, SC	
John Cowen	1814	Georgetown, DC	Date is desertion US army, aged 31
Patrick Curry	1791	Winchester, VA	Indentured servant
Lambert Emerson	1731	Philadelphia	Joiner and mirror maker
Hance Fairley	1796-1815	Charleston, SC	Born c, 1771 died 1815; from Belfast.
Francis Green	1850	Floyd Co., KY	
John Heffernan	1806-1819	Charleston, SC	
John Hourine	1819-1850	Cumberland Co., NC	Born Ireland; apprenticed US.
Thomas Jones	1771	New York, NY	Born Co Tipperary c1749
George Kingston	c1810	Savannah, GA	Died 1820, aged c, 30 years
John Maloney	1820	Person Co., NC	Census record
Terrence McAffrey	1810-12	Knoxville, TN	
Richard Montague	1819	Savannah, GA	Joiner; died 1819 aged 25
Josiah Murphy	1771	Charleston	date is date of death[584]
Joshua Neville	1794-1822	Charleston, SC	Born c, 1768
Newsam & Slater	1787	Winchester, VA	
John Powell	1772	Annapolis, MD	Indentured servant
Alexander Shaw	1795-c, 1808	Pendleton, SC	From Co. Antrim
Samuel Stuart	1820	Savannah, GA	Joiner; from Belfast; died 1820 aged 31
Robert Wells	1812	Marietta, OH	Apprenticed US
James Whelan	1816	Milledgeville, GA	Date is date he died.
Thomas Woods	1766	Anne Arundel Co., MD	Date broke out of jail
Charles White	1793	New York City	Date of naturalization
Shaw & Chisholm	1775-7	Annapolis[13] cf.	cf. Matthew Shaw, Dublin and Cabinetmaker, 1741-50[9]
B. Freeman	1784	Philadelphia	cf. Mr. Freeman Dublin, 1768-1775[9]
William Lloyd		Springfield, MA[518]	cf. William Lloyd Dublin, 1746-1749[9]
John & Thomas Seymour	1794-1820	Boston, MA[518]	cf. John Seymour, Youghall (sic) 1787-1795[9]

REFERENCES

1. Sheridan, P. *The Irish Immigrant in Pennsylvania 1840-1860*. 1950, State College, PA: Pennsylvania State College. p. 160.
2. Loomes, B. *Watchmakers and Clockmakers of the World*. Vol. 2. 1989, London: N.A.G. Press/Robert Hale.
3. Foley, P.J. *Willard's Patent Timepieces*. 2002, Norwell, Massachusetts: Roxbury Village Publishing.
4. Spittler, S.L., T.J. Spittler, and C.H. Bailey. *American Clockmakers and Watchmakers*. 2000, Fairfax, Virginia: Arlington Book Company, Inc.
5. Seaby, W. *An Unpublished List of Ulster Clockmakers*. Belfast Museum.
6. Stuart, W.G. *Watch and Clockmakers in Ireland*. 2000, Dublin: June Stuart, Kildrought House, Celbridge, Co Kildare, Ireland.
7. Fennell, G. *A List of Irish Watch and Clock Makers*. 1963, Dublin: National Museum of Ireland.
8. Baillie, G. *Watchmakers and Clockmakers of the World*. 3rd ed. 1951, London: N.A.G. Press Ltd.
9. FitzGerald, D. and J. Peill *Irish Furniture*. 2007, New Haven and London: Yale University Press.
10. Gilbert, J.T. *Calendar of Ancient Records of Dublin*. 1889, Dublin: Joseph Dollard.
11. Drepperd, C.W. *American Clock & Clockmakers*. 1947, New York, NY: Doubleday & Company, Inc.: 317.
12. Prime, A.C. *Colonial Craftsmen of Pennsylvania*. 1925, Philadelphia, Pennsylvania: Pennsylvania Museum.
13. Prime, A.C. *Arts and Crafts in Philadelphia, Maryland and South Carolina 1721-1785*. 1929, Topsfield, Massachusetts: Wayside Press, for Walpole Society.
14. Whisker, J.B. *Pennsylvania Clockmakers and Watchmakers, 1660-1900*. 1996, Lewiston, New York; Queenston, Ontario; Lampeter, Wales: The Edwin Mellen Press.
15. Whisker, J.B. *Clockmakers and Watchmakers of Maryland 1660-1900*. 1997, Lewiston, New York: The Edwin Mellen Press.
16. Whisker, J.B. *Virginia Clockmakers and Watchmakers, c.1660-1860*. 1999, Lewiston, New York: The Edwin Mellen Press.
17. Whisker, J.B., D.D. Hartzler, and S.P. Petrucelli. *Maryland Clockmakers*. 1996, Cranbury, New Jersey: Adams Brown Company.
18. Williams, C.M. *Silversmiths of New Jersey 1700-1825*. 1949, Philadelphia, Pennsylvania: George S MacManus Co.
19. Goldsborough, J.F. *Silver in Maryland*. 1984, Baltimore, Maryland: Museum and Library of Maryland History, Maryland Historical Society.
20. Caldwell, B.H. *Tennessee Silversmiths*. 1st ed. 1988, Winston-Salem, North Carolina: The Museum of Early Southern Decorative Arts.
21. Boultinghouse, M. *Silversmiths, Jewelers, Clock and Watch Makers of Kentucky 1785-1900*. 1980, Lexington, Kentucky: M Boultinghouse.
22. Burton, E.M. *South Carolina Silversmiths 1690-1860*. 1st ed. 1942, Charleston, South Carolina: The Charleston Museum.
23. Yoder, D., *Ireland and Pennsylvania: the folk-cultural legacy*. Béaloideas, 2006. 74: p. 1–63.
24. Myers, A. *Immigration of the Irish Quakers into Pennsylvania 1682-1750*. 1969, Baltimore, Maryland: Genealogical Publishing Society.
25. James, A.E. *Chester County Clocks and Their Makers*. 1947, West Chester, Pennsylvania: Chester County Historical Society.
26. Conrad, H.C., *Old Delaware Clockmakers*. Papers of the Historical Society of Delaware, 1898. XX: p. 3–34.
27. Harris, J.C. *The Clock and Watch Makers American Advertiser*. 1984: J. Carter Harris.
28. Myers, A. *Irish Quaker Arrivals to Pennsylvania 1682-1750; list of certificates of removal from Ireland, received at the Monthly Meetings of Friends in Pennsylvania, 1682-1750*. 1964, Baltimore, Maryland: Genealogical Publishing Company.
29. Records, Winterthur Museum, Wilmington, Delaware.

30. Greene, J.P. *American Furniture of the 18th Century*. 1996, Newtown, CT: The Taunton Press.
31. Jackson, C.J. *English Goldsmiths and their Marks. A History of the Goldsmiths and Plate Workers of England, Scotland and Ireland*. 1964, New York, New York: Dover Publications Inc.
32. Jordan, J.W., ed. *Colonial Families of Philadelphia*. Vol. 1. 1911, New York & Chicago: Lewis Publishing Co.
33. Archives, University of Pennsylvania. Available from: http://www.archives.upenn.edu/histy/features/1700s/people/syng_phil.html.
34. Gillingham, H.E., *The Cost of Old Silver*. The Pennsylvania Magazine of History and Biography, 1930. 54(1): p. 32–51.
35. Voss, W.E. *American Silversmiths*. 2008; Available from: http://freepages.genealogy.rootsweb.ancestry.com/~silversmiths/makers/silversmiths/261796.htm (accessed November 2013).
36. Eckhardt, G.H. *Pennsylvania Clocks and Clockmakers*. 1955, New York, New York: The Devin Adair Company/Bonanza Books.
37. Folliott, R., *Biographical Notes on Some Cork Clock and Watch Makers*. Journal of the Cork Historical and Archaeological Society, 1964. LXIX: p. 38–55.
38. Gibbs, J. *Pennsylvania Clocks and Watches*. 1984, University Park, Pennsylvania: Pennsylvania State University Press.
39. Prime, P.P. *Phildelphia Silver 1682-1800*. 1956, Philadelphia, Pennsylvania: The Philadelphia Museum of Art.
40. Anonymous. *Abstracts of Memorials*. Registry of Deeds Office: Dublin. p. 451.
41. Notice, in *Belfast Newsletter*. Belfast. 1767. August 11th, p. 1.
42. Notice, in *Pennsylvania Packet, published as Dunlap's Pennsylvania Packet or, the General Advertiser*. Philadelphia, Pennsylvania. 1774. October 3rd p. 3.
43. Notice, in *Pennsylvania Packet, published as Dunlap's Pennsylvania Packet or, the General Advertiser*. Philadelphia, Pennsylvania. 1775. March 20th, p. 3.
44. Notice, in *The Pennsylvania Evening Post*. Philadelphia, Pennsylvania. 1778. February 12th, p. 69.
45. Hazard, S. *Pennsylvania Archives*. 1853, Philadelphia, Pennsylvania.
46. Sellers, C.C., *Portraits and Miniatures by Charles Willson Peale*. Transactions of the American Philosophical Society New Series, 1952. 42(1): p. 1–369.
47. Pownall, T. *The Remembrancer, Or Impartial Repository of Public Events for 1777*. Vol. 5. 1778, London: J. Axmon.
48. Bell, D., *Personal Communication*. 2007.
49. Notice, in *Belfast Newsletter*. Belfast. 1780. September 1st, p. 3.
50. White, F. *The Philadelphia Directory*. 1785, Philadelphia, Pennsylvania.
51. MacPherson, J. *MacPherson's Directory for Philadelphia 1785*. 1785, Philadelphia, Pennsylvania.
52. Biddle, C. *The Philadelphia Directory*. 1791, Philadelphia, Pennsylvania.
53. Hardie, J. *The Philadelphia Directory and Register*. 1793, Philadelphia, Pennsylvania.
54. Hardie, J. The Philadelphia Directory and Register. 1794, Philadelphia, Pennsylvania.
55. Stephens, T. *Stephen's Philadelphia Directory*. 1796, Philadelphia, Pennsylvania.
56. Stafford, C.W. *The Philadelphia Directory for 1799*. 1799, Philadelphia, Pennsylvania: Cornelius Stafford.
57. Stafford, C.W. *The Philadelphia Directory for 1797*. 1797, Philadelphia, Pennsylvania: Cornelius Stafford.
58. Stafford, C.W. *The Philadelphia Directory for 1798*. 1798, Philadelphia, Pennsylvania: Cornelius Stafford.
59. Stafford, C.W. *The Philadelphia Directory for 1800*. 1800, Philadelphia, Pennsylvania: Cornelius Stafford.
60. Stafford, C.W. *The Philadelphia Directory for 1801*. 1801, Philadelphia, Pennsylvania: Cornelius Stafford.
61. Robinson, J. *The Philadelphia Directory for 1803*. 1803, Philadelphia, Pennsylvania: James Robinson.

62. Robinson, J. *The Philadelphia Directory for 1804*. 1804, Philadelphia, Pennsylvania: James Robinson.
63. Robinson, J. *The Philadelphia Directory for 1805*. 1805, Philadelphia, Pennsylvania: James Robinson.
64. Robinson, J. *The Philadelphia Directory for 1809*. 1809, Philadelphia, Pennsylvania: James Robinson.
65. Robinson, J. *The Philadelphia Directory for 1816*. 1816, Philadelphia, Pennsylvania: James Robinson.
66. Paxton, J.A. *The Philadelphia Directory and Register for 1818*. 1818, Philadelphia, Pennsylvania: John Adems Paxton.
67. Paxton, J.A. *The Philadelphia Directory and Register for 1819*. 1819, Philadelphia, Pennsylvania: John Adems Paxton.
68. Whitely, E. *The Philadelphia Directory and Register for 1820*. 1820, Philadelphia, Pennsylvania: Edward Whitely.
69. Forman, B.R., *Laurence Birnie and the Apprentice Griffith Owen*. Bulletin of the National Association of Watch and Clock Collectors, 2015. 57/2(March/April): p. 170–171.
70. Foley, P.J., *Personal communication*. 2014.
71. Records of the Museum of Early Southern Decorative Arts. Available from: http://www.mesda.org/research_sprite/mesda_craftsman_database.html.
72. Filby, P. and M. Meyer, eds. *Passenger and immigration lists index*. 1981, Detroit, Michigan: Gale Research Company.
73. Advertisement, in *The Pennsylvania Packet or the General Advertiser*. Philadelphia, Pennsylvania. 1783. July 5th, p. 2.
74. Robinson, J. *The Philadelphia Directory for 1811*. 1811, Philadelphia, Pennsylvania: James Robinson.
75. Kite, B.T. *Kite's Philadelphia Directory for 1814*. 1814. Philadelphia, Pennsylvania.
76. Notice, in *Belfast Newsletter*. Belfast. 1772. April 7th, p. 1.
77. Fee, A., et al. *The United Irishmen in East Tyrone*. The Bell - Journal of Stewartstown [County Tyrone] and District Local History Society, 1999(7): p. 3–43.
78. Lyons, J. *United Irishmen, Co. Tyrone, 1797*. 2013; Available from: http://www.from-ireland.net/history-united-irishmen-tyrone-1797 (Accessed November 2013).
79. Parkhill, T. *The Wild Geese of 1798: Emigrés of the Rebellion*. Seanchas Ardmhacha: Journal of the Armagh Diocesan Historical Society, 2003. 19(2): p. 118–135.
80. McDowell, R.B. *Proceedings of the Dublin Society of United Irishmen, Irish Manuscripts Commission*. Reproduction of 1949 edition of Analecta Hibernica No 17. ed. 1998, Dublin: Irish Manuscripts Commission.
81. Wilson. W. *Wilson's Dublin Directory*. 1780, Dublin.
82. Wilson. W. *Wilson's Dublin Directory*. 1784, Dublin.
83. Wilson. W. *Wilson's Dublin Directory*. 1786, Dublin.
84. Wilson. W. *Wilson's Dublin Directory*. 1787, Dublin.
85. Wilson. W. *Wilson's Dublin Directory*. 1788, Dublin.
86. Wilson. W. *Wilson's Dublin Directory*. 1789, Dublin.
87. Wilson. W. *Wilson's Dublin Directory*. 1790, Dublin.
88. Wilson. W. *Wilson's Dublin Directory*. 1791, Dublin.
89. Wilson. W. *Wilson's Dublin Directory*. 1792, Dublin.
90. Wilson. W. *Wilson's Dublin Directory*. 1793, Dublin.
91. Wilson. W. *Wilson's Dublin Directory*. 1794, Dublin.
92. Wilson. W. *Wilson's Dublin Directory*. 1795, Dublin.
93. Wilson. W. *Wilson's Dublin Directory*. 1796, Dublin.
94. Wilson. W. *Wilson's Dublin Directory*. 1797, Dublin.
95. Wilson, P. *Wilson's Dublin Directory*. 1760, Dublin.
96. Wilson, P. *Wilson's Dublin Directory*. 1762, Dublin.
97. Wilson, P. *Wilson's Dublin Directory*. 1764, Dublin.

98. Wilson, P. *Wilson's Dublin Directory*. 1766, Dublin.
99. Wilson, P. *Wilson's Dublin Directory*. 1767, Dublin.
100. Wilson, P. *Wilson's Dublin Directory*. 1768, Dublin.
101. Wilson, P. *Wilson's Dublin Directory*. 1770, Dublin.
102. Wilson. W. *Wilson's Dublin Directory*. 1798, Dublin.
103. Wilson. W. *Wilson's Dublin Directory*. 1800, Dublin.
104. Wilson. W. *Wilson's Dublin Directory*. 1801, Dublin.
105. Wilson, P. *Wilson's Dublin Directory*. 1802, Dublin.
106. Ferrar, J. *Ferrar's Limerick Directory of 1769*. 1769.
107. Dawes, E. *The Philadelphia Directory for 1817*. 1817, Philadelphia, Pennsylvania.
108. Davis, M.A. *Philadelphia Directory and Register*. 1822, Philadelphia, Pennsylvania: McCarty and Davis.
109. Desilver, R. *Philadelphia Index or Directory*. 1823, Philadelphia, Pennsylvania: Robert Desilver.
110. Desilver, R. *Philadelphia Directory and Strangers Guide*. 1828, Philadelphia, Pennsylvania: Robert Desilver.
111. Wilson, T. *Philadelphia Directory*. 1825, Philadelphia, Pennsylvania.
112. Desilver, R. *Philadelphia Directory and Strangers Guide*. 1833, Philadelphia, Pennsylvania: Robert Desilver.
113. McClroy, A. *A McElroy's Philadelphia City Directory*. 1837, Philadelphia, Pennsylvania: McElroy A. & Co.
114. Stewart, A. *James M. Orr, Watchmaker, and Jane Stewart, Belfast and Philadelphia*. 2012. Cited July 3, 2015. Available from: http://alison-stewart.blogspot.com/2012/08/james-m-orr-watchmaker-and-jane-stewart.html.
115. Orr, R. *Weavers & Watchmakers A Family Narrative History*. 2017: Roger Orr.
116. Harvey, B. *The Belfast and Province of Ulster Directory for 1870*. 1870. Belfast: Post Office.
117. *The Belfast and Province of Ulster Directory for 1877*. 1877, Belfast: News-Letter Office.
118. *The Belfast and Province of Ulster Directory for 1880*. 1880, Belfast: News-Letter Office.
119. *The Belfast and Province of Ulster Directory for 1884*. 1884, Belfast: News-Letter Office.
120. *The Belfast and Province of Ulster Directory for 1890*. 1890, Belfast: News-Letter Office.
121. *The Belfast and Province of Ulster Directory for 1894*. 1894, Belfast: News-Letter Office.
122. *The Belfast and Province of Ulster Directory for 1892*. 1892, Belfast: News-Letter Office.
123. *The Belfast and Province of Ulster Directory for 1896*. 1896, Belfast: News-Letter Office.
124. *The Belfast and Province of Ulster Directory for 1897*. 1897, Belfast: News-Letter Office.
125. *The Belfast and Province of Ulster Directory for 1899*. 1899, Belfast: News-Letter Office.
126. Palmer, B. *The Book of American Clocks*. 1950, New York, NY: Macmillan Co.
127. Notice. *The Pennsylvania Chronicle Philadelphia*. May 6th, 1771 p4.
128. Records, Charleston County, S.C. Inventory Book X, 1768 et seq. 1768, Charleston County, South Carolina. p. 352.
129. Robinson, K. *An unpublished list of Irish clock and watchmakers*. 2015: Winston-Salem, North Carolina.
130. Desilver, R. *Philadelphia Directory and Strangers Guide*. 1830, Philadelphia, Pennsylvania: Robert Desilver.
131. Adams, J.R.R. *Merchants in Plenty Joseph Smyth's Belfast Directories of 1807 and 1808*. 1991, Belfast: Ulster Historical Foundation.
132. *The Belfast and Province of Ulster Directory for 1852*. Belfast. Pub. Henderson J.A. 1852.
133. Bradshaw, T. *General Directory for Newry, Armagh etc for 1820*. 1819, Newry.
134. Matier, W. *Matier's Belfast Directory for 1835-6*. 1835, Belfast: William T. Matier.
135. Spittler, S.L., T.J. Spittler, and C.H. Bailey *American Clockmakers and Watchmakers*. 2011, Columbia, PA: National Association of Watch and Clock Collectors.
136. Egle, W.H., ed. *Pennsylvania Genealogies Chiefly Scotch-Irish and German*. Reprint 2003. Second Edition. 1896. Harrisburg, PA: Harrisburg Publishing Co. 1896.

137. Sweinhart, F.C., Early Pennsylvania Clocks and Their Makers. Bulletin of the Historical Society of Montgomery County Pennsylvania, Norristown. 1941. III: p. 42–52.

138. Beatty, G. *Beatty (George) and Heimer (John) Ledger*. 1841–1848, University of Southern Mississippi - McCain Library and Archives Manuscript Collection.

139. Waugh, B. *Pennsylvania Female College of Harrisburg - Papers Relating to Harrisburg Women*. 1861.

140. Roberts, C.R. *Grandfathers' Clocks*. Proceedings and Papers of the Lehigh County Historical Society, 1922: p. 29–33.

141. Orr, S.H. *Clockmakers, in Pennsylvania, of the 18th and 19th centuries*. Bulletin of the Historical Society of Montgomery County, Pennsylvania, 1937. I No 2(April): p. 81–85.

142. Wood, S.B.C., ed. *Clockmakers and Watchmakers of Lancaster County, Pennsylvania*. 1995, Lancaster, PA: Lancaster County Historical Society.

143. Anonymous. *Thomas H Burrowes, and the School System of Pennsylvania*. The American Journal of Education. Ed. Barnard H. 1859. 6: p. 107–124.

144. Meginness, J.F. *Biographical Annals of Lancaster County Pennsylvania containing Biographical and Genealogical Sketches of many Prominent and Representative Citizens and many of the Early Settlers*. 1903, Chicago, IL: J. H. Beers & Co.

145. Advertisement, in *Delaware Courant*. 1787. July 7th.

146. Langdon, J.E. *Clock and Watchmakers in Canada*. 1976, Toronto, Canada: Anson-Cartwright Editions.

147. Burrows, G.E. *Canadian Clocks and Clockmakers*. 1973, Oshawa, Ontario: G Edmond Burrows through Kalabi Enterprises Limited.

148. Loomes, B. *Painted Dial Clocks 1770-1870*. 1994, Woodbridge, Suffolk: Antique Collectors' Club.

149. Wood, S.B.C. *225 Years of Timepieces: A Lancaster County Legacy*. 1979, Columbia, Pennsylvania: National Association of Watch and Clock Collectors, Inc.

150. Wood, S.B.C. and S.E. Kramer. *Clockmakers of Lancaster County and their clocks 1750-1850*. 1977, New York, New York: Van Nostrand Reinhold Company.

151. Advertisement, in *The Pennsylvania Gazette*. Philadelphia, Pennsylvania. 1765. March 14th, p. 1.

152. Will Abstracts. Chester County Historical Society: Chester County.

153. Personal Communication, Chester County Historical Society. February 2007: West Chester PA.

154. Kincaide, N. Kincaid Pennsylvania Timeline. May 2015. Accessed April 3, 2020. http://freepages.rootsweb.com/~kincaide/genealogy/Kincaid%20Research/Kincaid%20Pennsylvania%20Timeline/kincaid%20pennsylvania%20timeline,%201680-1775.htm

155. Cescinsky, H. and M. Webster. *English Domestic Clocks*. 1976, Woodbridge, Suffolk: Antique Collectors Club.

156. Eckman, J. *The Kinkeads of Delaware as pioneers of Minnesota, 1856-1868: contemporary account of experiences in the Sioux Uprising, 1862, by Clara Janvier Kinkead: some genealogical history of the Kinkead and Janvier families*. 1949, Wilmington, DE: Printed for George W. Butz, Jr.

157. Dorman, C.G. *Delaware Cabinetmakers and Allied Artisans 1655-1855*. 1960, Wilmington, Delaware: Historical Society of Delaware.

158. Hoopes, P. *Connecticut clockmakers of the eighteenth century*. 2nd ed. 1974, New York, NY: Dover.

159. Zea, P., R. Cheney, and C. Sloat. *Clock Making in New England 1725-1825. An Interpretation of the Old Sturbridge Village Collection*. 1992, Old Sturbridge Village, Sturbridge, Massachusetts: Old Sturbridge Inc.

160. Kane, P.E. *Colonial Massachusetts Silversmiths and Jewelers*. 1998, New Haven, Connecticut: Yale University Art Gallery.

161. Dow, G.F. *The Arts & Crafts in New England 1704-1775 - Gleanings from Boston Newspapers*. 1927, Topsfield, MA: The Wayside Press.

162. Flynt, H.N. and M.G. Fales *The Heritage Foundation Collection of Silver with Biographical Sketches of New England Silversmiths, 1625 - 1825*. 1968, Old Deerfield: The Heritage Foundation.

163. Notice, in *The Boston Post-Boy & Advertiser*. Boston, Massachusetts. 1767. December 14th, 1767, p. 3.

164. Notice, in *The Boston-Gazette, and Country Journal*. Boston, Massachusetts. 1769. November 20th p. Supplement 1.
165. Norman, J. *Boston Directory*. 1789, Boston, Massachusetts: John Norman.
166. West, J. *Boston Directory*. 1796, Boston, Massachusetts: John West.
167. West, J. *Boston Directory*. 1798, Boston, Massachusetts: John West.
168. West, J. *Boston Directory*. 1800, Boston, Massachusetts: John West.
169. West, J. *Boston Directory*. 1803, Boston, Massachusetts: John West.
170. Cotton, E. *Boston Directory*. 1805, Boston, Massachusetts: Edward Cotton.
171. Cotton, E. *Boston Directory*. 1806, Boston, Massachusetts: Edward Cotton.
172. Cotton, E. *Boston Directory*. 1807, Boston, Massachusetts: Edward Cotton.
173. Cotton, E. *Boston Directory*. 1809, Boston, Massachusetts: Edward Cotton.
174. Cotton, E. *Boston Directory*. 1810, Boston, Massachusetts: Edward Cotton.
175. Cotton, E. *Boston Directory*. 1813, Boston, Massachusetts: Edward Cotton.
176. Cotton, E. *Boston Directory*. 1816, Boston, Massachusetts: Edward Cotton.
177. Cotton, E. *Boston Directory*. 1818, Boston, Massachusetts: Edward Cotton.
178. Frost, J.H.A., C. Stimpson, Jr. *Boston Directory*. 1820, Boston, Massachusetts: John H. A. Frost and Charles Stimpson Jr.
179. Wilson, W. *Wilson's Dublin Directory*. 1779, Dublin: William Wilson.
180. Wilson, W. *Wilson's Dublin Directory*. 1773, Dublin: William Wilson.
181. Wilson, W. *Wilson's Dublin Directory*. 1775, Dublin: William Wilson.
182. Wilson, W. *Wilson's Dublin Directory*. 1776, Dublin: William Wilson.
183. Wilson, W. *Wilson's Dublin Directory*. 1777, Dublin: William Wilson.
184. Wilson, W. *Wilson's Dublin Directory*. 1778, Dublin: William Wilson.
185. Wilson, W. *Wilson's Dublin Directory*. 1799, Dublin: William Wilson.
186. Corbet, W. *Wilson's Dublin Directory*. 1803, Dublin: William Corbet.
187. Corbet, W. *Wilson's Dublin Directory*. 1804, Dublin: William Corbet.
188. Corbet, W. *Wilson's Dublin Directory*. 1805, Dublin: William Corbet.
189. Corbet, W. *Wilson's Dublin Directory*. 1806, Dublin: William Corbet.
190. Corbet, W. *Wilson's Dublin Directory*. 1809, Dublin: William Corbet.
191. Corbet, W. *Wilson's Dublin Directory*. 1810, Dublin: William Corbet.
192. Corbet, W. *Wilson's Dublin Directory*. 1811, Dublin: William Corbet.
193. Corbet, W. *Wilson's Dublin Directory*. 1812, Dublin: William Corbet.
194. Corbet, W. *Wilson's Dublin Directory*. 1813, Dublin: William Corbet.
195. Corbet, W. *Wilson's Dublin Directory*. 1815, Dublin: William Corbet.
196. Corbet, W. *Wilson's Dublin Directory*. 1818, Dublin: William Corbet.
197. Corbet, W. *Wilson's Dublin Directory*. 1819, Dublin: William Corbet.
198. Corbet, W. *Wilson's Dublin Directory*. 1820, Dublin: William Corbet.
199. Corbet, W. *Wilson's Dublin Directory*. 1822, Dublin: William Corbet.
200. Corbet, W. *Wilson's Dublin Directory*. 1823, Dublin: William Corbet.
201. Corbet, W. *Wilson's Dublin Directory*. 1824, Dublin: William Corbet.
202. Notice, in *The Salem Gazette*. Salem, Massachusetts. 1795. December 29th, p. 4.
203. Notice, in *The Salem Register*. Salem, Massachusetts. 1802. October 4th, p. 3.
204. Notice, in *Essex Register*. Salem, Massachusetts. 1807. November 19th, p. 3.
205. Notice, in *Essex Gazette*. Haverhill, Massachusetts. 1839. April 5th, p. 1.
206. Foley, P.J., *Personal communication*. 2003.
207. Notice, in *The Salem Gazette*. Salem, Massachusetts. 1829. May 15th, p. 2.
208. Advertisement, in *Independent Journal*. New York. 1784. February 7th, p. 3.
209. Advertisement, in *New-Hampshire Gazette and Historical Chronicle*. Portsmouth, New Hampshire. 1769. September 1st, p. 3.

210. Advertisement, in *The New-York Gazette; and the Weekly Mercury*. New York. 1772. December 28th.
211. Advertisement, in *Rivington's New York Gazetteer, or the Connecticut, New-Jersey, Hudson's River, and Quebec Weekly Advertiser*. New York. 1773. July 1st, p 3
212. Atkins, C.E. *Register of Apprentices of the Worshipful Company of Clockmakers of the City of London*. 1931, London: Privately Printed.
213. Daniels, G. *Freemen of the Worshipful Company of Clockmakers 1631-1984*. 1984, Riversdale, Isle of Man: George Daniels.
214. Wilson, P. *Wilson's Dublin Directory*. 1752, Dublin: Peter Wilson.
215. Wilson, P. *Wilson's Dublin Directory*. 1753, Dublin: Peter Wilson.
216. Wilson, P. *Wilson's Dublin Directory*. 1763, Dublin: Peter Wilson.
217. Advertisement, in *The New-York Journal; or, The General Advertiser*. New York. 1775. May 25th Supplement, p. 2.
218. Advertisement, in *New-Hampshire Gazette, and Historical Chronicle*. Portsmouth, New Hampshire. 1768. December 23rd, p. 4.
219. Advertisement, in *New-Hampshire Gazette and Historical Chronicle*. Portsmouth, New Hampshire. 1770. May 18th, p. 3
220. Advertisement, in *New-Hampshire Gazette and Historical Chronicle*. Portsmouth, New Hampshire. 1770. June 22nd, p. 3.
221. Advertisement, in *The New-York Journal; or, the General Advertiser*. New York. 1770. August 23rd, p. 125.
222. Advertisement, in *The New-York Journal; or, the General Advertiser*. New York. 1771. June 20th, p. 375.
223. Advertisement, in *The New-York Journal; or, The General Advertiser*. New York. 1773. May 13th, p. Suppl 2.
224. Advertisement, in *The New-York Journal; or, The General Advertiser*. 1774. May 5th, p. 3.
225. Advertisement, in *The New-York Gazette; and the Weekly Mercury*. New York. 1774. June 13th, p. Suppl 1.
226. Advertisement, in *Rivington's New York Gazetteer; or Connecticut, Hudson's River, New-Jersey, and Quebec Weekly Advertiser*. New York. 1774. September 15th, p. 4.
227. Advertisement, in *The New-York Journal; or, The General Advertiser*. New York. 1775. May 25th, p. Suppl 2.
228. Advertisement, in *The New-York Journal; or, The General Advertiser*. New York. 1775. August 24th, p. 4.
229. Advertisement, in *The New-York Gazette; and the Weekly Mercury*. New York. 1776. April 29th, p. 3.
230. Advertisement, in *The New-York Gazetteer or Northern Intelligencer*. Albany, New York. 1783. May 19th, p. 4.
231. Advertisement, in *Loudon's New-York Packet*. New York. 1785. May 19th, p. 2.
232. Advertisement, in *Loudon's New-York Packet*. New York. 1785. June 9th, p. 4.
233. Bohan, P. and P. Hammerslough. *Early Connecticut Silver 1700-1840*. 1970, Middletown, Connecticut: Wesleyan University Press.
234. Carlisle, L.B. *Vermont Clock and Watchmakers, Silversmiths and Jewelers 1778-1878*. 1970, Burlington, Vermont: Burlington, VT: Distributed by the Stinehour Press, Lunenburg, VT; 1970.
235. Advertisement, in *Eastern Argus*. Portland, Maine. 1810. February 1st, p. 4.
236. Advertisement, in *New-Hampshire Patriot*. Concord, New Hampshire. 1810. August 21st, p. 3.
237. Advertisement, in *The Carolina Gazette*. Charleston, South Carolina. 1811. January 25th, p. 3.
238. Advertisement, in *Portland Gazette, and Maine Advertizer*. Portland, Maine. 1811. December 16th, p. 4.
239. Death Notice. *The Salem Gazette*. Salem, Massachusetts. 1819. July 20th, p. 3.
240. Gottesman, R.S. *The Arts and Crafts in New York 1800-1804*. 1965, New York: The New-York Historical Society.
241. Truxes, T.M., *Ireland, New York, and the Eighteenth-Century Atlantic World*. American Journal of Irish Studies, 2011. 8: p. 9–40.

242. Heron, I. *My own Memoirs; or the Life of Isaac Heron, a Loyalist on Pure Genuine Principles*. 1810, Waterford: John Bull (Printer).
243. Gottesman, R.S., *Isaac Heron, New York Watch Maker (1763 1778)*. American Collector, 1948. XVII(No 6): p. 5, 21.
244. Gottesman, R.S. *The Arts and Crafts in New York 1726-1776*. Da Capo Press 1970 ed. 1938, New York: New York Historical Society.
245. Advertisement, in *The New-York Gazette*. New York. 1766. May 5th, p. 3.
246. Stokes, I.N.P. *The Iconography of Manhattan Island 1498-1909*. 1915, New York: Robert H. Dodd.
247. Advertisement, in *The New-York Gazette; and the Weekly Mercury*. New York. 1770. July 23rd, p.4.
248. Jones, E.A. *A Literary, Political and Military Watchmaker in America*. Art in America, 1920. 8: p. 308–310.
249. Advertisement, in *The New York Journal; or, General Advertiser*. New York. 1772. December 24th, p. 813.
250. Advertisement, in *The New York Journal; or, General Advertiser*. New York. 1773. January 7th, p. 825.
251. Advertisement, in *Rivington's New York Gazeteer*. New York. 1775. November 23rd, p. 4.
252. LaFond, E.F. *Isaac Heron, The Outspoken Clockmaker*. Bulletin of the National Association of Watch and Clock Collectors, 1979. XXI(June): p. 291–307.
253. Advertisement, in *The New-York Gazette; and the Weekly Mercury*. New York. 1776. October 21st. p. 4.
254. Advertisement, in New-York Gazette, and Weekly Mercury. New York. 1777. February 3rd, p. 3.
255. Advertisement, in *The New-York Gazette; and the Weekly Mercury*. New York. 1777. June 9th, p. 3.
256. Advertisement, in *Royal Gazette*. New York. 1778. September 9th, p. 3.
257. Phillips, J. *Personal Communication*. 2014.
258. Heron, I. *Memorial to the Commission appointed by Act of Parliament for enquiring into the Losses and Services of the American Loyalists*, in *Public Records Office*. 1787: London. p. 203–206.
259. Government, *Decision*, in *Public Records Office*. 1787: London. p. 83–84.
260. Ffolliott, R. *Microfiche Index to Biographical Notices 1758 to 1821 for Waterford, Clonmel, Limerick and Ennis in the Possession of Waterford Library*. 1985: Waterford.
261. Morris, H.F. *The Waterford Herald 1791. Births, Marriages and Deaths*. The Irish Genealogist, 1980. 6: p. 24–37.
262. Heron, I. *To the following positive facts, stated for the information of Messrs. the Arbrtrators, between Smith, Heron, and Murphy --- Isaac Heron entreats attention.*, in *State Paper Office*. 1796: Dublin.
263. Heron, I. *Letter*, in *State Paper Office*. 1797: Dublin.
264. Inglis, B. *The Freedom of the Press in Ireland, 1784-1841*. Reprint ed. 1975, Westport, Connecticut: Greenwood Press, Publishers.
265. Aspinall, A. *Politics and the Press c. 1780-1850*. 1973, Brighton, England: The Harvester Press.
266. Advertisement, in *The Diary or Loudons Register*. New York. 1793. December 26th, p. 3.
267. Mollan, C. *Irish National Inventory of Historic Scientific Instruments*. 1995, Dublin: Samton Ltd.
268. Curtis, J. *Times Chimes & Charms of Dublin*. 1st Edition ed. 1992, Dublin: Verge Books Ltd.
269. Advertisement, in *The New-York Gazette and General Advertiser*. New York. 1798. August 24th, p. 4.
270. Notice, in *The New-York Gazette and General Advertiser*. New York. 1798. September 28th, p. 1.
271. Longworth, D. *Longworth's American Almanac, New-York Register and City Directory*. 1801, New York: D. Longworth.
272. Longworth, D. *Longworth's American Almanac, New-York Register and City Directory*. 1820, New York: D. Longworth.
273. Longworth, D. *Longworth's American Almanac, New-York Register and City Directory*. 1805, New York: D. Longworth.
274. Notice, in *American Citizen*. New York. 1805. December 25th, p. 3.
275. Notice, in *American Citizen*. New York. 1804. October 29th, p. 2.
276. Notice, in *Mercantile Advertiser*. New York, New York. 1809. April 13th, p. 2.
277. Advertisement, in *The Daily Advertiser*. New York. 1799. August 20th, p. 2.

278. Anonymous. *The James Arthur Lecture Series Past Topics and Presenters*. Cited October 12, 2014; Available from: tinyurl.com/y5etqd95.

279. Grant, J. and S. Jeronimo. *Guide to the Records of the James Arthur Collection of Clocks and Watches RG 42.1*. 2012. Accessed December 5, 2017; Available from: http://dlib.nyu.edu/findingaids/html/archives/jamesarthur/bioghist.html.

280. Arthur, J. *Time and its Measurement*. 1909, Chicago, IL: H.H. Windsor.

281. Arthur, J. *A Five Minute Repeater Clock*. Machinery, 1905. 11(March): p. 339–343.

282. Martin. *Martin's Belfast Directory for 1839*. 1839, Belfast. 172.

283. Cutten, G.B. *The Silversmiths, Watchmakers and Jewelers of the State of New York outside of New York City*. 1939, Hamilton, New York: G.B. Cutten, privately printed.

284. Notice, in *The Public Advertiser*. New York. 1808. February 6th, p. 3.

285. Notice, in *Orange County Patriot; or, The Spirit of Seventy-Six*. Goshen, New York. 1812. November 17, p. 3.

286. Notice, in *The Shamrock, or Hibernian Chronicle*. New York. 1811. April 13th, p. 1.

287. Downs, J.P. *History of Chautauqua County New York and Its People*. Editor-in-Charge J.P. Downs and Editor-in-Chief F.Y. Hedley. 1921, Boston, New York, Chicago: American Historical Society Inc.

288. Sperling, D., *John Nicholl, Clockmaker of Belvidere, New Jersey (1784-1862) Part I*. Bulletin of the National Association of Watch and Clock Collectors, 2005(February 2005): p. 81–83.

289. Notice, in *Belfast Newsletter*. Belfast. 1818. July 17th, p. 2.

290. Beckman, E.D. *An In-depth Study of the Cincinnati Silversmiths, Jewelers, Watch and Clockmakers*. 1975, Cincinnati: B. B. & Co. Cincinnati.

291. Gleeson, D.T. *The Irish in the South 1815-1877*. 2001, Chapel Hill and London: University of North Carolina Press.

292. Blethen, H.T. and C.W. Wood. *From Ulster to Carolina*. 1999 (revised). Raleigh: North Carolina Division of Archives and History.

293. Smith, J.W., *"A Large and Elegant Assortment:" a Group of Baltimore Tall Clocks, 1795-1815*. Journal of Early Southern Decorative Arts, 1987. XIII(November): p. 33-103.

294. *Irish Historic Towns Atlas Dublin 1610-1756*. Available from: http://www.logainm.ie/Eolas/Data/IHTA/dublin-2.pdf.

295. O'Brien, G. *The Economic History of Ireland in the Eighteenth Century*. 1977, Philadelphia, PA: Porcupine Press.

296. O'Brien, M. *A Hidden Phase of American History. Ireland's Part in America's Struggle for Liberty*. Dodd, Mead and Company: New York. 1919. https://archive.org/stream/hiddenphaseofame00obri/hiddenphaseofame00obri_djvu.txt

297. Lewis, M.H., *American Vernacular Furniture and the North Carolina Backcountry*. The Journal of Early Southern Decorative Arts, 1994. XX: p. 1-38.

298. Hurst, R.L. *Irish Influences on Cabinetmaking in Virginia's Rappahannock River Basin*. 1997; Available from: http://www.chipstone.org/publications/1997AF/Hurst/HurstIndex97.html (Accessed December 5, 2017).

299. Raley, R.L., *Irish influences in Baltimore decorative arts 1785-1815*. The Magazine Antiques, 1961. 79(March): p. 276-279.

300. Anonymous. *Maryland Queen Anne and Chippendale Furniture of the Eighteenth Century*. 1968, New York: October House Inc. for the Baltimore Museum of Art.

301. Wilson, W. *Wilson's Dublin Directory*. 1774, Dublin: William Wilson.

302. Rogers, J. *Eddies Extracts Faulkner's Dublin Journal -- 1725-1798*. Available from: http://freepages.genealogy.rootsweb.ancestry.com/~econnolly/extracts1700/fdj1725_98.html.

303. Advertisement, in *The Maryland Gazette: or, The Baltimore General Advertiser*. Baltimore, Maryland. 1783. November 28th, p. 3.

304. Advertisement, in *The Maryland Journal and Baltimore Advertiser*. Baltimore, Maryland. 1784. August 31, p. 1.

305. Advertisement, in *The Maryland Journal and Baltimore Advertiser*. Baltimore, Maryland. 1784. November 16th, p. 3.

306. Advertisement, in *The Maryland Journal and Baltimore Advertiser*. Baltimore, Maryland. 1785. May 3rd, p. 2.

307. Mullin, J. *The Baltimore Directory, for 1799, containing the names, occupations and places of abode of the citizens etc*. 1799, Baltimore, Maryland: John Mullin.

308. Matchett E. *The Baltimore Directory and Register, for 1816*. The Wanderer Office. Baltimore, Maryland.
309. Stafford, C. *The Baltimore Directory for 1803; &c.* 1803, Baltimore, Maryland: Cornelius Stafford.
310. Advertisement, in *The Maryland Journal and Baltimore Advertiser*. Baltimore, Maryland. 1786. January 17th, p. 3.
311. Advertisement, in *The Maryland Journal and Baltimore Advertiser*. Baltimore, Maryland. 1790. September 3rd, p. 3.
312. Advertisement, in *The Maryland Journal and Baltimore Advertiser*. Baltimore, Maryland. 1791. May 10th, p. 3.
313. Advertisement, in *Federal Intelligencer and Baltimore Daily Gazette*. Baltimore Maryland. 1794. November 22nd, p. 3.
314. Notice, *Baltimore County Register of Wills (Indentures) 1799-1800*. 1800, Baltimore Co., MD.
315. Notice, *Baltimore County Register of Wills (Indentures) 1811-1812*. 1812: Baltimore Co. MD.
316. Notice, in *Federal Gazette & Baltimore Daily Advertiser*. Baltimore, Maryland. 1804. September 17th, p. 3.
317. Notice, in *American & Commercial Daily Advertiser*. Baltimore, Maryland. 1806. February 27th, p. 3.
318. Advertisement, in Federal Gazette & Baltimore Daily Advertiser. Baltimore, Maryland. 1806. April 28th, p. 3.
319. Notice, in *American & Commercial Daily Advertiser*. Baltimore, Maryland. 1816. November 8th, p. 2.
320. Notice, in *Federal Republican and Baltimore Telegraph*. Baltimore, Maryland. 1817. November 26th, p. 2.
321. *Orphan's Court Proceedings No 10*. 1817–1819: Baltimore Co., Maryland. p. 48.
322. *Orphan's Court Proceedings No 10*. 1817–1819: Baltimore Co., Maryland. p. 51.
323. Pleasants, J.H. and H. Sill. *Maryland Silversmiths 1715-1830*. 1930, Baltimore, Maryland: J Hall Pleasants.
324. Notice, in *The Virginia Gazette, or the American Advertiser*. Richmond, Virginia. 1784. December 4th, p. 1.
325. Advertisement, in *The Maryland Gazette or the Baltimore General Advertiser*. Baltimore, Maryland. 1784. December 3rd, p. 3.
326. Advertisement, in *The Maryland Journal, and Baltimore Advertiser*. Baltimore, Maryland. 1787. May 18th, p. 3.
327. Advertisement, in *The Pennsylvania Packet, and Daily Advertiser*. Philadelphia, Pennsylvania. 1784. November 9th, p. 1.
328. Clarke, A. *The Maryland Gazette; or, the Baltimore Advertiser*. Baltimore, Maryland. 1789. May 12th, p. 3.
329. Advertisement, in *The Maryland Journal and Baltimore Advertiser*. Baltimore, Maryland. 1791. May 13th, p. 4.
330. Advertisement, in *The Baltimore Evening Post*. Baltimore, Maryland. 1792. December 20th, p. 3.
331. Notice, in *Federal Intelligencer and Baltimore Daily Gazette*. Baltimore, Maryland. 1795. April 14th, p. 3.
332. Notice, in *The Chestertown Gazette*. Chestertown, Maryland. 1793. September 27th, p. 4.
333. Notice, in *The Baltimore Daily Intelligencer*. Baltimore, Maryland. 1794. August 19th, p. 3.
334. Advertisement, in *The Baltimore Evening Post*. Baltimore, Maryland. 1810. May 15th, p. 3.
335. Notice, in *The Baltimore Evening Post*. Baltimore, Maryland. 1810. September 8th, p. 3.
336. Stafford, C. *The Baltimore Directory for 1802; &c.* 1802, Baltimore, Maryland: Cornelius Stafford.
337. Robinson, J. *The Baltimore Directory, &c.* 1804, Baltimore, Maryland: James Robinson.
338. M'Henry, J. *Baltimore Directory, and Citizens' Register, for 1807*. 1807, Baltimore, Maryland: James M'Henry.
339. Fry, W. *The Baltimore Directory for 1810, &c.* 1810, Baltimore, Maryland: William Fry.
340. Notice, in *Belfast Newsletter*. Belfast. 1767. May 8th, p. 3.
341. Bell, D., *The McCabes Watch and Clock Makers of Ulster Part II*. Antiquarian Horology, 2001. 26(March): p. 62-78.
342. Notice, in *Belfast Newsletter*. 1769. February 14th, p. 1.

343. Advertisement, in *The Maryland Journal and the Baltimore Advertiser*. Baltimore, Maryland. 1774. February 24th to March 3rd, p. 2.
344. Advertisement, in *Dunlap's Maryland Gazette; or The Baltimore General Advertiser*. Baltimore, Maryland. 1776. December 3rd, p. 3.
345. *The Baltimore Artificers Company*. Maryland Historical Magazine, 1907. 2(4): p. 367–368.
346. Notice, in *The Maryland Journal, and Baltimore Advertiser*. Baltimore, Maryland. 1778. July 28th, p. 4.
347. McCabe, J., *A United Irish Family*. The McCabes of Belfast. Familia Ulster Genealogical Review, 1997. 13: p. 1–24.
348. Hollan, C. *Virginia Silversmiths, Jewelers, Clock- and Watchmakers, 1607-1860, Their Lives and Marks*. 2010, McLean, Virginia: Hollan Press.
349. Robinson, J. *The Philadelphia Directory for 1807*. 1807, Philadelphia, Pennsylvania: James Robinson.
350. Advertisement, in *American & Commercial Daily Advertiser*. Baltimore, Maryland. 1811. December 5th, p. 3.
351. Advertisement, in *National Intelligencer*. Washington, DC. 1812. December 12, p. 4.
352. Advertisement, in *Daily National Intelligencer*. Washington, DC. 1813. October 18th, p.4.
353. Corkings, E., *Turning Cider into Wine*, in http://www.datamp.org/patents/displayPatent.php?id=47543. 1813, Ezra Corkings: USA.
354. Notice, in *Daily National Intelligencer*. Washington, DC. November 3, 1815. p. 4.
355. Advertisement, in *Frederick-Town Herald*. Frederick-Town, Maryland. 1814. September 24th, p. 1.
356. Advertisement, in *Winchester Gazette*. Winchester, Virginia. 1818. November 28th, p. 4.
357. Advertisement, in *Republican Constellation*. Winchester, Virginia. 1819. November 13th, p. 1.
358. Matchett, R.J. *Baltimore Directory and Register for the year 1842*. 1842, Baltimore, Maryland: R.J. Matchett.
359. Advertisement, in *Federal Gazette and Baltimore Daily Advertiser*. Baltimore, Maryland. 1796. August 31st, p. 3.
360. Advertisement, in *American and Daily Advertiser*. Baltimore, Maryland. 1801. October 31st, p. 3.
361. Advertisement, in *Federal Gazette and Baltimore Daily Advertiser*. Baltimore, Maryland. 1810. April 28th, p. 3.
362. Advertisement, in *American & Commercial Daily Advertiser*. Baltimore, Maryland. 1815. May 19th, p. 3.
363. Advertisement, in *American and Commercial Daily Advertiser*. Baltimore, Maryland. 1820. May 27th, p. 3.
364. Advertisement, in *Federal Gazette and Baltimore Daily Advertiser*. Baltimore, Maryland. 1805. April 29th, p. 3.
365. Pleasants, J.H. and H. Sill *Maryland Silversmiths 1715-1830*. 1972 (Republication), New York: Robert Allan Green.
366. Advertisement, in *American & Commercial Daily Advertiser*. Baltimore, Maryland. 1817. October 10th, p. 3.
367. Advertisement, in *American and Commercial Daily Advertiser*. Baltimore, Maryland. 1808. March 21st, p. 3.
368. Notice, in *Democratic Republican, and Commercial Daily Advertiser*. Baltimore, Maryland. 1802. June 24th, p. 3.
369. Notice, in *Democratic Republican, and Commercial Daily Advertiser*. Baltimore, Maryland. 1802. June 25th, p. 3.
370. Matchett, R.J. *Baltimore Directory and Register for the year 1853-54*. 1853, Baltimore, Maryland: R.J. Matchett.
371. Matchett, R.J. *Baltimore Directory and Register for the year 1855-56*. 1855–56, Baltimore, Maryland: R. J. Matchett.
372. Woods, J.W. *Woods' Baltimore Directory for 1856-57*. 1856–57, Baltimore, Maryland: J.W. Woods.
373. Advertisement, in *Baltimore Daily Repository*. Baltimore, Maryland. 1792. July 5th, p. 4.
374. Advertisement, in *Baltimore Daily Repository*. Baltimore, Maryland. 1793. February 20th, p. 1.
375. *Orphan's Court Proceedings No. 3. 1792-1798*. 1794: Baltimore Co., Maryland. p. 128.
376. *Orphan's Court Proceedings No. 3. 1792-1798*. 1796: Baltimore Co., Maryland. p. 197.
377. Advertisement, in *Federal Gazette & Baltimore Daily Advertiser*. Baltimore, Maryland. 1798. February 22nd, p. 4.

378. Barnes, R. *Marriages and Deaths from Baltimore Newspapers 1796-1816*. 1978, Baltimore, Maryland: Genealogical Publishing Co., Inc.
379. Pleasants, J.H., in *J. Hall Pleasants Research Files. The Frick Collection/Frick Art Reference Library Archives*: New York, New York.
380. Advertisement, in *The Maryland Gazette*. Annapolis, Maryland. 1764. March 22nd, p. 2.
381. Gibson, C.B. *The history of the county and city of Cork*. 1861, London: Thomas C Newby.
382. Cullen, L.M. *An economic history of Ireland since 1660*. 1972, London: B.T. Batsford.
383. Advertisement, in *The Maryland Gazette*. Annapolis, Maryland. 1764. August 30th, p. 1.
384. Gibbs, J.W. *Dixie Clockmakers*. 1979, Gretna, Louisiana: Pelican Pub Co.
385. Advertisement, in *The Maryland Gazette*. Annapolis, Maryland. 1768. May 19th, p. Supplement 1.
386. Notice, in *The Maryland Gazette*. Annapolis, Maryland. 1769. July 27th, p. 3.
387. Lanigan, L., *Charles Cudmore family early 1700's*. 2003. https://www.genealogy.com/forum/surnames/topics/cudmore/112/
388. Williams, C.T. *The influence of climate in the prevention and treatment of pulmonary consumption. Lettsomian lects., 1876*. 1877, London: Smith, Elder & Co.
389. Advertisement, in *The Maryland Gazette*. Annapolis, Maryland. 1766. March 13th, p. 4.
390. Diaries, *F. McParlin Papers*. 1763-1897; Available from: http://www.mdarchives.state.md.us/msa/refserv/bulldog/bull89/html/bull89a.html.
391. Letzer, M.B. and J.B. Russo, eds. *The Diary of William Faris*. 2003, Baltimore, Maryland: Baltimore Historical Society.
392. Advertisement, in *The Maryland Gazette*. 1804. August 23rd, p. 4.
393. Advertisement, in *The Maryland Gazette*. Annapolis, Maryland. 1809. May 31st, p. 3.
394. Advertisement, in *The Maryland Gazette*. Annapolis, Maryland. 1811. November 7th, p. 3.
395. Advertisement, in *The Maryland Republican*. Annapolis, Maryland. 1816. December 21st, p. 3.
396. Advertisement, in *The Maryland Gazette*. Annapolis, Maryland. 1819. December 30th, p. 4.
397. Richards, N.E. *A Most Perfect Resemblance at Moderate Prices. The Miniatures of David Boudon*. Winterthur Portfolio, 1974. 9: p. 77–101.
398. Advertisement, in *The Maryland Gazette*. Annapolis, Maryland. 1767. December 3rd, p. 2.
399. Advertisement, in *The Maryland Gazette*. Annapolis, Maryland. 1769. August 17th, p. 2.
400. *Supplying the Local Jeweler in late Colonial Annapolis: A Look into the Order and Letter Books of Wallace, Davidson and Johnson*. 2012. http://withwallacedavidsonjohnson.blogspot.com/2012/03/supplying-local-jeweler-in-late.html
401. Advertisement, in *The Maryland Gazette*. Annapolis, Maryland. 1769. August 3rd, p. 2.
402. Advertisement, in *The Maryland Gazette*. Annapolis, Maryland. 1773. May 13th, p. 3.
403. Advertisement, in *The Maryland Gazette*. Annapolis, Maryland. 1774. February 24th, p. 3.
404. Advertisement, in *The Maryland Gazette*. Annapolis, Maryland. 1777. November 27th, p. 1.
405. Advertisement, in *Dunlap's Maryland Gazette; or The Baltimore General Advertiser*. Baltimore, Maryland. 1777. May 6th, p. 3.
406. Force P. *Agree with William Whetcroft, Of Annapolis, to Import a Sufficient Number of Workmen to Make and Deliver Fifty Stand of Arms for the Province, Every Week, for Two Years. American Archives*. 4th series, Volume 3. Washington DC: St Clair Clarke and Force P. 1840; p. 1116 https://books.google.ie/books?id=mUcMAQAAMAAJ&pg=PR81&lpg=PR81&dq=Fifty+Stand+of+Arms+for+the+Province,+Every+Week,+for+Two+Years.,&source=bl&ots=xdkUiZ_gYH&sig=ACfU3U2pLLQbCqtLT4rTPQvt1ynrm4MJNw&hl=en&sa=X&ved=2ahUKEwi6-KfT8bPoAhWIZhUIHQxCDEEQ6AEwAHoECAgQAQ#v=onepage&q=Fifty%20Stand%20of%20Arms%20for%20the%20Province%2C%20Every%20Week%2C%20for%20Two%20Years.%2C&f=false
407. Advertisement, in *The Maryland Gazette*. Annapolis, Maryland. 1777. July 10th, p. 3.
408. Advertisement, in *The Maryland Gazette*. Annapolis, Maryland. 1775. December 7th, p. 2.
409. Advertisement, in *Dunlap's Maryland Gazette*. Baltimore, Maryland. 1778. May 26th, p. 6.
410. Convention, M. *Money Advanced to William Whetcroft, of Annapolis, to Assist Him in Erecting a Rolling, Sheeting, and Slitting Mill, Within Twenty Miles of Baltimore, Rank of Counties and Colonels established*. 1776. p. 740. https://archive.org/stream/proceedingsofcon00inmary/proceedingsofcon00inmary_djvu.txt

411. Advertisement, in *The Maryland Gazette*. Annapolis, Maryland. 1780. February 20th, p. 2.
412. Advertisement, in *Washington Gazette*. Annapolis, Maryland. 1797. March 15th-18th, p. 3–4.
413. Notice, in *The Telegraphe and Daily Advertiser*. 1799. August 8th, p. 3.
414. Advertisement, in *American & Commercial Daily Advertiser*. Baltimore, Maryland. 1813. June 21st, p. 3.
415. Advertisement, in *The Maryland Gazette*. Annapolis, Maryland. 1800. June 19th, p. 2.
416. Loomes, B. *Lantern Clocks and their Makers*. 2008, Ashbourne, Derbyshire: Mayfield Books.
417. *Dublin Main Drainage Scheme Souvenir Handbook; published by the authority of the Municipal Council to mark the inauguration of the Dublin main drainage, September, 1906*. 1906, Dublin: Sealy, Bryers and Walker.
418. Advertisement, in *The Maryland Gazette*. Annapolis, Maryland. 1771. May 23rd, p. 3.
419. Advertisement, in *The Maryland Gazette*. Annapolis, Maryland. 1783. October 8th, p. 2.
420. Baillie, G.H., C. Ilbert, and C. Clutton. *Britten's Old Clocks and Watches*. 9th ed. 1982, London: Methuen.
421. Notice, in *The New-England Courant*. Boston, Massachusetts. 1721. Monday November 6, to Monday November 13, 1721, p. 2.
422. Robinson, T. *The Longcase Clock*. 1995, Woodbridge, Suffolk: Antique Collectors' Club.
423. McCall, D.M., M.D. Farrell, and L.E. Alexander. *An early history of Charlestown, Maryland*. 1983, Charlestown, Maryland: Colonial Charlestown, Inc.
424. Chellar, K. and C. Chellar. *300 years of Irish Timekeeping*. 2010, Dublin: Timepiece Antique Clocks.
425. Advertisement, in *Kentucky Gazette*. Lexington, Kentucky. 1799. December 5th, p. 2.
426. Advertisement, in *Stewart's Kentucky Herald*. Lexington, Kentucky. 1799. November 19th, p. 3.
427. Ranck, G.W. *History of Lexington, Kentucky: Its Early Annals and Recent Progress, Including Biographical Sketches and Personal Reminiscences of the Pioneer Settlers, Notices of Prominent Citizens, Etc., Etc.* 1872, Cincinnati: Robert Clarke & Co.
428. Notice, in *Kentucky Gazette*. Lexington, Kentucky. 1810. November 13th, p. 3.
429. Advertisement, in *Argus of Western America*. Frankfort, Kentucky. 1819. March 19th, p. 3.
430. Pettigrew, Oulton. *The Dublin Almanac and General Register of Ireland*. 1842, Dublin: Pettigrew and Oulton.
431. Slater, I. *I. Slater's National Commercial Directory of Ireland*. 1846, Manchester & London: I. Slater.
432. Slater, I. *I. Slater's National Commercial Directory of Ireland*. 1856, Manchester: I. Slater.
433. Notice, in *Argus of Western America*. Frankfort, Kentucky. 1820. September 7th, p. 3.
434. Advertisement, in *Argus of Western America*. Frankfort, Kentucky. 1820. October 5th, p. 3.
435. Cutten, G.B. *The Silversmiths of Virginia from 1694 to 1850*. 1952, Richmond, Virginia: The Dietz Press, Incorporated.
436. Advertisement, in *The Times and Alexandria Advertiser*. Alexandria, Virginia. 1798. November 30th, p. 3.
437. Anonymous, *Necrology*. The Virginia Magazine of History and Biography, 1895. II: p. 331.
438. Notice, in *The Enquirer*. Richmond, Virginia. 1809. October 10th, p. 4.
439. Advertisement, in *The Virginia Patriot, and Richmond Daily Mercantile Advertiser*. Richmond, Virginia. 1817. July 16th, p. 3.
440. Advertisement, in *Richmond Enquirer*. Richmond, Virginia. 1825. September 30th, p. Suppl 1.
441. Pigot, J. *The Commercial Directory of Ireland, Scotland and the four most Northern Counties of England for 1821-22 & 23 etc.* 1820, Manchester: Pigot, J & Co.
442. Pigot, J. *City of Dublin and Hibernian Provincial Directory*. 1824, London, Manchester: Pigot, J & Co.
443. Maguire, M., *Watch and Clock Makers in Limerick City Trade Directories*. 2007, Unpublished.
444. Advertisement, in *Virginia Argus*. Richmond, Virginia. 1803. November 9, p. 2.
445. Bell, D.A., *The McCabes Watch and Clock Makers of Ulster Part I*. Antiquarian Horology, 2000. 25(December): p. 653-679.

446. Staunton Moore, M.E.J. *History and By-laws of Richmond Royal Arch Chapt NO. 3 A. F. & A. M. Richmond, Virginia, with a list of officers and members*. 1911, Richmond, Virginia: Williams Printing Company.
447. Anonymous. *McCabe grave*. Available from: http://www.findagrave.com/cgi-bin/fg.cgi?page=gsr&GSiman=1&GScid=52134&GSfn=&GSln=mccabe (accessed December 29, 2013).
448. Notice, in *The Enquirer*. Richmond, Virginia. 1804. June 9th, p. 3.
449. Advertisement, in *The Enquirer*. Richmond, Virginia. 1805. August 20th, p. 3.
450. Advertisement, in *The Enquirer*. Richmond, Virginia. 1811. December 7th, p. 3.
451. Advertisement, in *Virginia Argus*. 1812. March 2nd, p. 3.
452. Advertisement, in *The Daily Compiler*. Richmond, Virginia. 1814. September 8th, p. 2.
453. Advertisement, in *The Daily Compiler*. Richmond, Virginia. 1814. March 1st, p. 3.
454. Advertisement, in *Virginia Argus*. 1816. June 26th, p. 3.
455. Notice, in *Richmond Enquirer*. Richmond, Virginia. 1817. January 2nd, p. 3.
456. Gilbert, J.T. *A History of the City of Dublin (reprint)*. The Sackville Library Edition ed. Vol. 2. p. 259. 1978, Dublin: Gill & Macmillan Ltd.
457. Advertisement, in *The Virginia Gazette, or The American Advertiser*. Richmond, Virginia. 1785. April 23rd, p. 3.
458. Advertisement, in *The Virginia Gazette and Independent Chronicle*. Richmond, Virginia. 1785. May 21, p. 4.
459. Advertisement, in *Columbian Mirror and Alexandria Gazette*. Alexandria, Virginia. 1798. February 15th, p. 3.
460. Driggs, T.A. *Personal Communication* 2006.
461. Advertisement, in *Columbian Mirror and Alexandria Gazette*. Alexandria, Virginia. 1800. March 1st, p. 3.
462. Advertisement, in *Alexandria Daily Advertiser*. Alexandria, Virginia. 1806. November 15th, p. 3.
463. Advertisement, in *Norfolk Gazette and Publick Ledger*. Norfolk, Virginia. 1805. January 16th, p. 3.
464. Advertisement, in *Norfolk Gazette and Publick Ledger*. Norfolk, Virginia. 1809. April 15th, p. 3.
465. Advertisement, in *Norfolk Herald*. Norfolk, Virginia. 1811. June 17th, p. 3.
466. Advertisement, in *American Beacon and Commercial Diary*. Norfolk, Virginia. 1818. January 26th, p. 4.
467. Advertisement, in *Petersburg Intelligencer*. Petersburg, Virginia. 1808. September 27, p. 3–5.
468. Advertisement, in *Virginia Argus*. Richmond, Virginia. 1805. March 9th, p. 2.
469. Advertisement, in *Baltimore Whig*. Baltimore, Maryland. 1811. October 12th, p. 3.
470. Advertisement, in *The Virginia Gazette*. Williamsburg, Virginia. 1772. August 27th, p. 4.
471. Advertisement, in *The Virginia Gazette*. Williamsburg, Virginia. 1772. October 1st, p. 2.
472. *Edenton Woman's Club (N.C.)*. 1953, Edenton, North Carolina: Chowan Herald.
473. Advertisement, in *The State Gazette of North-Carolina*. Edenton, North Carolina. 1790. October 8th.
474. Advertisement, in *The State Gazette of North-Carolina*. Edenton, North Carolina. 1794. June 6th.
475. Advertisement, in *The State Gazette of North-Carolina*. Edenton, North Carolina. 1795. December 3rd.
476. Advertisement, in *The State Gazette of North-Carolina*. Edenton, North Carolina. 1796. October 27th.
477. Advertisement, in *South Carolina Gazette*. Charleston, South Carolina. 1753. September 24th, p. 4.
478. Anonymous. *Dublin Gazette for 15-18 August 1767*. 1767. Cited 2015; Available from: http://www.kildare.ie/ehistory/index.php/county-kildare-references-in-18th-century-newspapers-and-muniments-part-two-1766-1900/.
479. Revill, J. *A compilation of the original Lists of Protestant Immigrants to South Carolina 1763-1773*. 1981, Baltimore, Maryland: Genealogical Publishing Company.
480. Cook, J.L., *A Georgian Heritage: Charlestown Artisans and Chippendale Furniture in the Revolutionary Period*, in *Arts*. 1985, Wake Forest University.

481. Stuart, W.G. *Exhibition of Irish Clocks and Watches by Antiquarian Horological Society - Irish Section*. 1975. Dublin.

482. Notice, in *South Carolina Gazette*. Charleston, South Carolina. 1761. December 19 to December 26, p. 4.

483. Notice, in *South Carolina Gazette*. Charleston, South Carolina. 1769. June 22nd, p. 3.

484. *Land Records Miscellaneous, Pt 28*, Book QQ, 1755-1756. 1756: Charleston County, South Carolina. p. 651–659.

485. *Land Records Miscellaneous, Pt 50*, Book E4, 1773. 1773: Charleston County, South Carolina. p. 389–394.

486. Advertisement, in *South Carolina Gazette; and Country Journal*. Charleston, South Carolina. 1772. January 7th, p. 4.

487. Notice, in *South Carolina Gazette*. Charleston, South Carolina. 1772. May 21st, p. 3.

488. Advertisement, in *The City Gazette & Daily Advertiser*. Charleston, South Carolina. 1792. February 29th p. 3.

489. Negrin, J.J. *Negrin's Directory and Almanac for the year 1806*. 1806, Charleston, South Carolina: J.J. Negrin.

490. Shackleford, W. *The Directory and Stranger's Guide for the City of Charleston*. 1824, Charleston, South Carolina: A. E. Miller.

491. *Wills*. Volumes 24-26, 1786–1800: Charleston, South Carolina. p. 354.

492. *Wills*. No. 34, 1818–1826: Charleston, South Carolina. p. 97.

493. Boone, S.L. *Meanings Beneath the Skin: The Evolution of African-Americans*. 2011, Lanham, MD: Rowman & Littlefield Publishers.

494. Battison, E. and P. Kane. *The American Clock 1725-1865*. 1973, Greenwich, Connecticut: New York Graphic Society Limited.

495. Cromwell O. *Directory, or Guide to the Residences and Places of Business of the Inhabitants of the City of Charleston*. 1829, Charleston, South Carolina: O. Cromwell.

496. Goldsmith, M. *Directory and Strangers' Guide for the City of Charleston*. 1831, Charleston, South Carolina: Morris Goldsmith.

497. Cawley, M. *Information from Charleston Death Card File of Charleston County Public Library*. 2007: Charleston, South Carolina.

498. Honour, J.H. *Directory of the City of Charleston and Neck*, ed. J.H. Honour. 1849, Charleston, South Carolina: A. J. Burke.

499. Bagget, J.H. *Directory of the City of Charleston for the year 1852*, ed. J.H. Honour. 1851, Charleston, South Carolina: Edward Councell.

500. Gazlay, D. *The Charleston City and General Business Directory for 1855*. 1855, Charleston, South Carolina: David M. Gazlay.

501. Advertisement, in *The City Gazette or The Daily Advertiser*. Charleston, South Carolina. 1790. February 4th, p. 2.

502. Advertisement, in *Charleston Courier*. Charleston, South Carolina. 1806. August 11th, p. 3.

503. Schenck & Turner. *The Directory and Stranger's Guide, for the City of Charleston*. 1819, Charleston, South Carolina: Schenck & Turner.

504. Schenck, J.R. *The Directory and Stranger's Guide, for the City of Charleston*. 1822, Charleston, South Carolina: James R. Schenck.

505. Burton, E.M. and W. Ripley. *South Carolina Silversmiths 1690-1860*. Revised. ed. 1991. Charleston, South Carolina: The Charleston Museum.

506. Holcomb, B.H., in Naturalized Citizens Vol A 1802-1832 from *South Carolina Naturalizations 1783-1850*. p. 164.

507. Notice, in *City Gazette and Commercial Daily Advertiser*. Charleston, South Carolina. 1819. May 3rd, p. 4.

508. Advertisement, in *The Telescope*. Columbia, South Carolina. 1816. December 17th, p. 3.

509. Advertisement, in *City Gazette and Commercial Daily Advertiser*. Charleston, South Carolina. 1818. August 3rd, p. 4.

510. Henderson, J. *Henderson's New Belfast And Northern Repository For 1843-1844*. 1843, Belfast: John Henderson.

511. Henderson, J. *Henderson's Belfast Directory And Northern Repository 1846-1847*. 1846, Belfast: John Henderson.

512. Henderson, J.A. *The Belfast and Province of Ulster Directory for 1852*. 1852, Belfast: James Alexander Henderson.

513. Henderson, J.A. *The Belfast and Province of Ulster Directory for 1858-9*. Vol. IV. 1858, Belfast:

James Alexander Henderson.
514. Henderson, J.A. *The Belfast and Province of Ulster Directory for 1863-4*. Vol. VI. 1863, Belfast: James Alexander Henderson.
515. Pettigrew, Oulton. *The Dublin Almanac and General Register of Ireland*. 1840, Dublin: Pettigrew and Oulton.
516. Thom, A. *Thom's Irish Almanac and Official Directory of the United Kingdom of Great Britain and Ireland for the year 1860*. 1860, Dublin: Alexander Thom.
517. Watson, J. *Gentleman and Citizen's Almanack*. 1732, Dublin: John Watson.
518. Robey, J. *The Longcase Clock*. 2001, Ashbourne, Derbyshire, England: Mayfield Books.
519. Loomes, B. *Brass Dial Clocks*. 1998, Woodbridge Suffolk: Antique Collectors Club.
520. Robinson, K., *Dublin Clocks*. Bulletin of the National Association of Watch and Clock Collectors, 2003. 45/4(August): p. 445–461.
521. Robinson, K., *Dublin Clocks*. Bulletin of the National Association of Watch and Clock Collectors, 2003. 45/5(October): p. 583–597.
522. Loomes, B. *Grandfather Clocks and their Cases*. 1985, Newton Abbot & London: David & Charles.
523. Rogers, M.R. *Philadelphia via Dublin: Influences in Rococo Furniture, in Philadelphia Furniture and its Makers*, J.J.S. Jr, Editor. 1975, Universe Books: New York. p. 74–77.
524. Curran, C.P. *Dublin decorative plasterwork of the seventeenth and eighteenth centuries*. 1967, London: Alec Tiranti.
525. Theus, C.M. *Savannah Furniture 1735-1825*. 1967, Savannah (?): Unknown - possibly private.
526. Bivins, J.J. *The Furniture of Coastal North Carolina 1700-1820*. 1988, Winston-Salem: The Museum of Early Southern Decorative Arts.
527. Berkley, H.J., *A Register of the Cabinet Makers and Allied Trades in Maryland as shown by the Newspapers and Directories, 1746 to 1820*. Maryland Historical Magazine, 1930. XXV(No 1): p. 1–27.
528. Prime, A.C. *Arts and Crafts in Philadelphia, Maryland and South Carolina 1786-1800 Series 2*. 1932, Topsfield, MA: The Walpole Society.
529. Gusler, W.B. *Furniture of Williamsburg and Eastern Virginia 1710-1790*. 1979, Richmond, Virginia: Virginia.
530. Hornor, W.M. *Blue Book Phildelphia Furniture William Penn to George Washington*. 1st ed. 1988, Alexandria, Virginia: Highland House Publishers.
531. Trump, R.T., *Joseph B. Barry, Philadelphia Cabinetmaker, in Philadelphia Furniture and its Makers*, J.J.S. Jr, Editor. 1975, New York: Main Street/Universe Books.
532. Thorpe, A.L.P. Personal communication to author January 18th 2020: *Our Suber-Thorpe Ancestors*. 2000; Available from: https://www.ancestry.com/family-tree/person/tree/21183993/person/1042434906/facts.
533. Lahikainen, D. *Samuel McIntire - Carving an American Style*. 2007, Salem, MA: Peabody Essex Museum.
534. Naeve, M.M. *John Glinn's clock case of 1750 for Henry Bromfield of Boston, Massachusetts*. Furniture History, 1992. 28: p. 22–34.
535. Robinson, K., *An unpublished list of trades-people possibly associated with Irish clock and watchmakers*. 2015: Winston-Salem.
536. Lucas, R. *The Cork Directory for the Year 1787*. Journal of the Cork Historical and Archaeological Society (reprinted). 1967. LXII.
537. Lucas, R. *The Limerick Directory for the Year 1788*. 1788. Accessed May 31, 2015. Available from: http://www.from-ireland.net/1788-lucas-directory-limerick-richard-lucas/.
538. Loomes, B. *White Dial Clocks. The Complete Guide*. 1981, Newton Abbot: David & Charles.
539. Foley, P.J., *James Harden and William Jones Philadelphia Painted Tall Clock Dials 1816-1845*. Bulletin of the National Association of Watch and Clock Collectors, 2014. 56/1(January/February): p. 3–11.
540. Seaby, W.A., *James Wilson Clockmaker of Belfast*. Antiquarian Horology, 1983(June 1983): p. 133–155.
541. Robey, J.A. *An Irish Pull-Repeat Mechanism*. Horological Journal, 1997: p. 415–419.
542. Van Winkle Keller, K., *Musical Clocks of Early America*. Bulletin of the National Association of Watch and Clock Collectors, Inc., 1982. XXIV(June): p. 253–316.
543. Miller, E.G. *American Antique Furniture - A Book for Amateurs*. First ed. 1937, Section 187, p.

920. New York: M. Barrows & Company, Inc.

544. Clark, D. *The Irish in the American Economy*, in *The Irish in America: Emigration, Impact and Assimilation*, P.J. Drudy, Editor. 1984, Cambridge University Press: Cambridge, London, New York.

545. Advertisement, in *The Pennsylvania Gazette*. Philadelphia, Pennsylvania. 1748. May 5th, p. 3.

546. Hensel, W.U. *Jacob Eichholtz Painter: Some loose leaves from the ledger of an early Lancaster artist. An address delivered at the opening of an exposition of the evolution of portraiture in Lancaster County Pennsylvania under the auspices of the Lancaster County Historical Society and the Iris Club Woolworth Building November 22 1912*. Historical Papers and Addresses of the Lancaster County Historical Society, 1911. Volume 15. https://archive.org/stream/jstor-20085625/20085625_djvu.txt

547. Advertisement, in *The Pennsylvania Packet, and General Advertiser*. Philadelphia, Pennsylvania. 1784. May 15th, p. 3.

548. Craig, M. *Dublin 1660-1860*. 1952 Reprinted 1980, Dublin: Allen Figgis Ltd Dublin.

549. Gilbert, J.T. *A History of the City of Dublin (reprint)*. The Sackville Library Edition ed. Vol. 1. p. 33, 1978, Dublin: Gill & Macmillan Ltd.

550. Dukes, F. *Campanology in Ireland*. 1994, Dublin, Ireland: Samton.

551. Georges, J. *George Beatty*. 2014. Available from: http://www.findagrave.com/cgi-bin/fg.cgi?page=gr&GRid=90056787.

552. Notice, in *Dunlaps Pennsylvania Packet or the General Advertiser*. Philadelphia, Pennsylvania. 1774. February 7th, p. 1.

553. Notice, in *Ballymena Observer*. 1881. April 30th, p. 2.

554. Notice, in *Belfast Newsletter*. 1884. October 1st, p. 3.

555. Notice, in *The Salem Gazette*. Salem, Massachusetts. 1796. March 15th, p. 4.

556. Emsley, C., T. Hitchcock, and R. Shoemaker. *London History - Currency, Coinage and the Cost of Living*. 2015. 31 March 2015; version 7.0: Available from: http://www.oldbaileyonline.org/static/Coinage.jsp.

557. Burnett, J. and A. Morrison-Low. *"Vulgar and Mechanick." The Scientific Instrument Trade in Ireland 1650-1921*. 1989, Dublin: National Museums of Scotland, Royal Dublin Society.

558. Unknown. Christies Auctioneers. Cited May 15, 2015. Available from: https://digitalcollections.nypl.org/items/52c83270-52e5-0135-68ed-053cf01a19c5

559. Robinson K. Personal observation. Clock dial seen at the *Ulster Folk & Transport Museum*. 1998.

560. Spear, D.E. *American Watch Papers With a Descriptive List of the Collection in the American Antiquarian Society*. 1952, Worcester, MA: American Antiquarian Society.

561. Patterson, M.R. *Thomas Andrew McParlin, Colonel, United States Army*. 2007. Cited 2014 October 19, 2014. Available from: http://www.arlingtoncemetery.net/tamcparlin.htm.

562. Advertisement, in *Virginia Chronicle & General Advertiser*. Norfolk, Virginia. 1794. July 31st, p. 3.

563. American Anti-Slavery Society. *Slave Market of America*.1836. Available from: http://www.loc.gov/pictures/item/2008661294/.

564. Notice, in *Advertiser and Commercial Intelligencer*. Alexandria, Virginia. November 15th 1806. p. 3.

565. Advertisement, in *American Beacon and Norfolk & Portsmouth Daily Advertiser*. Norfolk, Virginia. 1820. May 24th, p. 3.

566. Melvin, P. *Captain Florence O'Sullivan and the Origins of Carolina*. The South Carolina Historical Magazine, 1975. 76(No. 4): p. 235–249.

567. Pettigrew, Oulton. *The Dublin Almanac and General Register of Ireland*. 1849, Dublin: Pettigrew and Oulton.

568. Corbet, W. *Wilson's Dublin Directory*. 1821, Dublin: William Corbet.

569. https://lists.rootsweb.com/hyperkitty/list/kincaid@rootsweb.com/thread/2253565/. Available from: https://lists.rootsweb.com/hyperkitty/list/kincaid@rootsweb.com/thread/2253565/

570. Kincaid PA. Documents pertaining to the Kinkeads of Barons Court, County Tyrone. Available from: http://www.kyncades.org/papers/Baronscourt_2016.

571. Dyke, S. *Clock-makers of Lehigh and Northampton Counties compiled from tax records in the court houses*. 1967, Allentown, Pennsylvania: The Lehigh County Historical Society.

572. Hardiman, N. and M. Kennedy, eds. *A Directory of Dublin for the Year 1738*. 2000/ Dublin: Dublin

Corporation Public Libraries.
573. Corbet, W. *Wilson's Dublin Directory*. 1829, Dublin: William Corbet.
574. Corbet, W. *Wilson's Dublin Directory*. 1830, Dublin: William Corbet.
575. Folds, W. *Wilson's Dublin Directory*. 1832, Dublin: William Folds.
576. Cutten, G.B. *The Silversmiths of Georgia Together with Watchmakers and Jewelers 1733-1850*. Second Revised ed. 1984, Savannah, Georgia: The Oglethorpe Press.
577. Dowling, D. *The Charleston Directory and Register for 1835-6*. 1835, Charleston, South Carolina: Daniel Dowling.
578. Motts, A. *Charleston Directory and Strangers' Guide*. 1816., Charleston, South Carolina: Abraham Motts.
579. Burges, J.S. *Directory or Guide to the Residences and Places of Business of the Inhabitants of the City of Charleston*. 1829, Charleston, South Carolina: James S. Burges.
580. Keenan, C. *Baltimore Directory and Register for the year 1822 & 1823*. 1822–23, Baltimore, Maryland: C. Keenan.
581. Matchett, R.J. *Baltimore Directory for 1831*. 1831, Baltimore, Maryland: R.J. Matchett.
582. Matchett. *Baltimore Directory corrected up to 1833*. 1833, Baltimore, Maryland.
583. Bordes, M.J. *Baltimore Federal Furniture in The American Wing*. 1972, New York: Metropolitan Museum of Art. 18 pages.
584. Burton, E.M. *Charleston Furniture 1700-1825*. 1955, Charleston, South Carolina: The Charleston Museum.

Index

Abbott, Wes(t)ley 64
Aicken, James 77
Allen, Charles 30
Allen, Joseph 31
Amie, Slave 92
Andrews, David 60
Arthur, James 52, 53, 54, 55, 56, 57
Ashwin and Co. 104

Bagnall, Thomas 105
Bailey, William 119
Baker, Alexander 120
Baker, Matthias 71
Baldwin, Jabiz 21
Baltimore, Lord 61
Bankson, Harriet 77
Barklie, Thomas 69
Barkley, Joseph 64, 68
Barnes, Abraham 311
Barrett & Sherwood 111
Barrington, Benjamin 121
Barrington, Isaac 121
Barrington, Isaac Jr. 121
Barrington, J 121
Barrington, Joseph 121
Barry, John 120
Barry, Joseph 115, 120
Barry, Lavallin 120
Barry, Robert 120
Barry, Spranger 120
Barry, William 120
Barry, Standish 64
Beatty, George 20
Beatty, Nancy 20
Bell, Joseph 120
Bennett, Alfred 119

Berkley, Henry 116
Bigger, Gilbert 63, 64, 65, 66, 67, 68, 118
Bigger, Elizabeth 64
Bigger, Hugh 68
Bigger, William 68
Birnie, Alexander 7
Birnie, John 7
Birnie, Laurence 7, 8, 26, 113
Birnie, Samuel 7
Birnie, William 7
Bob, Slave 105
Booth, James 122
Boudon, David 79
Bowers, George 119
Bowlin, Mr 89
Boyd, Alexander 108
Bradley, Zebul 37
Brouggy, Sarah 92
Brown, Alfred 108
Burrage, John 79
Burrowes, Isaac B 24, 25
Burrowes, Mrs 23
Burrowes, Thomas 23, 24, 25, 114

Burrowes, Thomas H. 24
Bush, Charles 124
Butler, John 31

Calder, James 124
Calderwood, Andrew 12, 13, 14, 37
Calderwood, William 12
Calvert Family 61
Campbell, Moses 90
Carr, Adam 53
Carson, Kit 81
Cashell & Lagary 70, 71
Cashell, Randall 70, 71
Casey, Samuel 31
Cass, Slave 84
Cassells or Castles, Joseph 13
Cattle, Barsheba 105
Chandlee, Benjamin 3, 4, 87
Chandlee, Benjamin Jr 3
Chandlee, Ellis 3
Chandlee, Isaac 3
Chandlee, John 87
Chapman, Benjamin 111
Chapman, James 111
Chapman, Joseph 111
Chapman, Julia Ann 111
Chapman, William 111
Cherry, James 119
Church, Ann 92
Clarke, Ambrose 13, 63, 68, 99
Clarke, Christopher 63
Clark, David 108
Claude, Abraham 78, 84, 87
Cling, Widow 100
Coleman, James 119
Coleman, John 119
Cooke, William 121
Corkings, Ezra 70
Cottey, Abel 3
Cottey, Sarah 3
Cowen, John 124
Coyle, David 123
Craig, Charles 63
Craig, James 101
Crampton, John 88
Creighton, John 58
Croker, James B 98, 100
Crowley or Crawley, John 13

Cudmore, Frances 77
Cunningham, John 21
Currie, William 103
Curry, Patrick 124

Dalrymple, Hannah 32
Dalrymple, James 32, 33
Dalrymple, John 32, 33, 39
Davis, John 41, 120
Davis, William 31
Dease, John 121
Dermont, Henry 123
Dogood, Charles 19
Doherty, Cornelius 33
Donahue, Robert 122
Dougherty, Christopher 123
Dougherty, John 117, 123
Dowling, Mary 49
Doyle, John 123
Down, Samuel 56
Duffield, Edward 115
Durkin, John 60

Ebbe, John 87
Egan, Daniel 71
Egan, Robert 77, 98, 100, 101
Egan, Sarah 102
Eichholtz, Jacob 23, 24
Elliott, Francis 110
Emerson, Lambert 124
Evans, William 121

Fairley, Hance 124
Fallon, Thomas 60
Faris, Charles 78, 80
Faris, William 78, 80, 81, 82
Farqu(h)ar, James 56
Farr, John 16
Fenny, John – see Finney
Ferris, Benjamin 20
Févret de Saint-Mémin, Charles B. J. 43
Findlay see Finley
Finlay, Christopher see also Finley 123
Finley, Hugh 123
Finley John 123
Finney of Liverpool 46
Finney, Cathren (sic) 85
Finney, Elizabeth 85

Finney, John 85, 87, 88
Finney, Mary 85
Finney, Susannah 85
Fitzgerald, Desmond 113, 116
Fitzgerald, Edward 122
Fitzgerald, Richard 122
Fitzgerald, William Bolster 122
Foley, John 123
Foley, Timothy 123
Franklin, Benjamin 6
Frazer, Alexander 88, 89
Frazer, David 89
Frazer, James 88, 89
Frazer, John 89
Frazer, Oliver 87, 89
Frazer, R 90
Frazer, Robert 86, 87, 88, 89
Frazer, Robert Jr 89
Frazer, William 89
Freeman, Mr 117
Freeman, B 124
French, Calfrey 87
French, James M 87

French, James Ormsby 84, 87
French, Paulgry 87
French, Robert 87
French, William 87

Garvey, Matthew 56
Gibbs, James 98, 105
Gibson, William 16
Gilbert, B 68
Gilliam, Edward 111
Gird, Henry Hatton 99
Gird, Henry Jr 99
Gird, William 97, 99
Glinn, Bernard 117
Glinn, George 117
Glinn, John 117
Godshalk, Jacob 9
Gottesman, Rita 41
Goodwin, Widow 100
Gordon, George 56
Gordon, James 56
Gordon, Joseph 56
Gordon, Thomas 56

Gowdey, Thomas 122
Grattan, Henry 49
Grattan, Miss 49
Green, Francis 124
Gregory, William 21
Gregson, Pierre 97
Griffith, Nathaniel Sheaffe 35
Guy, Francis 50

Hadlock, Robert 119
Hadlock, William 119
Hagan, Bernard 93
Hagan, Joseph 93
Hammond, AG 72, 73
Harden & Ryding 117
Harden, James 117, 118
Harper, Richard 32
Haunt, Catherine 90
Haunt, Mary 90
Haunt, Peter 90
Haunt, Thomas H 90
Harris, William 123
Hay, Anthony 115
Hayes, Mr 68
Heckscher, M.H. 15
Heffernan, John 124
Heimer, John 21
Hemphill, James 22
Hering, Daniel W. 54
Heron, Edward 41,
Heron, Isaac 35, 41, 43, 44, 45, 46, 47, 48
Herschel, A. S. 52
Hickey, John 31
Hill, Samuel 20
Hind, Mary 99
Hinklin, John 122
Hoff, John 21
Hogan, James 64
Hogan, McCutcheon (or M'Cutchan) & Co. 64, 116
Hourine, John 124
Hughes, Christopher 62
Hughes, Philip 62
Hughes, Thomas 117
Hughes, William 62
Humphries, Richard 6, 7

Jackson, Anthony 4
Jackson, George 5
Jackson, Isaac 4
Jackson, John 4, 5
Jeffereys, Samuel 19
Jenkins & Hatch 121
Jenkins, Henry 121
Jenkins, Newth 121
Jenkins, Thomas 121
Jenkins, William 121
Johnson, David 31
Johnston, John 38
Johnston, Robert 105
Johnston, Thomas 38
Jones, George 116
Jones, Theophilus 116
Jones, Thomas 124
Jones, William 117
Joyce, Robert 48, 49, 50, 51, 52

Keddie, James 69
Kelly, Michael 111
Kennedy, Samuel 123
Kennedy, William 115
King, Josias 86
King, William 76
Kingston, George 124
Kinkead, Alexander 29, 30
Kinkead, Charles 26
Kinkead, Christopher 119
Kinkead, Clara Janvier 30
Kindead, David 26
Kinkead, James 26, 27, 28, 29
Kinkead, John 26, 119
Kinkead, Joseph 29, 30
Kinkead, Samuel 26
Kinkead, Sarah 29
Kinkead, Thomas 30
Kinkead, William 29
Knapp (nee Cudmore), Frances 77, 79
Knapp, Edmond or Edwin 77
Knapp, John 77
Knapp, William 75, 76, 77, 78, 79, 82
Kock, Captain 102

LaFond, Edward Jr 46, 118
Lahee, Margaret 99
Lahee, Samuel 99
Lamb, William 92, 93
Lampe, John 86
Latham & Clark 104
Latham, Gilbert 108
Latham, James 56, 118, 120
Latham, Joseph 105, 108
Leatham, John 120
Leban, Lucy 63
Lee, John 123
Lee, Robert E 81
Lemon, Charles 116
Lemon, John 116
Lemon, William 116
Lloyd, William 124
Long, George 118
Long, Leonard 118
Loomis, Warham 89, 90
Loomis & Fowler 89
Loomis & Ralph 89

index 147

Lowry, John 111
Luke, Samuel 50
Lynch, Arthur 73
Lynch, Benjamin 74
Lynch, Farrell 73
Lynch, James 73
Lynch, John 70, 71, 72, 73, 74, 120
Lynch, Robert 73
Lynch, Thomas 73

McCabe, James 69, 94
McCabe, John 13, 68, 69, 70, 71, 94, 95, 118
McCabe, Phebe 70
McCabe, Patrick 69, 94
McCabe, Thomas 94, 123
McCabe, William (possibly also M'Cay or M'Cabe) 93, 94, 95, 96, 97, 98
McAffrey, Terrence 124
McCalmont, John 122
McCartney, John N 111
McClure, John 120
McClure, Joseph (possibly also McClurg) 120
McConaghy, Hugh 121
McConnell, Thomas 120
McCormick, James 116, 117
McCrow, Thomas 87
McCullough, John 111
McElwee, James 20
McFadden, Mr 123
McFadon, Alexander 86
McFarland, William see McParlin
McGann, Jane Rebecca 105
McGann, Patrick see Magann
McGuire, Bernard 34
McHinch, Robert 51, 53
McKay, William 120
McKee, Andrew 108
McKee, Jane 108
McKee, John (South Carolina) 26, 106, 107, 108, 109, 110
McKee, Julia Felicia 106
McKee (nee Hayden), Mary 106, 109
McKee, Mary Ellen 106
McKinley, Edward 20
McLean or M'Lane, John 31, 118
McParlin, Thomas 81
McParlin, William 78, 79, 80, 81, 82
McQuaide, Thomas 21

McSweeney, Paul 123
Magan & Latham 108
Magan(n), Patrick see also McGann 103, 104, 105, 117
Mahve or Maher, Matthew 19
Maloney, John 124
Marshall, William 88
Martin, John 120
Martin, Samuel 49, 50, 51, 52, 53, 77
Martin, George 49

Martin, Thomas 50
Martin, Young 50
Massey, John or Joseph 121
Mears, John 120
Mears, Josias 120
Merriman, Marcus 37
Mesick, John F Rev. 21
Miller, George 113, 117
Molineux, Joseph 120
Molyneux, Joseph 120
Montgomery, Robert 120
Montague, Richard 124
Moore, Ambrose 13
Moore, John 62
Morphy, Johannes 23
Mulliken, Joseph 32
Murphy & Pollard 98
Murdock, Abigail 6
Murphy, J.H. 121
Murphy, James 119
Murphy, James 119, 120
Murphy, John (Pennsylvania) 23, 119
Murphy, John (Virginia) 98, 100, 119
Murphy, John B 121
Murphy, Josiah 124
Murphy, Mary 100
Murphy, Thomas 119

Narney, John 101, 103
Narney, Teresa 103
Narney, William 103
Nathan, Slave 72, 73
Neill, James 111
Neill, Robert 105

Nelson, James 57
Nelson, Joseph 57
Nelson, Robert 57
Nelson, Samuel 57
Neville, Joshua 124
Newsam & Slater 124
Nicholl, John 57, 58, 59, 60
Nixon, Elias 36
Nolen and Curtis 51

O'Connell, John 34
O'Donnell, John 82
O'Flaherty, Mr 47
O'Neil, Charles 37
O'Neill, Charles 37, 58
Oliver, Nancy 89
Orr, Jane 18
Orr, James Armstrong 19
Orr, James Malcolm 16, 17, 18
Orr, James S 17
Orr, Samuel 17, 18
Orr, Thomas 16
Orr, William 13
Orr, William Stewart 18, 19
Owen, Griffith 8, 113

Palmer, B 105
Pangborn and Brinsmaid 38
Parker, George 68
Patton and Jones 15
Peale, Charles Willson 8, 81
Peill, James 113, 116
Penn, William 3
Perkins, Jedidiah or James 38
Phalon, Timothy 123
Physick, Edward 6
Pickering, John 15
Pitt, Mr 81
Pollard, Lewis 98, 100
Pool(e), James 121
Powell, John 124
Price, Montmorency 81
Purcell, Ann 92
Purcell, Anna Maria 92
Purcell, Charles 91, 92, 93
Purcell, James 92
Purcell, John 91, 92
Purcell, William 92

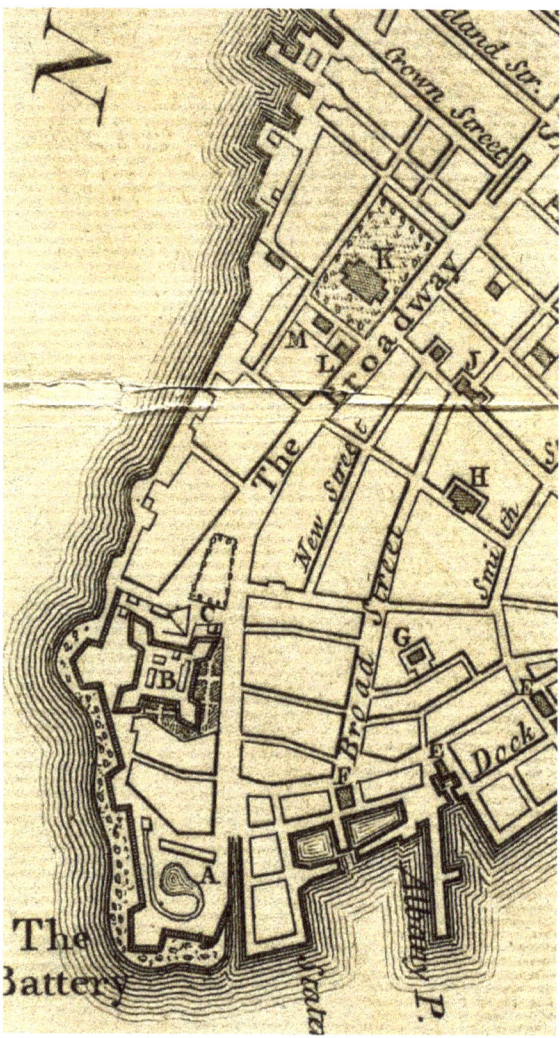

Richardson, Captain 97
Rider, Job 105
Riley, John 10, 120
Roach, Patrick 77
Robey, John 115
Roberts, Charles 23
Robinson, Alexander 121
Robinson, Andrew 121
Rolain, Martha 108
Russell, Mary 89
Russell, Robert 89
Ruttle, Daniel 90
Ryan, Mary 92
Ryan, William 92

Sandell, Edward 65
Sanderson, Thomas 114
Schurman, E.W. 15
Scott, Upton 82
Sedley, Francis 123
Sewell, Samuel 31
Seymour, John 124
Seymour, Thomas 124
Sharman, William 43
Sharpe, Horatio 82
Shaw & Chisholm 82, 124
Shaw, Alexander 124
Shaw, Matthew 124
Shaw, Pigot 64, 65
Sherrard, H & L.J. 56
Sherwood, Robert 111
Shivery, George 89
Shrom, Catherine 22
Shrom, Sarah Smith 22
Simnet or Simnel, John 34, 35, 36, 37
Simpson, James 122
Sinclair, William 119
Slover and Kortwright 48
Smith, Ann 24
Smith, Charles 68
Smith, Charles Conolly 102
Smith, Pat 88
Spalding, John 71
Spence, James 25, 26
Spence, David 26
Spotswood & Clarke 68
Spotswood, George 68
Spotswood, William 68

Pyper, John 16

Raley, R.L. 123
Ralph & Loomis 89, 90
Ralph, Patrick 90
Ralph, Samuel 90
Ranck, George Washington 87
Reiley and Co 12, 120
Reily, John 10, 99, 119
Reilly, John 95, 99
Reil(l)y, Phillip 119
Reynolds, Charles 68
Rice & Co 69
Rice, Joseph 64
Rice, Sally 64

Spratt, Samuel 120
Stearns, Dr 33
Stedman, Henry 121
Stedman, John C 121
Stewart & King 76
Stewart, G 76, 120
Stewart, James 75, 77, 117, 120
Stewart, Jane 16
Stewart, John 76, 120
Stuart, Samuel 124
Stevenson, John 63
Stoner, Rudy 114
Sullivan, Eugene 121
Sullivan, John 25
Sullivan, William F 121
Sweeney, Paul 123
Syng, Abigail 6
Syng, Philip 6
Syng, Philip Jr 6, 7

Taylor, John 26
Terlau, Henry 90
Thompson, John 46
Tompion, Thomas 34
Tryon, Lt General William 45

Underwood, Alexander 58
Underwood, Charles 58
Underwood, William 58

Van Wagenen Family of New York 9

Waddill, William 99
Waldo, Major 33
Wallace, Davidson & Johnson 82
Walker, Mr 97
Walker, Thomas 21
Walsh, Elizabeth 63
Walsh, John 122
Washington, George 12
Webster, Mr 34
Wells, Robert 119, 121, 124
Wells, Thomas 119
Welsh, Robert 58
Whelan, James 124
Whetcroft, Burton 84
Whetcroft, Letitia 86
Whetcroft, William 79, 81, 82, 83, 84, 86

White, Charles 124
White, Elizabeth 22
Willard Brothers 97
Williams, Charles 21
Woods, Thomas 124
Woodward, Cassandra 81
Wooldridge, John 89
Worge and Smith 47

index 151

About the Author

Killian Robinson has been a member of the National Association of Watch & Clock Collectors (NAWCC) since 1998. Graduating in Medicine from the University of Dublin, Trinity College in 1978, he trained as a cardiologist and practiced in the United States for nearly 25 years. Now Professor Emeritus of Cardiology at Wake Forest University, he is semi-retired in Ireland. He became interested in studying Irish clocks when he purchased a tall case clock made by Sanderson of Dublin. At that time, relatively little had been published on the subject of Irish clockmakers, which piqued his interest in researching this area further. A move to Winston-Salem, North Carolina, placed the magnificent resources of the staff and the databases of the Museum of Early Southern Decorative Arts at his ready disposal for the research for this book. As well as numerous medical publications, he has authored several peer-reviewed papers on Irish horology published in the *Watch & Clock Bulletin* of the NAWCC and elsewhere. This is his first book dedicated to horology. He is married with two daughters, both living in Chicago.

Time is a gift. Embrace the present.
Join the NAWCC

Become a member today by applying at nawcc.org or calling toll free 877.255.1849 (US and Canada) or 717.684.8261

Join the National Association of Watch and Clock Collectors, Inc., the largest international association dedicated to preserving and stimulating interest in horology, the art and science of time and timekeeping.

Our members are enthusiasts, students, educators, collectors, businesses, and professionals, who love learning about the clocks and watches they collect, preserve, and study.

Your dues support:
- World's leading research library on horology
- Largest public collection of timepieces in the Americas
- Educational programs that teach watchmaking and clockmaking skills as well as art and history of timekeeping

Your membership gives you:
- Six issues of the *Watch & Clock Bulletin*, an educational journal, and the *Mart & Highlights*, an advertising supplement and chapter magazine
- NAWCC's Library and Research Center's resources and assistance
- Webinars and workshops
- Online access to articles, videos, and archival materials
- Regional buying and selling venues
- Camaraderie at meetings, dinners, and events
- Free admission to the National Watch and Clock Museum in Columbia, PA
- Free or discounted admission to more than 250 museums and science centers

The National Association of Watch and Clock Collectors is a 501(c)(3) nonprofit organization.

www.ingramcontent.com/pod-product-compliance
Lightning Source LLC
Chambersburg PA
CBHW040929240426
43667CB00026B/2992